Radical Inclusivity

NEW PERSPECTIVES ON LANGUAGE AND EDUCATION
Founding Editor: Viv Edwards, *University of Reading, UK*

Series Editors: Phan Le Ha, *University of Hawaii at Manoa, USA*, Joel Windle, *Monash University, Australia* and Kyle R. McIntosh, *University of Tampa, USA*.

Two decades of research and development in language and literacy education have yielded a broad, multidisciplinary focus. Yet education systems face constant economic and technological change, with attendant issues of identity and power, community and culture. What are the implications for language education of new 'semiotic economies' and communications technologies? Of complex blendings of cultural and linguistic diversity in communities and institutions? Of new cultural, regional and national identities and practices? The New Perspectives on Language and Education series will feature critical and interpretive, disciplinary and multidisciplinary perspectives on teaching and learning, language and literacy in new times. New proposals, particularly for edited volumes, are expected to acknowledge and include perspectives from the Global South. Contributions from scholars from the Global South will be particularly sought out and welcomed, as well as those from marginalized communities within the Global North.

All books in this series are externally peer-reviewed.

Full details of all the books in this series and of all our other publications can be found on http://www.multilingual-matters.com, or by writing to Multilingual Matters, BLOCK, The Fairfax, Pithay Ct, Bristol, BS1 3BN, UK.

The policy of Multilingual Matters/Channel View Publications is to use papers that are natural, renewable and recyclable products, made from wood grown in sustainable forests. In the manufacturing process of our books, and to further support our policy, preference is given to printers that have FSC and PEFC Chain of Custody certification. The FSC and/or PEFC logos will appear on those books where full certification has been granted to the printer concerned.

NEW PERSPECTIVES ON LANGUAGE AND EDUCATION: 134

Radical Inclusivity

Critical Language Awareness in the Language and Writing Classroom

Edited by
Gloria Park, Quanisha Charles, Shannon Tanghe and Marie Webb

MULTILINGUAL MATTERS
Bristol • Jackson

DOI https://doi.org/10.21832/PARK0345
Library of Congress Cataloging in Publication Data
A catalog record for this book is available from the Library of Congress.
Names: Park, Gloria G., editor | Charles, Quanisha, editor |
   Tanghe, Shannon, editor | Webb, Marie, editor
Title: Radical Inclusivity: Critical Language Awareness in the Language
   and Writing Classroom/Edited by Gloria Park, Quanisha Charles, Shannon
   Tanghe and Marie Webb.
Description: Bristol; Jackson: Multilingual Matters, 2026. | Series: New
   Perspectives on Language and Education: 134 | Includes bibliographical
   references and index. | Summary: "This book blends theory and practice
   to share the hows and whys of implementing radical inclusivity in the
   language and writing classroom. It is designed to provide teachers and
   graduate students with theoretical background and practical activities
   that can be integrated into language teacher education, as well as
   writing and language classrooms"—Provided by publisher.
Identifiers: LCCN 2025021698 (print) | LCCN 2025021699 (ebook) | ISBN
   9781836680338 paperback | ISBN 9781836680345 hardback | ISBN
   9781836680369 pdf | ISBN 9781836680352 epub
Subjects: LCSH: English language—Rhetoric—Study and teaching | Critical
   pedagogy | Language awareness | Social justice and education |
   Educational change | English language--Study and teaching—Foreign
   speakers | Language teachers—Training of | LCGFT: Essays
Classification: LCC PE1404 .R34 2026 (print) | LCC PE1404 (ebook)
LC record available at https://lccn.loc.gov/2025021698
LC ebook record available at https://lccn.loc.gov/2025021699

British Library Cataloguing in Publication Data
A catalogue entry for this book is available from the British Library.

ISBN-13: 978-1-83668-034-5 (hbk)
ISBN-13: 978-1-83668-033-8 (pbk)

Multilingual Matters
UK: BLOCK, The Fairfax, Pithay Ct, Bristol, BS1 3BN, UK.
USA: Ingram, Jackson, TN, USA.
Authorised Representative: Easy Access System Europe – Mustamäe tee 50, 10621
Tallinn, Estonia, gpsr.requests@easproject.com.

Website: https://www.multilingual-matters.com
X: Multi_Ling_Mat
Bluesky: @multi-ling-mat.bsky.social
Facebook: https://www.facebook.com/multilingualmatters
Blog: https://www.channelviewpublications.wordpress.com

Copyright © 2026 Gloria Park, Quanisha Charles, Shannon Tanghe, Marie Webb
and the authors of individual chapters.

All rights reserved. No part of this work may be reproduced in any form or by any
means without permission in writing from the publisher.

Typeset by Techset Composition India(P) Ltd, Bangalore and Chennai, India.

Contents

	Contributors	vii
	Foreword: Seeds of Transformation: The Power of Critical Language Awareness and Radical Inclusivity *Shawna Shapiro and Shenika Hankerson*	xiii
	Introduction: Critical Incidents in the Classroom: Realizing CLA and Radical Inclusivity Intersections *Quanisha Charles, Shannon Tanghe, Marie Webb and Gloria Park*	xix

Part 1: What Does Radical Inclusivity Look Like in the Preparation of Undergraduate Writers?

1	Critical Language Awareness (CLA) Reading: Radical (and Rhetorical) Engagement with Texts *Laura Aull and Shawna Shapiro*	3
2	Fictional 'Truths' about Language: Using Creative Fiction for Radical Inclusion and Critical Language Awareness *Sean Oros*	17
3	Toward Radical Inclusivity in First Year Composition: A Lesson for CLA, Translingual Writing and Metacognitive Development *Sophia Minnillo*	30
4	Radically Inclusive Teaching: A Lesson Utilizing the Learning about Written Languages (LaWL) Approach *Marie Webb*	39

Part 2: What Does Radical Inclusivity Look Like in the Preparation of Language and Writing Teachers?

5	Critical Language Awareness and Translingual Pedagogies in the Language Teacher Education Classroom: An Enactment *Havva Zorluel Ozer*	51

6 Linguistic Landscapes, Discussion Forums and *Conscientização*:
   A Pedagogical Ensemble to Address Linguistic Glottonormativity
   in Language Teacher Education   68
   Sílvia Melo-Pfeifer and Vander Tavares

7 Critical Language Awareness in Language Teacher Education:
   How Can Critical Autoethnographic Narrative Help?   84
   Bedrettin Yazan, Ceren Kocaman and Kristen Lindahl

8 Increasing Pre-Service ESOL Teachers' Critical Language
   Awareness through Dialectical Variation   97
   Brian Hibbs

9 Radical Inclusivity in Language Teacher Education:
   Addressing Linguistic Bias and Linguistic Discrimination   111
   Shannon Tanghe

Part 3: What Does Radical Inclusivity Look Like in Community Engagement?

10 Metrolingual Maps: Exploring Multilingual Practices in the
   Community   125
   Nils Olov Fors

11 The Dialogic Griot: Advocating for Communities through
   Story Mapping   136
   Valerie A. Gray

Part 4: What Does Radical Inclusivity Look Like in Institutional and Programmatic Contexts?

12 Exploring NCTE Position Statements as Opportunities for
   Critical Awareness and Inclusivity   155
   Kristene K. McClure and Rodrigo Martinez

13 Trauma-Informed Practice in a Radically Inclusive Classroom   168
   Elizabeth S. Coleman

14 Sparking Critical Awareness of Language Variation, Accent
   and Ideology through an Allyship Approach   181
   Vance Schaefer and Tamara Warhol

15 Partnering with Students with Disabilities: Informed Practices
   and Support Networks   196
   *Abir Ward, Carroll Beauvais, Amy Bennett-Zendzian,
      Jessica Kent and Marie Satya McDonough*

   Afterword: Moving Forward with Shared Understanding and
   Responsibility   212
   *Gloria Park, Quanisha Charles, Shannon Tanghe
      and Marie Webb*

   Index   216

Contributors

Editors

Quanisha Charles https://orcid.org/0000-0001-5875-2924
is an Associate Professor of English, teaching first-year writing seminars and linguistic courses at North Central College in Naperville, IL. She has more than 15 years of experience teaching EFL, ESL, and Composition Studies collectively in the US, South Korea, China, Vietnam, and virtually in Lebanon. Her research interests include critical digital theory, racialized ideologies, intercultural communication, and teacher identity in English language education. Her publications can be found in the *TESOL Journal*, *International Journal of Language Arts and Linguistics* and the *Journal of English Language Teaching and Linguistics*.

Gloria Park https://orcid.org/0000-0001-8759-7564
is a Professor in the Graduate Studies in Composition & Applied Linguistics at Indiana University of Pennsylvania. Her teaching and scholarship focus broadly in the areas of language teacher identities as they connect to teacher agency and practices. Her work appears in internationally recognized journals such as *TESOL Quarterly*, *TESOL Journal*, *Journal of Language, Identity and Education*, *Race, Ethnicity and Education*, *ELT Journal*, and *L2 Journal*. She has co-edited special themed issues in *TESOL Quarterly* (2016) and in *TESOL Journal* (2014, 2023). Her monograph, *Narratives of East Asian Women Teachers of English: Where Privilege Meets Marginalization*, was published in 2017 by Multilingual Matters. Gloria served as a section editor for *TESOL Journal* (2010–2015), and in 2015, she edited the Teacher Education and Professional Development volume of *TESOL-Wiley English Language Teaching Encyclopedia* (2017). In 2023, Gloria co-edited *Critical Pedagogy in Language and Writing Classroom*, published by Routledge. Gloria continues to serve the Fulbright Office as a national screener for ETA applications to South Korea, and in 2023, she was invited to facilitate a workshop with over 300+ Foreign Language Teaching Associates sponsored by Fulbright/Institute of International Education.

Shannon Tanghe https://orcid.org/0000-0001-8759-7564
is an Assistant Professor in ESL teacher education in the School of Urban Education at Metro State University in Minneapolis, MN. Shannon has

taught in several countries, including 16 years in teacher education in South Korea. Her main research interests include teacher education/collaboration, reflective teacher inquiry, and World Englishes.

Marie Webb https://orcid.org/0000-0002-4950-4336
is a continuing lecturer in the English for the Multilingual Students program and the TESOL minor in the Department of Linguistics at the University of California at Santa Barbara. Her research interests include TESOL leadership, critical language pedagogies, professional identities of applied linguistics and L2 writing teacher-scholars/language teacher identity, flipped classroom instruction, and online/CALL/TELL instruction. Outside of California, Marie has taught in South Korea, Macau, China and Japan in a variety of English language, writing, and teacher education programs.

Authors

Laura Aull https://orcid.org/0000-0001-8306-1180
is Professor of English and Director of the English Department Writing Program at the University of Michigan. She is the author, most recently, of *How Students Write: A Linguistic Analysis* (MLA, 2020) and *You Can't Write That: 8 Myths about Correct English* (Cambridge UP, 2024).

Carroll Beauvais https://orcid.org/0009-0009-5627-7504
and First-Year Writing Studio Coordinator in Kilachand Honors College at Boston University. She is interested in expanding inclusion and accommodations to include strength-based supports, eschewing the traditional deficit model. She is the author of the poetry collection *Preverbal* (Lit Fox Books, 2025).

Amy Bennett-Zendzian https://orcid.org/0009-0006-0312-1440
is a Lecturer and Writing Center Coordinator in the Writing Program at Boston University, where she teaches first-year writing and research seminars on fairy tales. She writes about children's and young adult literature, and recently co-authored (with Theodora Goss) a chapter in the collection *Fairy Tales in the College Classroom*.

Elizabeth S. Coleman https://orcid.org/0000-0002-9227-7984
took an unusual route into language teaching arriving in ELT with a background in gender and environmental activism. She has a special interest in diversifying classroom practice and views education as a socially transformative tool. Elizabeth engages in research around social constructions, gender, and minority representation.

Nils Olov Fors https://orcid.org/0009-0006-5990-0347
has taught writing, linguistics, and pedagogy for over 20 years at universities in the US, China, South Korea, Sweden, Vietnam and Japan, and works with internationalization of higher education, cross-cultural pedagogy, and academic practices. Olaf is currently teaching at Kanda University of International Studies in Japan.

Valerie A. Gray https://orcid.org/0009-0001-2464-3647
is Professor of English at Harrisburg Area Community College, teaching courses in composition, business writing, technical writing, professional writing, and literature. Additionally, she is an author, presenter, and consultant, focusing on topics that pertain to belonging, diversity, equity, inclusion, English studies, history, and technology.

Shenika Hankerson https://orcid.org/0000-0003-0496-8417
is Assistant Professor of Applied Linguistics and Language Education in the Department of Teaching and Learning, Policy and Leadership at the University of Maryland-College Park. Her research explores the intersection of race, language, equity, and justice with a focus on Black Language and college writing.

Brian Hibbs https://orcid.org/0009-0005-0894-1555
is an Associate Professor of Education/ESOL at Dalton State College, USA. He teaches courses in applied linguistics, language teaching methodology, and culture and education. His scholarly interests include children's and adolescent literature, educator preparation, faculty development, intercultural competence, second language acquisition, study abroad, and teacher research.

Jessica Kent https://orcid.org/0009-0000-9552-4218
is Senior Lecturer and Associate Director of the Writing Program at Boston University, where they teach writing and research seminars on graphic memoirs. Their research interests include alternative assessment, comics, queer literature, trauma-informed pedagogy, knowledge transfer, and accessibility in higher education.

Ceren Kocaman https://orcid.org/0000-0002-3003-0871
is a lecturer and a PhD candidate in the Department of Teaching English as a Foreign Language at the University of Potsdam, Germany. She has worked with feminist and LGBTQ civil society organizations and as an instructor of academic English prior to her current position. Her current research focuses on critical, identity-oriented language teacher education practices.

Kristen Lindahl https://orcid.org/0000-0003-2123-2743
is an Associate Professor of TESL/Applied Linguistics in the Department of Bicultural-Bilingual Studies at the University of Texas at San Antonio. She has over 20 years of experience working with and preparing educators to work with multilingual students. Lindahl's research focuses on language awareness, content and language integrated learning, and identity approaches to teacher education.

Rodrigo Martinez https://orcid.org/0009-0006-9256-2730
is a Peace Corps Volunteer as an ESL educator at the Universidad Tecnológica de San Juan del Río de Jalpan in Querétaro, México. His study, research, and practical focus at Georgia Gwinnett College revolved around ELA and ESL education, earning him a BA in English Education and TESOL certification.

Kristene K. McClure https://orcid.org/0009-0001-1053-8774
is an Associate Professor of English and Director of the Integrative Studies Program at Georgia Gwinnett College, where she regularly mentors English Language Arts teacher certification candidates and teaches first-year and corequisite college writing, as well as English courses in linguistics, teaching writing, and TESOL, among others.

Marie Satya McDonough https://orcid.org/0009-0006-1520-5932
is a Senior Lecturer in the Writing Program and the Women's, Gender, and Sexuality Studies Program at Boston University. Her research and teaching interests include comics, feminist and gender theory, Indigenous and critical race studies, and equitable assessment. She is the translator of Michel Foucault's *Binswanger and Existential Analysis* (Columbia UP, 2025) and of *Young Foucault* (Columbia UP, 2022).

Sílvia Melo-Pfeifer https://orcid.org/0000-0002-7371-3293
is Full Professor of Foreign Language Teacher Education at the University of Hamburg (Germany). She carries out research on pluralistic approaches to language learning and teaching (with particular emphasis on intercomprehension across languages of the same linguistic family), heritage language education, and foreign language teacher education.

Sophia Minnillo https://orcid.org/0000-0002-8962-7920
is a PhD Candidate at University of California, Davis in Linguistics with an emphasis in Writing, Rhetoric, and Composition Studies. She teaches first year composition and multilingual writing courses, and her research focuses on multilingual writing development and language learning.

Sean Oros https://orcid.org/0009-0007-1597-9804
is a PhD candidate in the Composition and Applied Linguistics Program at Indiana University of Pennsylvania. He currently serves as a Lecturer

of English and Coordinator of the First-Year Curriculum at Thiel College. He teaches first year composition and creative writing courses, and his research and pedagogy focus on combining narrative theory and growth mindset in composition classrooms.

Havva Zorluel Ozer https://orcid.org/0000-0003-2919-0613
is an Assistant Teaching Professor in the Department of Writing Studies, Rhetoric, and Composition at Syracuse University. Her research focuses on translanguaging practices in writing and language ideologies within the discourses of language and literacy education.

Vance Schaefer https://orcid.org/0000-0002-4801-7114
is an Associate Professor of Applied Linguistics and TESOL in the Department of Modern Languages at the University of Mississippi. His work focuses on second language phonology (accent), pronunciation pedagogy, teaching language variation, and translation pedagogy.

Shawna Shapiro https://orcid.org/0000-0001-7080-6649
is Professor of Writing and Linguistics at Middlebury College in Vermont (USA). Her research focuses on college transitions and innovative pedagogies for multilingual/L2 writers. Shapiro has published in numerous peer-reviewed journals and her latest book is *Cultivating Critical Language Awareness in the Writing Classroom* (Routledge, 2022). http://clacollective.org/

Shannon Tanghe https://orcid.org/0000-0001-8759-7564
is an Assistant Professor in ESL teacher education in the School of Urban Education at Metro State University in Minneapolis, MN. Shannon has taught in several countries, including 16 years in teacher education in South Korea. Her main research interests include teacher education/collaboration, reflective teacher inquiry, and World Englishes.

Vander Tavares https://orcid.org/0000-0002-9954-4141
is an Associate Professor of Education at Inland Norway University of Applied Sciences and holds a PhD from York University, Canada. His research interests include language teacher education, critical second language education, and the internationalization of higher education.

Abir Ward https://orcid.org/0000-0002-7234-4289
Before joining Boston University's College of Arts and Sciences Writing Program in 2022, Dr Ward taught at the American University of Beirut (AUB), where she led the editorial team for a 700-page academic reader and founded 2Rāth, a social justice initiative focused on the politics of representation. Her research focuses on justice-oriented pedagogy.

Marie Webb https://orcid.org/0000-0002-4950-4336
is a continuing lecturer in the English for the Multilingual Students program and the TESOL minor in the Department of Linguistics at the University of California at Santa Barbara. Her research interests include TESOL leadership, critical language pedagogies, professional identities of applied linguistics and L2 writing teacher-scholars/language teacher identity, flipped classroom instruction, and online/CALL/TELL instruction. Outside of California, Marie has taught in South Korea, Macau, China and Japan in a variety of English language, writing, and teacher education programs.

Tamara Warhol https://orcid.org/0000-0002-1955-5909
is an Associate Professor of Applied Linguistics and TESOL in the Department of Modern Languages at the University of Mississippi. A discourse analyst, her research explores professional discourse, language variation, language and linguistics pedagogy, and language teacher education.

Bedrettin Yazan https://orcid.org/0000-0002-1888-1120
is a Professor in the Department of Bicultural-Bilingual Studies at the University of Texas at San Antonio. His research focuses on language teacher learning and identity, collaboration between ESL and content teachers, language policy and planning, and world Englishes. Methodologically he is interested in critical autoethnography, narrative inquiry, and qualitative case study.

Foreword: Seeds of Transformation: The Power of Critical Language Awareness and Radical Inclusivity

Shawna Shapiro and Shenika Hankerson

> *All of us in the academy and in the culture as a whole are called to renew our minds if we are to transform educational institutions—and society—so that the way we live, teach, and work can reflect our joy in cultural diversity, our passion for justice, and our love of freedom.* (bell hooks, *Teaching to Transgress* [1994]: 34)

> *[We need] to perpetuate and foster—to sustain—linguistic, literate, and cultural pluralism as part of the democratic project of schooling, and as a needed response to demographic and social change.* (Django Paris & H. Samy Alim, 2014: 88)

We were delighted to accept the invitation from the editors of this volume to write a Foreword that would frame some of the concepts, issues, and questions that undergird the work in this groundbreaking collection. We teach at very different types of institutions: Shawna is at a small, liberal arts college, while Shenika works at a large, public university. But we both have found ways to incorporate Critical Language Awareness (CLA) pedagogy into writing courses that include students from a range of language backgrounds, including multilingual immigrant and international students, as well as multidialectal students from US Communities of Color. We have also incorporated CLA into our curriculum development, professional learning for teachers and administrators, and other institutional service and leadership work.

We have structured this Foreword around three guiding questions:

(1) What are the historical and ideological roots for CLA as an intellectual movement and pedagogical approach?
(2) How does CLA intersect with the concept of radical inclusivity?
(3) What are some common features of CLA approaches to writing/language education?

We hope that our exploration of these questions deepens the learning experience for readers and inspires them to take up CLA in their own work toward diversity, equity, and (radical) inclusion in the classroom and beyond.

(1) The Roots of CLA

The term 'Critical Language Awareness' was coined in the late 1980s by linguists and literacy specialists in the United Kingdom who were looking to bring insights about the social and political aspects of language into writing/literacy curricula (Carter, 1997; James, 1999; Janks, 2010). Part of what motivated that work was the publication of the UK's first National Curriculum for public schools in 1988, which stipulated that 'knowledge about language' should be included in the (L1 or 'mother tongue') English curriculum – i.e. what US educators usually call 'English Language Arts'. A group of experts convened by Parliament to flesh out this portion of the new curriculum chose to put forth a new vision for English education: They knew that notions of 'correctness' with language are often overly simplistic and often harmful to multilingual and multidialectal students. They wanted teachers and students to understand how language, identity, power, and privilege intersect. In other words, they wanted all students to develop Critical Language Awareness, or CLA.

Sadly, most of the politicians saw this vision as too radical, and so CLA was never fully integrated into the UK's English curriculum at the national level. (For a more detailed account of how all of this played out, see Chapter 3 of Carter, 1997, and Chapter 2 of Shapiro, 2022). However, CLA became the impetus for an intellectual and pedagogical movement, taken up in a variety of contexts, including L1 education, English to Speakers of Other Languages (ESOL), world/heritage language instruction, and language/writing teacher education. Representations of the range of CLA work can be found in Fairclough (1992/2014) and Lorimer Leonard and Shapiro (2023), as well as in the current volume.

Ideologically, CLA tends to straddle a pragmatic and a progressive orientation, teaching what students need to be successful in schools and society as they exist today while also working actively toward more equitable and inclusive schools and society for the future (see Pennycook, 1997, for more on this ideological orientation). Shapiro (2024, forthcoming) has identified four central values and goals from pedagogical case studies, building on work from Janks (2000, 2010) and other CLA scholars:

- **Access:** Helping students to understand how language works in their lives and how power operates in and through language.
- **Agency:** Preparing all students to use language in powerful ways, to achieve their academic, professional, and civic goals and potential.

- **Asset:** Recognizing and building on the linguistic experiences and resources that each student and teacher brings to the classroom.
- **Advocacy:** Understanding how educational structures, policies, and practices can be harmful to students from multilingual and multidialectal backgrounds and working toward transformational change.

The values of access and agency remind us not to lose sight of students' real-world goals and needs when it comes to language/writing instruction. The values of asset and advocacy are aimed at changing our classrooms, programs, and institutions to promote linguistic justice, which is of course tied to other forms of social justice.

(2) CLA and Radical Inclusivity

CLA offers many pedagogical affordances that can facilitate a more culturally, racially, and linguistically just educational environment. One of these affordances is the promotion of radical inclusion, which has been conceptualized by Sengeh (2023) as a transformative approach that ensures persistent inclusion and positive experiences for *all* students in *all* aspects of education. This approach seeks to fundamentally transform and reshape the educational experience to make it more inclusive and truly welcoming for all. To achieve this vision there must be deliberate efforts to include individuals who have been historically excluded from education – exclusion that can be traced back to choices made by people, intentionally or unintentionally, that lead to unjust societal norms or institutional policies and practices. The overarching goal of radical inclusion (or radical inclusivity) is to ensure that everyone is fully and meaningfully seen, heard, and counted in education and ultimately, in society.

Teachers, administrators, and other staff committed to radical inclusivity work actively and intentionally to foster a more democratic and equitable learning environment for all students. They seek to remove barriers that prevent full participation for historically marginalized groups, such as material inequities (e.g. lack of necessary resources), structural opportunity gaps (e.g. policies and program structures that hinder access for some students), and deficit-oriented pedagogies that overlook the aspirations and assets of certain groups of students (e.g. Carter & Welner, 2013; Shapiro, 2014). But even more so, they seek to build learning spaces and school cultures where those barriers do not exist in the first place, so that all students feel valued, respected, and supported, regardless of their backgrounds. In this larger commitment, radical inclusivity intersects with critical pedagogy, social justice education, and decolonizing methodologies, highlighting the need for institutions and educators to challenge and transform the norms and structures that perpetuate systemic inequality in education. Some of the most prominent scholarship on writing, literacy, and language education promotes such a radical and transformative vision, including work by Alim *et al.* (2016), Haddix (2015), and Paris and Alim (2017), among others.

Bringing CLA and radical inclusivity together helps to ensure that teachers, administrators, and students understand the role of *language* as a factor in educational equity and justice work. CLA aims to disrupt persistent and systemic linguistic inequities in educational environments, whereas radical inclusivity seeks to transform these environments to fully include *all* students in all aspects of schooling, especially students from historically marginalized and oppressed groups. Together, CLA and radical inclusivity ensure that all students – regardless of their language, as well as of their race, culture, ethnicity, gender, sexuality, class, ability, or any other characteristic – have equitable and just access to educational opportunities and resources.

(3) Features of a CLA Approach to Writing/Language Education

Now that we have defined and linked our central concepts, we turn to questions of pedagogical praxis: What are the foundational features of a CLA approach to writing/language education? Below are five key features that are most salient in extant scholarship and are also visible throughout this collection.

A CLA approach…

- **Applies to a wide range of educational contexts**: As noted earlier, CLA pedagogy has been taken up in a wide range of educational contexts. It has been used with both children and adults, and in primary, secondary, postsecondary, and even professional education classrooms around the world (Fairclough, 1992/2014; Lorimer Leonard & Shapiro, 2023). This volume alone includes case studies from college composition (with both L1 and L2 writers), English as Foreign Language (EFL), and language/literacy teacher education. Authors in this collection are also working in a variety of geographic and demographic settings: Germany, Japan, and several regions of the United States.
- **Affects both macro and micro levels of instruction:** One of the affordances of a CLA approach is that it has relevance to all aspects of instruction, from lesson planning to curriculum design to teacher professional development and institutional advocacy work. All of these components of educational work must be considered, in fact, in order to achieve the vision for radical inclusivity outlined above. The current collection reflects this versatility, offering case studies of educational innovation at the level of assignments and activities, as well as broader curricular, programmatic, and institutional approaches.

- **Centers both students' immediate goals and long-term transformational change:** Although long-term, systemic change is a key objective for a CLA approach with the goal of radical inclusivity, practitioners need a 'both/and' orientation that does not lose sight of students' more immediate academic, professional, and civic aspirations. We can see this progressive yet pragmatic orientation in many of the instructional activities presented in this collection, including self-reflection (for both students and teachers), textual and linguistic analysis, storytelling and story-mapping, place-based projects, and other forms of experiential learning and embodiment. These pedagogical innovations increase students' access and agency in pursuing their goals, while also increasing our own efficacy in recognizing student assets and advocating for equity, inclusion, and justice.
- **Builds on other research-based pedagogical practices**: A CLA approach does not replace other approaches and commitments that inform our teaching. CLA meshes well, in fact, with universal/inclusive design, culturally and linguistically sustaining (or responsive) instruction, antiracist pedagogy, and other social justice pedagogies, bringing a more explicit focus on *language* within those approaches.

    We (the Authors) have done this meshing work in many of our own courses: For example, Shawna teaches writing courses that include high numbers of multilingual/L2 writers. She has found in her research that integrating CLA into English for Academic Purposes (EAP) courses helps to deepen students' understanding of the origin and power of academic literacy conventions, so that those students are better prepared to decide *for themselves* when (and how) to follow or resist those conventions (e.g. Shapiro, 2022, forthcoming; Aull & Shapiro, this volume). In her own courses, which include high numbers of Black Language speakers, Shenika weaves CLA and Afrocentricity, as a way to honor, value, and center those students' social and cultural linguistic experiences. Her research has found that the integration of these two approaches helps to foster Black Language users' critical consciousness about the rhetorics, discourses, and grammars available to them, resulting in stronger college writing skills and better overall well-being (see e.g. Hankerson & Obiri-Yeboah, 2024; Hankerson *et al.*, 2024). Both of us have also integrated CLA into professional development workshops and teacher education courses – an endeavor exemplified in many of the chapters in this collection as well.

We hope that this chapter has provided helpful grounding for engaging with the remainder of this volume. Moreover, we hope it has inspired readers to take up CLA and radical inclusivity in their own pedagogical praxis. There is much work to be done, and collections like this one remind us that we do not do that work alone. Onward!

References

Alim, H.S., Rickford, J. and Ball, A. (eds) (2016) *Raciolinguistics: How Language Shapes Our Ideas about Race*. Oxford University Press.
Carter, R. (1997) *Investigating English Discourse: Language, Literacy and Literature (Chapter 3: Politics and knowledge about language: The LINC project)*. Routledge.
Carter, P.L. and Welner, K.G. (eds) (2013) *Closing the Opportunity Gap: What America Must Do to Give Every Child an Even Chance*. Oxford University Press.
Fairclough, N. (1992/2014) *Critical Language Awareness*. Routledge.
Haddix, M.M. (2015) *Cultivating Racial and Linguistic Diversity in Literacy Teacher Education: Teachers Like Me*. Routledge.
Hankerson, S. and Obiri-Yeboah, M.A. (2024) Language, ideologies, discrimination, and Afrocentric-focused, critical language awareness writing curricula for African American Language and Akan Language speakers. In C. Shei and J. Schnell (eds) *The Routledge Handbook of Language and Mind Engineering* (pp. 404–417). Routledge.
Hankerson, S., Martin, K., Charity Hudley, A. and Mallinson, C. (2024) Critical metalinguistics in U.S. writing instruction: Fostering linguistic agency for Black Language users. In R. Love and P. Proctor (eds) *Pursuing Language and Metalinguistic Awareness in K-12 Classrooms: A Framework for Critical Engagement* (pp. 67–82). Routledge. https://doi.org/10.4324/9781003334804
hooks, b. (1994) *Teaching to Transgress: Education as the Practice of Freedom*. Routledge.
James, S. (1999) Language awareness: Implications for the language curriculum. *Language, Culture and Curriculum* 12 (1), 94–115.
Janks, H. (2000) Domination, access, diversity and design: A synthesis for critical literacy education. *Educational Review* 52 (2), 175–186.
Janks, H. (2010) *Literacy and Power*. Routledge.
Lorimer Leonard, R. and Shapiro, S. (eds) (2023) Critical Language Awareness as a lens for looking backward, outward, and forward in L2 writing. *Special issue of the Journal of Second Language Writing* 60 (1).
Paris, D. and Alim, H.S. (2014) What are we seeking to sustain through culturally sustaining pedagogy? A loving critique forward. *Harvard Educational Review* 84 (1), 85–100.
Paris, D. and Alim, H.S. (eds) (2017) *Culturally Sustaining Pedagogies: Teaching and Learning for Justice in a Changing World*. Teachers College Press.
Pennycook, A. (1997) Vulgar pragmatism, critical pragmatism, and EAP. *English for Specific Purposes* 16 (4), 253–269.
Sengeh, D. (2023) *Radical Inclusion: Seven Steps to Help You Create a More Just Workplace, Home, and World*. Flatiron Books.
Shapiro, S. (2014) 'Words that you said got bigger': English language learners' lived experiences of deficit discourse. *Research in the Teaching of English* 48 (4), 386–406.
Shapiro, S. (2022) *Cultivating Critical Language Awareness in the Writing Classroom*. Routledge.
Shapiro, S. (2024) Access, asset, agency, and advocacy: Four pillars of linguistic and cultural inclusion in higher education. *Language, Culture, Justice, and Hub* (July). https://lcjh.bard.edu/july-2024-access-asset-agency-and-advocacy-four-pillars-of-linguistic-and-cultural-inclusion-in-higher-education/
Shapiro, S. (forthcoming) Unpacking the 'C' in CLA: Enacting our commitment to linguistic access, asset, and agency. *Journal of Multilingual Theories and Practices*.

Introduction: Critical Incidents in the Classroom: Realizing CLA and Radical Inclusivity Intersections

Quanisha Charles, Shannon Tanghe, Marie Webb and Gloria Park

The inspiration for this book originated through an example of a radically inclusive action. It began with three mentees and a mentor who have become co-collaborators. Three of the co-editors (Quanisha, Shannon and Marie) had all been doctoral students and mentees of Gloria Park at different times. In 2020, Gloria first brought us together by inviting us to collaborate on a book chapter on female leadership identity in TESOL. As we were becoming more comfortable with each other, we engaged in a duoethnographic study where we each posed specific questions to one another. As we asked, responded, questioned, reflected and grew, we quickly learned from each other and also discovered our shared passions and commitments to fostering radically inclusive environments where all learners, and particularly multilingual learners, were encouraged to thrive and grow. As we collaborated on writing projects and presentations, we engaged deeper in critical reflexivity about our identity construction as female leaders in applied linguistics and TESOL in order to reimagine ourselves as collective and embodied leaders (Webb *et al.*, 2024).

Studying our critical reflexive practices led us to understand our shared goal of enacting humanizing practices, such as creating mentoring opportunities to help increase the visibility of our teaching, scholarship, and service early on in our academic careers. We then set out to further explore this shared goal by studying how our intentions intersect with our personal and professional identities. We detailed our lived experiences of how our native intersections, colonial contestation, and combative dispositions toward relations of power brought us closer to our individual and collective goals (Charles *et al.*, 2024). We considered ways we are practicing what we preach and engaging in antiracist, trauma-informed, critical language awareness in our own classrooms and what that might entail in classrooms around the world, and also how we are living up to our proposed next steps (Webb *et al.*, 2024). These reflections challenged us to consider how we are endeavoring humanizing practices as leaders within the TESOL discipline. As we collectively and individually become more aware of possibility, we continue to try new endeavors, sharing with each other what we do and its impact, both on learners, as well as ourselves.

Quanisha began leading curriculum development, critical thinking, and inclusive learning workshops for Lebanese English teachers. In doing so, she began considering what it means to practice inclusivity in virtual contexts and also learned the many ways in which concepts of inclusivity are challenged and conceptualized within a context in the Middle East. Furthermore, Quanisha started understanding that the work she puts forward stems from her philosophy of L.O.V.E. (Charles, 2024) and built upon this concept in her teaching and multilingual leadership endeavors. Specifically, these endeavors may include not only championing epistemologies and foresight of nonnative speakers but also working alongside nonnative speakers to co-create epistemologies and best practices.

Shannon began returning to South Korea each summer, a place where she had lived and taught for 16 years, in order to reconnect with a global initiative for university students from around the world. As she leads courses on English language teaching she is intentionally exploring what radical inclusivity looks like at the global level while preparing students for the complex intersectionalities associated with transnational English language teaching.

Marie joined a language program leadership certificate course and cross-campus DEI co-mentorship to bring about further collaborations inside her department regarding the curriculum and development of DEIB initiatives. This formal mentoring opportunity inspired several other co-mentorships including one to implement and study the teaching of decolonized ELT perspectives in her introductory TESOL course as well as a co-mentorship on equitable assessment of writing for students and second language (L2) writing teachers. She also co-mentored and collaborated with a colleague to design a collaborative podcast paper for multilingual students utilizing a critical language awareness (CLA) lens.

Gloria has taken on more intentional mentoring roles, helping teachers and scholars to continue expanding their teacher-scholar identities. She recently co-authored a journal article to define intentional mentorship practices by exploring her lived experiences as language teacher educator alongside her mentees. She has encouraged us all to further engage with the authors of this edited book by supporting us in collaborative conference proposals of how we are integrating CLA-informed instruction and DEIB perspectives into our teaching.

At the core of our collaborations have been ongoing question chains. We first began by creating formal questions, asking and sharing our beliefs, processes, ways of knowing, and enactments of these in our classrooms. As we dialogued, new questions emerged. How do we invite and live these principles and pedagogies in our classrooms? Our professional and personal lives? What does it look like to be radically inclusive in school communities? How and from whom can we learn more about this? How can we share what we are learning? We recognize that many colleagues have been going through similar collaborative endeavors to reinvigorate their courses with equitable and inclusive pedagogies and materials. At the same time, we acknowledge that opportunities for increasing the visibility of our radical approaches to education in our language and writing classrooms remain limited, especially for early career colleagues. Without the leadership and coaching of early teacher-scholar applied linguistics and writing studies professionals, our voices and exceptional materials often remain confined within our classrooms and academic contexts. On occasion, some of us have the privilege of taking a break from our busy academic lives to attend conferences or workshops where DEIB theory and practice are bridged. At these presentations or within smaller communities of practice we may dive deep into the materials we have created and explored within our classrooms. More often than not though, our lessons remain confined to our classrooms, and the literature on reducing colonial harm and engaging in critical self-reflexive practices often remains focused on theory.

What Does it Mean to be Radically Inclusive?

Through our dialogues, we (Gloria, Quanisha, Marie and Shannon) all shared critical incidents that prompted us to embark on this journey of embracing radically inclusive teaching. In spring of 2023, we gathered together for a four-day writing retreat. During this time we continued talking, questioning, and reflecting. We recognized the ways our own community-building had opened new doors and perspectives for us, and began to envision how much more we could learn and grow from a larger community. As we dug deeper into our own visions and ideas, we wanted to seek insights and to learn from a broader community of educators also engaging with this work. Before the retreat was over, we had drafted and opened a call for proposals for the book with the shared goal of bringing multilingual advocates from all stages of their academic lives together to bridge the theory-to-practice divide and showcase various ways of creating engaging classroom lessons and activities to embrace radical inclusivity and critical language awareness in their contexts. In our call for proposals, we drew upon the Chief Minister of Sierra Leone David Moinina Sengeh's (2023) framework of radical inclusion that was guided by seven principles:

(1) Identify the exclusion.
(2) Listen, to understand and learn.
(3) Define your role – why you, why now?
(4) Build a coalition.
(5) Advocacy and action.
(6) Adapting to a new normal.
(7) Beyond inclusion (always working further to identify the next exclusion, working towards a more just society by identifying new areas of exclusion and dismantling them through radical inclusion).

These guiding principles aligned with the work we had been doing and piqued our interest in studying more about what this means for connecting with communities and people via CLA specifically in the language and writing classroom. For example, in Sengeh's book he discusses how individuals often engage in social 'code-switching' in which they change who they are, how they talk, dress, or show up, *'so they can feel seen and feel a sense of belonging'* (2023: 9). Yet this solution carries a high emotional cost, and it is a temporary solution to a permanent problem – a problem that may look differently according to the individual – that requires identifying the inclusion to sustain inclusivity. This guiding framework emphasizes a commitment to continually identifying and addressing individuals' unique concerns in order to dismantle exclusions and foster a community where each individual can feel a growing sense of belongingness. Our working definition of radical inclusivity refers to an approach that aims to fully include and value all individuals, particularly those from marginalized or historically excluded groups. It involves not just accommodating diversity but fundamentally rethinking systems, practices, and structures to ensure that everyone is genuinely recognized and included.

As language teacher educators, we wanted to merge these concepts of radical inclusivity specifically with critical language awareness, 'to focus on the intersections of language, identity, power, and privilege, with the goal of promoting self-reflection, social justice, and rhetorical agency' (Shapiro, 2022: 4). Radical inclusivity explores the vital role of CLA in fostering inclusive language and writing practices within the classroom. The purpose of this edited book is to share a collection of chapters that blend theory and practice to share the how's and why's of radical inclusivity in the language and writing classroom through real examples of educators who are doing this work. Broadly, this edited collection seeks to highlight the experiences and practices of global K-20 teachers and teacher educators by sharing the many ways they promote these radically inclusive practices in their classrooms. 'Radical inclusion is radical because it involves a commitment to intentional and persistent action and seeks to help all people who have been excluded, directly or indirectly, due to the tides of history, current actions or inactions, unjust laws, systemic inequities, or reasons that are hard to pinpoint but nonetheless exist' (Sengeh, 2023: 12). Because these systems of inequity manifest in different ways and across different spectrums, as language teachers, we sought to explore what our colleagues are doing in the classroom to tackle these systems of oppression to bring forth awareness and/or action.

What does this look like in our classrooms? How do we share this information with others? Do we? Can we do more?

In our last collaborative book chapter (Charles *et al.*, 2024), we ended by recognizing the need to do more to share this information, and intend for this book to be a step forward in that direction. We know there are many doing this work and this book highlights specific theory-to-practice examples in a variety of contexts. We believe that by dialoguing about our intersectional identities first, we were able to come to new understandings of ourselves as multilingual advocates. This transformative practice of engaging in a duoethnography ultimately led to our shared goals for this book to further understand how we define and enact radical inclusivity in and beyond our classroom spaces.

But how does teaching writing and language classes actually dismantle exclusions and work beyond advocacy and action through students' work?

As we practice radical inclusivity in classroom teaching contexts, we feel hopeful and inspired by the extensions we see occurring as students embrace this into their own lives. We see students questioning normalized assumptions and practices, and asking more questions.

- Why do we insist on 'English only' classrooms?
- ¿Por qué las familias y los padres no se sienten bienvenidos en el aula? '(*Why don't families and parents feel welcome in the classroom*')?
- How do I show others I value multilingualism as an asset?
- Why are many still resisting the normalization of pronoun use in classrooms, despite the clear need for respect and inclusivity toward diverse gender identities?

Guiding Questions for Readers

This edited book is our effort at organizing ourselves as female co-editors, into an intentional community of practice to help us grow alongside other language and writing teachers. bell hooks (2018) reminds us that both love and healing are best learned and practiced in community with others rather than in isolation. We believe there is no better place to learn the art of loving our students and our colleagues than in a community of radical inclusivity. It is our hope that this book is one effort of many to share that commitment with the community.

As we began and continue our own learning journeys based on questioning and inquiry-based approaches, we invite readers to consider these questions while engaging with the experiences of the teacher-scholars throughout the book:

- How does CLA intersect with radical inclusivity in your own context?
- What can you do to strengthen this connection?

Contributors and Contributions

Anchored by the foundational Foreword by Shawna Shapiro and Shenika Hankerson, alongside the Introduction, we briefly introduce the contributors and their work in promoting radical inclusivity.

Part 1: What Does Radical Inclusivity Look Like in the Preparation of Undergraduate Writers?

In Chapters 1, 2, 3 and 4, authors argue that undergraduate writing courses become a fertile ground for introducing critical language awareness and radical inclusivity. In Chapter 1, **Laura Aull and Shawna Shapiro** offer a rationale and case study for rhetorical reading with a CLA lens, integrating both sociocultural and linguistic levels of text used in undergraduate writing courses. In **Chapter 2, Sean Oros** focuses on using creative fiction assignments to challenge the Standard American English (SAE) ideology, a pedagogical strategy of building critical language awareness (CLA) into an existing course. Within the context of first year composition (FYC) lessons, **Chapter 3** by **Sophia Minnillo** argues for the effective utility of pedagogical practices that support students' development of three areas: CLA, translingual writing strategies, and metacognition. In **Chapter 4, Marie Webb** introduces the Learning about Written Languages (LaWL) Approach, which is grounded in CLA. Specifically, Webb designs a collaborative writing podcast script about students' learning of social inequities via a CLA lens.

Part 2: What Does Radical Inclusivity Look Like in the Preparation of Language and Writing Teachers?

In Chapters 5, 6, 7, 8 and 9, the authors discuss the ways that teacher education courses can guide teacher candidates to reflect further on what it means to practice inclusivity in their own practices. **Chapter 5** by **Havva Zorluel Ozer** chronicles a teacher educator's journey in working with teacher candidates to promote activities designed to deconstruct their socialization into dominant ideologies and foster their critical engagement with language. In **Chapter 6, Sílvia Melo-Pfeifer** and **Vander Tavares** argue for the pedagogical potential of the linguistic landscape in developing student teachers' criticality lens, specifically linguistic glottonormativity. In **Chapter 7** authored by **Bedrettin Yazan, Ceren Kocaman** and **Kristen Lindahl**, they argue for using critical autoethnographic narrative (CAN) as a form of radical inclusivity. In particular, the authors use CAN to pedagogize identity in language teacher education and highlight how the personal is also political. In **Chapter 8, Brian Hibbs** designs lesson plans outlining linguistic variation using the following concepts: inclusivity, radicality, critical language awareness, and heteroglossia. **Chapter 9** by **Shannon Tanghe** describes pedagogical activities that embed CLA and radical inclusivity into language teacher preparation, highlighting their impact on language teachers, their identities and practices.

Part 3: What Does Radical Inclusivity Look Like in Community Engagement?

Chapters 10 and 11 argue that our communities can become a space for learning about a diverse set of linguistic resources – a place-based learning as part of radical inclusivity.

In **Chapter 10, Nils Olov Fors** introduces Metrolingual Maps as a course project for students to seek out linguistic resources in their communities, thereby finding ways to navigate a diverse sociolinguistic landscape. **Chapter 11** by **Valerie Gray** also focuses on students' communities via a transformative dialogic assignment that uses Esri/ArcGIS StoryMap as the cornerstone media in an undergraduate African American literature course.

Part 4: What Does Radical Inclusivity Look Like in Institutional and Programmatic Contexts?

Chapters 12, 13, 14 and 15 challenge how educators can work toward building more inclusivity and criticality in institutional and programmatic contexts. **Kristene K. McClure** and **Rodrigo Martinez** in **Chapter 12** focus on critiquing NCTE position statements as part of a teacher education course assignment. Through the design of integrated activities, student teachers are encouraged to explore those that prioritize links between critical language awareness and DEI considerations such as race, gender, sexual orientation, and language status. In **Chapter 13, Elizabeth Coleman** presents an activity that allows learners to share their truths and represent their authentic selves, which serves to bring together trauma-informed methods as radical inclusive positioning. **Vance Schaefer** and **Tamara Warhol** in **Chapter 14** describe an Allyship Approach as part of radical inclusivity, specifically connecting the pedagogical practices in language variation, accent, and ideology around Englishes. In the **final chapter,**

Abir Ward, Carroll Beauvais, Amy Bennett-Zendzian, Jessica Kent and **Marie Satya McDonough,** faculty in the Writing Program at Boston University, argue for a more inclusive learning environment where all constituents of a university can explore how inclusive practices and support networks can be improved through informed strategies – specifically highlighting the importance of universal design, trauma-informed pedagogy, and self-care practices. We now turn to the chapters.

References

Charles, Q. (2024) Transnational Black feminism: L.O.V.E. as a practice of freedom, equity, and justice in English language teaching. *TESOL Journal* 15(1), e831. https://doi.org/10.1002/tesj.831

Charles, Q., Tanghe, S., Webb, M. and Park, G. (2024) Intersectionality as a duo-ethnographic process: Four transnational English language teachers (re)storying critical incidents as multilingual leaders. In E. Trinh, L.C. de Oliviera and A. Fuad Selvi (eds) *Multilingual Leadership in TESOL* (pp. 153–171). Routledge.

hooks, b. (2018) *All About Love*. New Visions.

Sengeh, D.M. (2023) *Radical Inclusion: Seven Steps to Help You Create a More Just Workplace, Home, and World*. Flatiron Books.

Shapiro, S. (2022) *Cultivating Critical Language Awareness in the Writing Classroom* (1st edn). Routledge.

Webb, M., Charles, Q., Henderson-Lee, S., Tanghe, S. and Park, G. (2024) Reimagining women leadership in TESOL: Advocating for change, harnessing reflexivity, and humanizing practices. In D. Rashed and D. Suarez (eds) *Reimagining Influence in TESOL: Global Perspectives on Female Leadership Identity* (pp. 109–131). Brill.

Part 1

What Does Radical Inclusivity Look Like in the Preparation of Undergraduate Writers?

Part I

What Does Radical Inclusivity
Look Like in the Preparation
of Undergraduate Writers?

1 Critical Language Awareness (CLA) Reading: Radical (and Rhetorical) Engagement with Texts

Laura Aull and Shawna Shapiro

Introduction

Though it is not a new approach, critical language awareness (CLA) pedagogy is gaining visibility in writing studies as a radically inclusive approach to literacy learning. As Smitherman (2017: 10) explains it, CLA pedagogy 'seeks to develop in students a critical consciousness about language, power, and society' through fostering students' awareness of the stakes of language attitudes and policies and through imparting knowledge about students' own language, including its social and linguistic rules. Shapiro (2022) describes CLA pedagogy in writing classrooms similarly, as an approach that promotes self-reflection, social justice, and rhetorical agency.

One important way that CLA fosters inclusion is in its commitment to unpacking and challenging standardized language norms and ideologies. It is equally a way to foster rhetorical agency, so that student writers learn to make informed language choices and to evaluate the choices of others. Thus, CLA calls for a stance of criticality toward academic literacy vis-à-vis both reading and writing.

Nevertheless, much of the pedagogical scholarship on CLA to date has emphasized writing more heavily than reading (e.g. di Gennaro *et al.*, 2023; Lorimer Leonard, 2021; Shapiro, 2022; Shapiro *et al.*, 2022; Tran & Batacharya, 2023). Furthermore, even as CLA has clearly gained much inspiration from critical discourse analysis (CDA), CLA scholarship that addresses reading often focuses on macro-level and sociocultural concerns rather than micro-level linguistic patterns (e.g. Dar *et al.*, 2010; Flowerdew, 2012; Wallace, 1999). Yet, as will be discussed below, attention to both macro and micro-level features of texts is necessary in order to empower students as rhetorical readers.

In this chapter, we discuss why and how rhetorical reading should incorporate a CLA lens, integrating both sociocultural and linguistic levels of text. First, we review recent scholarship on innovative approaches to reading in writing classrooms, including mindful reading (Carillo, 2017), critical reading (Horning, 2024), and antiracist reading (Inoue, 2020). Then, we offer some principles that link CLA to rhetorical reading, as a language-focused complement to these other approaches. From there, we illustrate these principles with a CLA reading activity sequence centered around Vershawn Ashanti Young's (2010) 'Should Writers Use They Own English?' We describe the use of this sequence in a first-year writing course at a large public university, underscoring the approach to reading that takes a pluralist, rhetorical, and descriptivist stance toward English which helps build students' awareness of – and ability to question – social and linguistic norms of written English. We conclude by offering brief considerations for incorporating CLA reading into writing curricula.

Critical and Rhetorical Reading

The trend of prioritizing writing more than reading in CLA scholarship is reflected in writing studies more broadly. As Horning and Kraemer (2013) point out, the vast majority of explicit reading instruction US students receive is in primary grades. Once students reach secondary and postsecondary levels, the dominant assumption is that they have the foundational skills necessary to engage with a range of text types. Extant research proves this assumption to be patently false, in several ways. First, the texts that students engage with in postsecondary courses become more linguistically dense (Biber & Gray, 2016). In addition, the strategies students are often taught in early years (e.g. 'skimming for the main idea') are often not sophisticated enough for students to engage confidently with complex texts (Thelin, 2009). Moreover, students are expected to do more with the texts – not just summarizing or writing a personal response, but also evaluating, synthesizing, and applying texts to other cases or contexts. Thus postsecondary reading requires a broader set of reading strategies, as well as more nuanced disposition toward texts themselves.

The approach we introduce here brings together CLA scholarship with earlier work on critical approaches to reading. These approaches encourage students to see reading as a social and dialogic process in which they actively co-create meaning with the author (e.g. Wilkinson & Son, 2011; also Flower, 1990). Implementing critical reading often involves diversifying the kinds of texts students read, as well as broadening the strategies they use while reading (Horning & Kraemer, 2013). Finally, critical approaches to reading often encourage more attention to aspects such as author identity and values, audience, historical and social context, and genre than to linguistic features.

In their survey of college student reading practices, however, Haas and Flower (1988) found that very few undergraduate students use these sorts of strategies, compared with graduate students, who presumably have more disciplinary knowledge and other contextual information to bring to the texts (Haswell *et al.*, 1999). Critical reading is therefore a skillset that secondary and postsecondary students need to be taught. Carillo (2015) found that although many college writing instructors employed some amount of rhetorical reading in their classes, most instructors were not adept at infusing criticality into that rhetorical reading.

One way scholars have tried to unite critical and rhetorical approaches is through an emphasis on pacing and mindfulness, encouraging readers to slow down their reading of the text in order to attend to their own cognitive, emotional, and physical reactions. Carillo (2017) calls this 'mindful reading'. Other scholars have applied Krista Ratcliffe's notion of 'rhetorical listening' to readings that are challenging intellectually or emotionally (e.g. Rivera-Mueller, 2020).

Inoue (2020) views these mindful strategies as tools for antiracist pedagogy. He argues that slower, mindful reading creates opportunities for students to recognize their own reactions to an author or text, and to reflect on beliefs and experiences that underlie those reactions – including problematic racial ideologies that most of us are steeped in at school and in society more broadly. Other scholars, such as Carmichael (2021) and Suh (2022) have found this mindful approach to be a helpful means of scaffolding students' critical engagement with texts – and with each other.

However, although the scholarship on critical, mindful reading often touches on language as one of the themes or aspects of texts that might be examined, extant case studies tend to focus much more on what texts say about language (i.e. at the macro-level), than on the linguistic choices made by the authors, and the rhetorical impact of those choices. In other words, a mindful, critical approach to reading may still be incomplete if it does not include opportunities for students to notice and interpret authors' linguistic choices – i.e. to engage critically with language *use* as well as ideas.

Infusing CLA into Critical, Rhetorical Reading

CLA offers helpful strategies for critically approaching both macro and micro-level aspects of texts, with attention to the intersections among language, identity, power, and privilege (e.g. Shapiro, 2022). A CLA approach to reading helps students consider and respond to authors' linguistic and rhetorical choices, taking into account sociocultural contexts and power relations. This in turn builds students' confidence and skill as agentive language users in their own writing and other communication. Such an approach is particularly helpful in engaging students with the tensions around linguistic norms and conventions (see e.g. Janks & Ivanič, 1992).

Perhaps the most lengthy discussion of CLA approaches to reading comes from Wallace (1999: 104–105), who highlights the importance of 'literacy practices in social settings', which she frames as a macro-level focus, alongside micro-level 'effects in specific texts'. Wallace is explicit in saying that this type of reading does not need to be 'oppositional' toward authors and texts – and in fact, often responds 'more tentatively and reflectively', with the goal of 'raising questions and dilemmas rather than offering solutions to problems' (1999: 104). Approaching texts in this way, Wallace explains, helps to build students' 'capacity to gain some distance from their own identities, experiences and circumstances' (1999: 104) as well as their 'understanding of the nature of disadvantage and injustice beyond that personally experienced' (1999: 104).

A Framework for CLA-Informed Rhetorical Reading

We see four key features that CLA brings into critical, rhetorical reading instruction:

(1) **An explicit focus on language** as both a medium of communication and (often) a topical theme in the text itself. In other words, a CLA approach looks in particular for texts that involve 'languaging about language'.
(2) **Links between micro and macro-level authorial choices.** Students use what Shapiro (2022) calls 'linguistic sleuthing' to notice and evaluate the writer's linguistic choices. In this way, students engage more fully with the links between text and context.
(3) **A pluralist and rhetorical orientation to language difference.** In other words, linguistic choices that diverge from what is conventional (e.g. use of varieties other than standardized US English or academic discourse) are not simply 'celebrated' as an end in itself. Rather, CLA investigates with students the likely reason for this rhetorical 'resistance' and their reactions to it.
(4) **An emphasis on students' agency as writers.** As they become more aware of the linguistic and other rhetorical choices made by other writers – including choices that may go against convention – students develop an increased understanding of their own rhetorical potential. They gain confidence in making informed choices in their writing, including choices that may align with convention and others that might resist. As Clark (1992/2014: 136) framed it in one of the earliest publications about CLA as a pedagogical approach: 'I see my job as facilitating the students' examination of the conventions of the academic discourse community they are operating within…providing them with as much knowledge as possible so that they can make their own informed decisions'.

As with the antiracist reading discussed earlier, this approach encourages students to recognize and complicate their assumptions about language, including in their responses to the text. In the next sections, we offer an illustration of CLA reading in an example activity, first describing the context for the first-year writing course in which it took place.

Curricular context

The first-year writing curriculum at the University of Michigan (UM) centers on critical language awareness, specifically through a focus on examining ideas about language and practicing linguistically-informed reading and analysis of diverse forms of written English. A premise of this approach is that we need language knowledge to advance inclusivity and linguistic justice; in other words, we need awareness of linguistic and rhetorical patterns at the level of lexis (e.g. vocabulary), grammar (e.g. subject-verb agreement), and genre (e.g. student papers; text messages) to advance a mission for writing education in which language variation is valued and diverse language users are empowered to use diverse writing knowledge to make informed choices (Aull, 2024). Though many critical approaches in writing studies focus more on language ideologies than on language itself, there are also rich examples of how linguistic knowledge and analysis can support linguistic justice (Aull, 2023; Perryman-Clark, 2013; Shapiro, 2022; Smitherman, 1993).

In support of these goals, Laura's fall 2023 first-year writing course began with a unit that invited students to read like writers and reflect on their own writing experiences. In this unit, students began reading about and identifying writing strategies, including rhetorical moves and linguistic patterns in informal and formal writing, and they reflected on rules and beliefs commonly associated with them. Students applied this knowledge in their engagement with Young's article, which provided an example of how authors can blend dialectal and rhetorical features and which invited students to reconsider some of their linguistic assumptions.

More specifically, in a course meeting twice per week for 80 minutes, the first four sessions of class were structured as follows: During the first class session, students freely wrote about their perceptions and/or what they had learned constitutes 'good writing', and they were introduced to the course, the syllabus, and the course language acknowledgment (see Aull, 2023). During the second class session, students engaged with a book excerpt that maps different registers and genres on a written English continuum (Aull, 2024 – see Figure 1.1 below).[1]

To help inform the discussion, students brought in a piece of their own writing, such as from informal digital writing (e.g. texting) or formal academic writing (e.g. essays and papers). During class, students discussed the continuum reading as a class; then, in pairs, they annotated linguistic and rhetorical patterns that signaled to them where their example writing

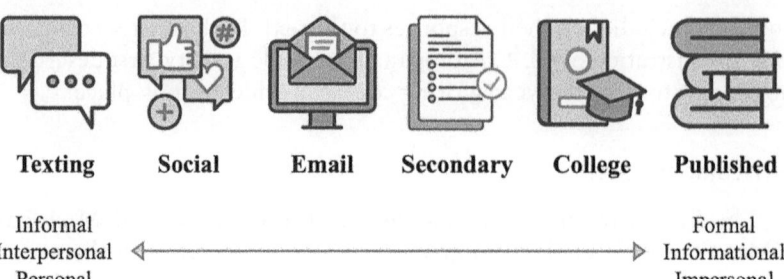

Figure 1.1 English writing continuum

fell on the continuum of interpersonal and informational, informal and formal, and personal and impersonal patterns. We also discussed, in pairs and as a class, what students had heard and experienced with writing across the continuum, drawing, for example, from the first-day freewrite on 'good writing'. Many students, for instance, suggested that they had learned that the informal, interpersonal side of the continuum is 'lazy' or 'incorrect', and this allowed us to talk about a point the continuum reading illustrates, which is that all dialects and registers are rule-governed, grammatically meaningful, and responsive to (and used in) communities.

In the third class session, we shifted from categorizing different types of writing patterns to rhetorical moves made across disciplines and genres in published writing (Swales, 1990) and in student writing (see e.g. Chang, 2023; Gere *et al.*, 2013). Students read an excerpt from Chapter 7 in Swales' *Genre Analysis* along with accessible supplemental representations (for example, on Purdue's OWL website or in USC's library guides).[2] In this model, the first move 'establishes a territory', or introduces a topic. The second move introduces a gap or 'niche' in the territory noted in move 1. The third move 'occupies the niche', by e.g. offering a new proposal or otherwise clarifying what the unfolding piece of writing will offer as a response to the niche noted in move 2. These moves matter not only because they help students recognize common rhetorical options in informational introductions, but also because by moving from more familiar ideas to a less familiar niche, introductory moves ease the processing burden for readers. The linguistic cues associated with each move can further support reader access in that they display how sentences relate to one another.

In the third class session, students discussed the moves and identified them in several different texts. These included relatively popular articles (e.g. 'How Did We Get Here? 163 Years of *The Atlantic*'s Writing on Race and Racism in America' by Gillian B. White; 'Deep Learning: Understanding Neural Networks' by AI Today) and the continuum reading they read for the last class, in order to showcase a range of genres that use introductory moves. These application activities happened in small groups and full class discussion. As they discussed moves and linguistic cues in the texts, the discussion included connections between writing choices and reader understanding: how the moves and words led readers from one point to another, and how they supported the writers' ideas and arguments.

In effect, during the first three classes, students read about and practiced recognizing patterns, including introductory rhetorical moves, in a few kinds of writing. In preparation for the fourth class, students read Vershawn Ashanti Young's (2010) 'Should Writers Use They Own English?', the focus of the CLA reading sequence described in the next section.

Description of the CLA-oriented reading activity sequence

Vershawn Ashanti Young's (2010) 'Should Writers Use They Own English?' is an engaging piece for practicing CLA reading as both readers (for ideas) and writers (for rhetorical strategies). In this 12-page article, Young argues that using multiple dialects and languages, including in the same rhetorical situation, is common and beneficial to all language users, because it expands everyone's rhetorical knowledge and helps reduce linguistic prejudice. Specifically, Young illustrates the prevalence and value of what he calls code meshing – 'blendin two or mo dialects, languages, or rhetorical forms into one sentence, one utterance, one paper', sometimes intentionally and sometimes unintentionally, which allows writers and speakers to 'bridge multiple codes and modes of expression'. These codes, Young shows, are deemed disparate and unmixable by Stanley Fish and other standardized prescriptivists (2010: 116). As he develops his argument, Young code-switches between more standardized/conventional language and elements of African American Vernacular English or Black Language (see Baker-Bell, 2020); this blend is often new to students as a strategy in academic writing.

In Laura's course, reading this piece like CLA readers meant considering how narrow ideas about correctness misconstrue and limit language variation. Reading like CLA writers meant analyzing its introductory moves and considering the writing choices Young makes to advance his ideas and offer information and interpersonal connection to his audience. We considered student responses to seeing multiple dialects in a piece of writing they were reading for school, and how the fact that it was a new experience for some students helped make Young's point that constraining language to one kind limits what we encounter and whom we empower in schools. In the case of the activities below, in preparation for class, students annotated Young's text for the introductory rhetorical moves in the text and linguistic cues they saw as they read from the continuum, as they had done with other texts in prior class meetings. In class, we covered the following activity sequences, which each took about 20–25 minutes.

First, in class, the students began by comparing annotations in small, randomly-selected (e.g. numbered-off) groups. As they did in earlier classes, each group first discussed their annotations and then made notes on their group's section of a shared Google document. They noted where they see each move beginning (i.e. where in the text), how (i.e. what linguistic cues signaled the move), and why (i.e. how the section of text achieves the rhetorical goal of the move). As the groups worked, they were reminded to be as concrete as possible, making sure their notes included specific linguistic and rhetorical patterns and moves they were seeing Young using in order to e.g. introduce his main ideas in move 3. Identifying the three rhetorical moves was important not only so that students continued applying past knowledge but also so that they annotated evidence that Young's code-meshing discourse did not make his essay any less complex rhetorically, even by traditional definitions.

In the second activity, each student group engaged with the other groups' notes on the shared class document before a full class discussion that addressed each move in an effort to come to a class consensus about each one. For example, move 3 (occupying the niche, or responding to a lingering question or issue) was annotated in more than one way, including (a) a long move 3 over two paragraphs, beginning with the sentence 'But don't nobody's language, dialect, or style make them "vulnerable to prejudice"', with the countering cue *but don't nobody's*, and ending with the sentence 'And that's my exact argument'; or, (b) a shorter move 3, consisting only of the sentence, 'And that's my exact argument, that we should all know everybody's dialect, at least as many as we can, and be open to the mix of them in oral and written communication' (Young, 2010: 110–111), with the cue *my exact argument*.

The discussion thus allowed students to build language knowledge by discussing moves and patterns they were observing and why, and to consider together how Young moves from naming a problem to responding to it, and how. The goal of the discussion was not to find a single 'right' answer but rather to practice recognizing where writers signal different kinds of information and connection with their audience. Ultimately, the students labeled the introductory moves where they begin in the excerpts below, as well as particular cues that help signal the moves, bolded in the excerpts.

Young, 'Should Writers Use They Own English?' (2010: 110–11)
[Move 1: Establishing the territory] Cultural critic Stanley Fish **come talkin bout** – in his three-piece **New York Times 'What Should Colleges Teach?'** suit – there only one way to speak and write to get ahead in the world, that writin teachers should 'clear [they] mind of the orthodoxies that have taken hold in the composition world' (Part 3). **He say** don't no student have a right to they own language if that language make them 'vulnerable to prejudice'; that 'it may be true that the standard language is a device for protecting the status quo, but that very truth is a reason for teaching it to students'....

[Move 2: Establishing the niche] **Lord, lord, lord! Where do I begin,** cuz this man sho tryin **to take the nation back** to a time when we were less tolerant of linguistic and racial differences. Yeah, I said racial difference, tho my man Stan be talkin explicitly bout language differences. The two be sho nuff intertwined… Fish himself acquiesce to this linguistic prejudice when he come saying that people make theyselves targets for racism if and when they don't write and speak like he do. …

[Move 3: Occupying the niche] **But don't nobody's** language, dialect, or style make them 'vulnerable to prejudice'. It's ATTITUDES. **It be the way** folks with some power perceive other people's language. […] And **that's my exact argument**, that we all should know everybody's dialect, at least as many as we can […] Everybody mix the dialect they learn at home with whateva other dialect or language they learn afterward….

Discussing the moves and choices that students highlighted included discussing Young's writing choices and their rhetorical effects. Drawing from the continuum reading, students noticed, for instance, the informational use of noun phrases to name phenomena (*linguistic and racial differences*; *linguistic prejudice*; *common language system*; *rhetorical and grammatical features*), and they noticed interpersonal addresses to the audience (*where do I begin*) and personal references (*to me*) and exclamations (e.g. *lord, lord, lord*, usage common in African American communities – see e.g. Kamwangamalu, 2010). We also discussed usage that many students said they had never seen in a published academic piece of writing, including zero-g verbs and adjectives (*talkin, writin*) and third person zero-s singular (*he say*), a common subject-verb agreement pattern in Black English and in English as a *lingua franca* (MacKenzie, 2014; Smitherman, 1973). These discussions engaged the 'slowing down' of mindful reading, to consider beliefs about, and responses to, familiar and unfamiliar dialects of English, including who and what has shaped those beliefs.

The discussions also allowed us to try applying our terminology and concepts from the continuum reading along with a new term from Young, *code meshing*. Such terminology included English *registers* and *dialects*, all of which are linguistically, though not socially, equal: they are all equally rule-governed and grammatically possible and meaningful in English. This terminology furthermore avoided common prescriptive and hierarchical labels such as *incorrect* or *sophisticated* in favor of descriptive labels such as *interpersonal* and *informational*. This discussion, in other words, offered the class the chance to consider social and linguistic responses to the reading and to apply descriptive terminology.

The third and final activity was comprised of two tasks that students completed in groups before a full class discussion: (a) finding places where they saw the main ideas from the introductory moves (especially move 3) echoed throughout the piece, and (b), mapping the piece onto the written English continuum discussed earlier. To do the first task, students found places in the text that exemplify Young's argument (e.g. each group labeled at least two paragraphs or sections according to their topic and examples, and how and where they link back to the idea in move 3). To do the second task, students considered informational, interpersonal, and other patterns noted in their annotations and our discussions so far.

These small group and ultimately full-class discussions included students' critical confrontation with assumptions they had about academic writing, argument, formal writing, and informal writing. For example, one group of first-year students suggested the piece was on the informal side of the continuum; when asked for more detail, they mentioned shortened words (*sho*, *sayin*) and double negation (*don't nobody's*). Another group countered that the piece had all of the patterns of formal, informational writing, e.g. introductory moves, references to another piece of informational writing via direct quotes and paraphrasing, long noun phrases, and so on. This allowed us to return to descriptive terminology: dialect (which can include informal, formal, written, and spoken registers), register (formal, informal, written, or spoken) and genre (e.g. more interpersonal more informational). It also allowed us to see the ways that Young's writing choices were making his argument: he had more to work with, rather than less, due to his ability to draw from multiple language codes.

Some students also discussed that as Young developed ideas, his choices slid along the continuum differently: some evidence and explanation moves were especially informational, using dense noun phrases. Then, some analysis or inference moves were more interpersonal, using language directly addressing the reader as he offered a response to the evidence. One student group took us to a paragraph on page 113 in the article by way of illustration:

> But here what Fish don't get: standard language ideology insist that minority people will never become an Ivy League English department chair or president of Harvard University if they dont perfect they mastery of standard English. At the same time the ideology instruct that white men will gain such positions, even with a questionable handle of standard grammar and rhetoric (I think here of the regular comments made about former President Bush's bad grammar and poor rhetoric). Fish respond that this the way our country is so let's accept it. I say: 'No way, brutha!'

Once the group took us to this paragraph, we discussed and annotated it together as a class. It has clear development moves:[3] first, the topic (what Fish don't get about the paradoxes and limitations of standardized language ideology), then the examples with explanations (e.g. George W. Bush as president despite being criticized for his language use), and then the analysis: Fish's and Young's response, at the end of the paragraph. In these development moves, Young labels phenomena in the noun-heavy, informational style of formal academic writing; e.g. in noun phases including 'standard language ideology', 'minority people', 'mastery of standard English', and 'questionable handle of standard grammar and rhetoric'. His analysis is more interpersonal in nature, characterized by simpler and more personally oriented subjects, and more of a balance between nouns and verbs: *Fish respond that this the way our country is so let's accept it. I say: No way, brutha!* The group that focused on this paragraph suggested they felt it was a rhetorically successful way to both introduce ideas in ways academic readers might expect, as well as draw them in conversationally. Two students said they wanted to try doing that kind of informational and interpersonal blend in their own writing, and could they do so in class (to which naturally the answer was: try it!).

Ultimately, the class discussed that an 'informal' designation seemed to be a misunderstanding of dialect difference. Instead, the evidence the groups amassed in their analysis suggested that Young draws from multiple dialects, and from interpersonal and informational patterns; and the article is a formal piece of writing (in other words, it is in the formal register, with a blend of dialects and interpersonal and informational language patterns). Several students noted that they found the piece 'hard to read', which they ultimately felt likewise made Young's point: if, as Young argues, they had been taught 'what it take to understand, listen, and write in multiple dialects simultaneously' (2010: 116), then reading the piece would have gone differently. The assessment of students' learning in this case was informal and rooted in their engagement with one another and the text, but checks for understanding were important because we continued to return to the Young piece throughout the term. This included in the students' first assignment in which they analyze patterns in multiple genres they use in their own writing, because many of the students chose to integrate Young's piece as they wrote about the codes they use.

Reflecting on the activity

In this article, we have endeavored to delineate CLA reading and to describe an example activity that takes an inclusive, linguistically-informed stance toward the productive diversity already present in written English. The activity connects reading to moves, a rhetorical focus familiar to many writing studies instructors. Still, we know that any new recommendations can feel like even more to do for already-overwhelmed instructors and curricula. We want to close, therefore, with considerations that have helped us incorporate CLA reading independent of specific activities.

(1) **Promoting quality over quantity of reading.** Consider how much every student – with multiple courses, jobs, family responsibilities, and otherwise – can read and annotate well. Consider assigning less reading, with engaged reading expectations for what you do assign that includes criticality toward ideas and writing strategies. Students might

engage with the reading, for instance, through discussion posts about what moves and linguistic cues students expect and don't expect in college reading and why; student-led discussion in which students lead their peers through key ideas, moves, and linguistic cues in the reading; or social annotation reading tool so that you can provide individual or overall feedback on how students are reading and annotating.

(2) **Questioning language beliefs and language itself.** Whatever reading you assign, include linguistically as well as socioculturally diverse texts, and consider how you might help students notice their language beliefs and their responses to language used in the texts. Questions they might consider, for instance, include: what kinds of language do they expect to see in college reading? Who or what has shaped those expectations, and what are their implications?

(3) **Prioritizing metalinguistic talk.** In order to foster criticality about ideas and writing itself, consider language knowledge and terminology as time well spent, even if it means taking time during several classes to discuss and come to a class consensus on shared understandings about terms such as *dialect, register, moves, cohesion, subject/verb agreement, interpersonal discourse*, and *informational discourse*. These terms can help us work on shared understandings that avoid impressionistic – and often hierarchical and discriminatory – labels such as *incorrect, slang, lazy/broken*, or *sophisticated*. Likewise, these terms can help us emphasize what Shawna calls choice versus voice, by underscoring the range of options that writers use in different texts and how we might make informed choices about them.

(4) **Emphasizing practice versus 'mastery'.** CLA reading is about practicing a mindset that recognizes and critically considers diverse social and linguistic norms of language use and their implications. When our students (or we) want to get something 'right', it can be helpful to note that noticing and practicing are the ultimate goals, and we become more able to see, name, and critically consider language patterns the more we make space to do so.

Notes

(1) This book is available open access, but the excerpt Laura uses in first-year writing is also available here: https://docs.google.com/document/d/1CgA3-1jfgTDSfWb71aLMKTbmOkOxUrAfxCVo9HbPj64/edit
(2) See Purdue's OWL website description here: (https://owl.purdue.edu/owl/general_writing/the_writing_process/organization_CARS_Model.html) and USC's library guide description here: (https://libguides.usc.edu/writingguide/CARS).
(3) In the UM class, students annotate for development moves – the moves that focus particular paragraphs and sections of writing on a topic move (or T move), an evidence and explanation move (or E move), an analysis or inference move (or A move), and, sometimes, a move that links the smaller topic to the main ideas of a piece of writing (or L move) (Aull, 2020).

References

Aull, L. (2020) How students write: A linguistic analysis. Modern Language Association.
Aull, L. (2023) Attention to language in composition. *Composition Forum* 51 (Spring).
Aull, L. (2024) *You Can't Write That: 8 Myths about Correct English*. Cambridge University Press.
Baker-Bell, A. (2020) *Linguistic Justice: Black Language, Literacy, Identity, and Pedagogy*. Routledge.
Biber, D. and Gray, B. (2016) *Grammatical Complexity in Academic English: Linguistic Change in Writing*. Cambridge University Press.
Carillo, E.C. (2015) *Securing a Place for Reading in Composition: The Importance of Teaching for Transfer*. University Press of Colorado.
Carillo, E.C. (2017) *A Writer's Guide to Mindful Reading*. University Press of Colorado.
Carmichael, F.A. (2021) Teaching anti-racist reading practices in first-year writing. *Writing Program Administration* 44 (3), 138–145.
Chang, T.S. (2023) A move analysis of Chinese L2 student essays from the sociocognitive perspective: Genres, languages, and writing quality. *Assessing Writing* 57, 100750.
Clark, R. (1992/2014) Principles and practice of CLA in the classroom. In N. Fairclough (ed.) *Critical Language Awareness* (pp. 117–140). Routledge.
Dar, Z.K., Shams, M.R. and Rahimi, A. (2010) Teaching reading with a critical attitude: Using critical discourse analysis (CDA) to raise EFL university students' critical language awareness (CLA). *International Journal of Criminology and Sociological Theory* 3 (2), 457–476.
di Gennaro, K., Choong, K.W.P. and Brewer, M. (2023) Uniting CLA with WAW via SLA: Learning about written language as a model for college writing courses. *Journal of Second Language Writing* 60, 100967.
Flower, L. (1990) *Reading-to-Write: Exploring a Cognitive and Social Process*. Oxford University Press.
Flowerdew, J. (2012) *Discourse in English Language Education*. Routledge.
Gere, A.R., Aull, L., Escudero, M.D.P., Lancaster, Z. and Vander Lei, E. (2013) Local assessment: Using genre analysis to validate directed self-placement. *College Composition & Communication* 64 (4), 605–633.
Haas, C. and Flower, L. (1988) Rhetorical reading strategies and the construction of meaning. *College Composition and Communication* 39 (2), 167–183.
Haswell, R.H., Briggs, T.L., Fay, J.A., Gillen, N.K., Harrill, R., Shupala, A.M. and Trevino, S.S. (1999) Context and rhetorical reading strategies: Haas and Flower (1988) revisited. *Written Communication* 16 (1), 3–27.
Horning, A.S. (2024) *The Case for Critical Literacy: A History of Reading in Writing Studies*. University Press of Colorado.
Horning, A.S. and Kraemer, E.W. (eds) (2013) *Reconnecting Reading and Writing*. Parlor Press.
Inoue, A.B. (2020) Teaching antiracist reading. *Journal of College Reading and Learning* 50 (3), 134–156.
Janks, H. and Ivanič, R. (1992/2014) CLA and emancipatory discourse. In N. Fairclough (ed.) *Critical Language Awareness*. Routledge.
Kamwangamalu, N.M. (2010) African American vernacular English, religion and ethnicity. In T. Omoniyi (ed.) *The Sociology of Language and Religion: Change, Conflict and Accommodation* (pp. 190–204). Palgrave Macmillan.
Leonard, R.L. (2021) The role of writing in critical language awareness. *College English* 84 (2), 179-198.
MacKenzie, I. (2014) *English as a Lingua Franca: Theorizing and Teaching English*. Routledge.

Perryman-Clark, S.M. (2013) African American language, rhetoric, and students' writing: New directions for SRTOL. *College Composition and Communication* 64 (3), 469–495.

Rivera-Mueller, J. (2020) Enacting rhetorical listening: A process to support students' engagement with challenging course readings. *Journal on Empowering Teaching Excellence* 4 (2). https://doi.org/10.26077/0845-bae3

Shapiro, S. (2022) *Cultivating Critical Language Awareness in the Writing Classroom*. Routledge.

Shapiro, S., Gere, A.R., Curzan, A., Hammond, J.W., Hughes, S., Li, R., Moos, A., Smith, K., Van Zanen, K., Wheeler, K.L. and Zanders, C.J. (2022) Interchanges: A Kairotic moment for CLA? Response to Anne Ruggles Gere et al.'s 'Communal Justicing: Writing Assessment, Disciplinary Infrastructure, and the Case for Critical Language Awareness'/Response. *College Composition and Communication* 74 (2), 373–387.

Smitherman, G. (1973) 'God don't never change': Black English from a Black perspective. *College English* 34 (6), 828–833.

Smitherman, G. (1993) 'The Blacker the Berry, the Sweeter the Juice': African American Student Writers and the National Assessment of Educational Progress. Annual Meeting of the National Council of Teachers of English, Pittsburgh, PA, 17–22 November.

Smitherman, G. (2017) Raciolinguistics, 'mis-education', and language arts teaching in the 21st century. *Language Arts Journal of Michigan* 32 (2). https://doi.org/10.9707/2168-149X.2164

Suh, E.K. (2022) Teaching reading as raciolinguistic justice: (Re)Centering reading strategies for antiracist reading. *Teaching English in the Two-Year College* 50 (2), 116–131.

Swales, J. (1990) *Genre Analysis: English in Academic and Research Settings*. Cambridge University Press.

Thelin, W.H. (2009) The peculiar relationship to reading in college curriculum. *Open Words: Access and English Studies* 3, 1–4.

Tran, P.M. and Batacharya, S. (2023) Using CLA pedagogy to examine an asynchronous supplemental English for academic writing program: Curriculum design and pilot results. *Journal of Second Language Writing* 60, 101020.

Wallace, C. (1999) Critical language awareness: Key principles for a course in critical reading. *Language Awareness* 8 (2), 98–110.

White, G.A. (2020) How did we get here? 163 years of *The Atlantic*'s writing on race and racism in America. *The Atlantic*, 16 June. https://www.theatlantic.com/education/archive/2020/06/atlantic-reader-race-and-racism-us/613057/

Wilkinson, I.A. and Son, E.H. (2011) A dialogic turn in research on learning and teaching to comprehend. In M.L. Kamil, P.D. Pearson, E.B. Moje and P. Afflerbach (eds) *Handbook of Reading Research, Volume IV* (pp. 359–387). Routledge.

Young, V.A. (2010) Should writers use they own English? *Iowa Journal of Cultural Studies* 12 (1), 110–117.

2 Fictional 'Truths' about Language: Using Creative Fiction for Radical Inclusion and Critical Language Awareness

Sean Oros

Introduction

Creative fiction also provides a pathway for reimaging existing systems to be more inclusive, as called for by Sengeh in *Radical Inclusion* (2023). To me, radical inclusion is not just reimagining the inclusivity of my own classrooms; as an educator, I also have the privilege and duty to create a ripple effect of language inclusion across society. Teaching Critical Language Awareness (CLA) is a key step towards building linguistic radical inclusivity across society, as CLA helps students recognize the need for radical inclusion in writing classrooms and beyond. Many documented approaches exist for using nonfiction writing and reading exercises to build Critical Language Awareness (see, for instance, Canagarajah, 2013; Sánchez-Martín, 2022), but few have explored creative fiction. This chapter adds to overlooked areas of research by examining use of a creative fiction assignment as a tool to build CLA at a small, rural northeastern United States college, in a Standard American English (SAE) dominant section of ENG 284: Creative Fiction. This assignment is designed to open the door for discussion and introduction of CLA concepts to build a more radically inclusive understanding of language, especially when teaching rural audiences that may be somewhat resistant to both.

I argue that creative fiction writing is a way for monolingual students to engage with CLA and develop greater language awareness and empathy, which we urgently need in all language classes. Scholars noted at the turn of the millennia that the number of families in the US primarily speaking a non-English language at home was at 8.7% of the total population

(Kubota & Ward, 2000), spurring on the need for a more inclusive language-teaching approach. However, the 2021 census estimated that this number increased to 21.6% (US Census Data, n.d.), meaning that this need has only increased. This is not restricted to the US, as scholars have identified a global need for accessible critical pedagogies in all educational contexts (Park *et al.*, 2023). In current composition debates, Shapiro and other scholars from the University of Michigan discuss the role of CLA as a way to balance the rigidity of composition and standards with the 'fluid, dynamic, shifting quality of language' in what Shapiro terms 'communal justicing' of the discipline (Shapiro *et al.*, 2022). This type of radical inclusion is necessary, but, unfortunately, not all populations are receptive to these lessons. I propose that creative fiction can help bridge this divide.

My approach to this CLA assignment is rooted in established translingual principles. While Canagarajah and most other scholars on translingualism (i.e. the individual/collective adoption of translanguaging practices) attest to the spread of the international internet and pop culture as one of translingualism's driving forces (Canagarajah, 2013), these studies are often kept to the fields of music, social media, and other multimedia forms of culture. This approach overlooks the many creative writing outlets young people enjoy, ranging from fan-fiction forums to the expanded field of self-publishing (Black, 2009). This appetite for creative fiction can help illustrate – or negotiate – the translingual nature of language to students. Furthermore, even in an SAE-dominant setting, this can provide ways to answer Canagarajah's call to 'scrutinize institutional practices influenced by and maintaining monolingualism' (Lee & Canagarajah, 2019) by expanding students' understanding of language beyond the stratification of language and even the binary concept of native English speakers and non-native English speakers. However, students coming from many US rural areas are often some of the most in need of accessible CLA, and yet, in my experience, the most resistant to it. Many of these students, especially those at institutions where they are the dominant population, are often monolingual in SAE and politically opposed to truly inclusive language diversity in education and society. Creative fiction provides a way to partially bypass this and open the door to CLA discussions in ways that nonfiction cannot, allowing SAE-monolingual classrooms to engage with CLA in creative and engaging ways.

Translingual scholarship has a proven record of success in centering CLA, which itself can be used to promote radically inclusive understandings of language. Translingual theory and pedagogy have been steadily growing and informing each other over the past decades (Cummins, 2019: 23), leading to a variety of classroom practices. Many, although not all, of these translanguaging practices rely on having some element of multilingual students in class (see, for instance, Canagarajah, *Literacy as Translingual Practice*, 2013). However, as Zhang-Wu (2021) states, translingualism requires action from all, including the collective of native English speakers. Not teaching even a cursory overview of these concepts in rural schools is a disservice to students in our increasingly interconnected world. Creative fiction also lends itself readily to linguistic radical inclusivity. It already has a demonstrated role in giving students their own voice in deconstructing 'literacy normative' practices that further marginalized populations (Johnson, 2017), and the creative work of students and their imagination is an 'integral part of their lives' (Black, 2009). Additionally, many current creative-nonfiction pedagogies rely on non-native SAE students, as the exercises center around shared experiences of language from different language or dialect backgrounds. This poses a challenge for more rural or dialect-dominant locations. It is possible to use other language learning experiences to help address this gap, but, as this is still rooted in a single dominant language, I argue that getting students to contemplate a full language barrier is necessary for building linguistic radical inclusivity.

In the following pages, I provide a scholarly backdrop to this discussion, exploring creative fiction as a tool for radical inclusion, as well as examining the role of the creative process of fiction as a way to develop CLA. Afterwards, I describe the course I taught and its context, providing examples and student responses from both in-class and from a pre- and post-survey. I conclude with a discussion of results and implications, exploring possibilities for integration of creative fiction to build CLA and radical inclusion within creative fiction assignments and classes.

Creative Fiction as Radical Inclusion

Stories have power; they share perspectives and increase CLA. Some world literature scholars teach about translingualism through focusing on the 'lived experience of multilingualism' (Heng Hartse *et al.*, 2018: 90) in world literature. As Cristina Sánchez-Martín says in her review of three different immigrant story collections, 'systemic transformation requires deep and sustained reflexive work at the individual and collective level' (2022: 172). One way to build this perspective in students is by exposing them to stories of different language backgrounds and lived experiences – an effective tool for developing their own compass of cultural justice and inclusivity.

Creative writing already has a proven record of 'negotiating' realities. In particular, this is evident in forms of student inclusion. Creative writing classes and clubs have considerable pull with some marginalized identities already, including at the high school level; giving students their own voice in creative writing helps to deconstruct 'literacy normative' practices that further marginalizes populations (Johnson, 2017). However, although great progress has been made pedagogically, formal academic language is still based in privileged traditions, such as patriarchal, heteronormative, and SAE bases. Creative writing, however, comes with a different set of presuppositions, many of them from student experience online. If these classes already draw marginalized groups thanks to the genre's ability to negotiate realities and express themselves in experimental or artistic ways, then it stands to reason that this could be further encouraged and refined into developing a sense of CLA even in a monolingual class.

In today's technologically and pop-culturally literate world, the creative work of students and their imagination is an 'integral part of their lives' (Black, 2009) that gives them important forms of expression in a variety of mediums. Fanfiction writing and websites are one popular format of this that pushes the boundaries of 'what counts as good writing' (Black, 2009) and blurs the lines between native and non-native English speakers. Although we canonize and enshrine established fields of literature and maxims such as 'good writing is timeless / universal / etc.', the side effect is that we are reinforcing the marginalization that students feel when they are not represented among literature's 'great works' (Sumpter, 2016). As such, creative writing opens yet another door for radical inclusion by allowing students a voice in the matter. Creative writing remains a growing area of negotiated meaning-making and constructive culture. Online pop culture has given a common language that people from many diverse cultures can communicate within – and, perhaps more importantly, gives them a reason to want to communicate.

This desire for creative expression lends itself well to CLA, as creative nonfiction has long, as a discipline, mixed finesse in creative expression with rigor of writing and honesty (Mays, 2018) and more artistic 'truths' in fiction; this provides students a chance to present their own truths in an expressive way and encourages experimentation with language. Engaging in this can help demonstrate the critical nuances of language and create more radically inclusive classrooms in English disciplines. We can use this same framework to help reshape our classrooms and heal the inequities of our society, one story at a time.

On the Creative Process

I argue that Matsuda's idea of Composition and ELL being 'symbiotic' fields, rather than separate (2003: 28), should also include elements of the field of Creative Writing. Tying translingualism to first year composition courses is not unusual; the University of Washington has a webpage on their English department that highlights several courses that take this approach ('Syllabi – Materializing Translingualism') as public resources. This is in keeping with the calls from many scholars that 'translingualism must be reimagined as a lived reality for all language users' (Zhang-Wu, 2021: 126), but this call is mostly sounded in just the halls of compositionists and applied linguists. Broadening this to other writing classes could help enhance student encounters with CLA and introduce these concepts to monolingual and rural communities in 'palatable' ways to more resistant student populations (Canagarajah, 2011).

A combination of creativity and composition has been successfully applied in ELL classes. Sui (2021) regards 'fictionality as being almost synonymous with creativity itself' (2021, "Fictionality") and created a structured writing course focused on telling short stories in (China English) as a way to help Chinese students gain more skills in English; he concluded that a well-structured writing course that includes creative writing results in deeper and more holistic comprehension of language. Sui states that creative production engages the 'imaginative, inventive, and productive potentials' of students (2021, "Tellability'), giving them a more holistic experience with language. Furthermore, it has been an increasing trend of scholars to use creative freewriting as a way to have students engage with translanguaging strategies, as demonstrated by Nicolarakis and Mitchell (2023), though these are normally relegated to just introductory writing assessments. However, the students engage readily in these activities *because* of their preexistent enjoyment of creative writing; as one ASL student stated in the prior study, 'I enjoy poetry, I like to play with words, and I like experimenting with writing' (Nicolarakis & Mitchell, 2023: 141). Again, the intent here was to engage students in the cross between ASL (which is actually closer to Romance-language grammar systems than Germanic ones) and written English; the student interest in creative writing is present, but the translingual element relies on the bilingual nature of the students.

Given this success in other classes, though, it can be surmised that creative writing has a demonstrated role in encouraging translanguaging practices thanks to the fluidity and experimentation it encourages; however, in bridging this to monolingual students, one of the typical elements is missing. However, creative fiction can bridge this gap and introduce monolingual SAE classrooms to the nuances of language and begin developing a more radically inclusive mindset.

Course Background

I designed a course module based on intersectionality with translingual concepts in a SAE-dominant creative writing fiction class, utilizing a two-week lesson segment, a specific short story built on translingual negotiation, and a set of pre- and post-assignment questions. The purpose of this module is to create a way to raise an awareness of diverse options of language without setting unfair expectations or divergent course requirements (Canagarajah, 2011), providing students in this class the creative writing development they want while integrating it meaningfully with practical and beneficial lessons in CLA and modeling radical inclusivity. Asking students to 'write an essay' in an objective, academic style on language barriers of an immigrant or refugee is one thing; asking students to put themselves in the point-of-view of a language minority and creatively exploring the negotiation and psychology of those situations is more engaging and challenging. As this is paired with readings from immigrants and other language minorities, students are naturally led to discussion of language justice and immigrant experiences to build empathy and more inclusive mindsets.

There are, of course, limitations to this study. The course is a required rotation of our department and one of our major/minor electives. As it was taught in 2023, but had not been taught since 2017 due to faculty staffing shortages, there was a substantial appetite for the course and its content. Students predominantly signed up for this course as an English major/minor elective. Students frequently seek out creative writing opportunities (my institution also has a thriving creative writing club), and so there is an ethical need to address the content that they signed up for (e.g. the best practices of written storytelling, genres of fiction, and possibly publication outlets). However, I framed the module with this in mind, basing it around principles that serve them as writers in any context and reminding them that writers constantly write about perspectives not their own. The instructor was a white, heterosexual male. Specific student demographics for the class were not collected; other than that all students were white or white-passing and only fluently spoke SAE, being effectively all monolingual, save for one exchange student from South Korea.

I incorporated this lesson into a two-week segment scheduled before midterms, building from prior dialogue lessons (which already play on the miscommunication of meaning), followed by an examination of the interplay of languages in global English short stories, and finally culminating in a week on CLA and translanguaging practices. Their task was to write a flash fiction story (750–1500 words for the purposes of our class) in which the protagonist is a language minority and cannot communicate verbally to people. One of the goals was to incorporate 'psychological realism', encouraging them to get into the thoughts and emotions of someone in a situation like this. To provide inspiration and points of reference, I provided various short stories or brief travel accounts that ranged from poignant, such as the cases of real-life refugees, to humorous travel misunderstandings. Students could take whichever tonal approach they wanted but were required to engage with the idea of language barriers.

Pre- and post-survey questions were designed to address CLA questions and to provide a space for student responses. Students were told that this part of the classroom assignment was voluntary, anonymous, and had no impact on their grade either way; they were also told that the survey results would be used in research and had received IRB approval prior to the start of the semester. All students in the class opted in. These surveys were designed as a general gauge of their understanding of the topics and an attempt to map their development of CLA and radical inclusion as writers.

Description of Class Assignment

The class lesson and corresponding written assignments took place over two weeks in four 80-minute class segments; Tuesdays were dedicated to lecture and discussion, while Thursdays were used for workshopping and group work. The week prior, week four, was dedicated to dialogue exercises to set the stage for this segment. Additional readings were intended to complement the lessons, but these were not successfully employed due to logistical time constraints. There were two written activities as part of this assignment: a 'creative' literacy narrative, in which students reflected on their exposure to stories over their lives, in week five; and the primary subject of this chapter, the language minority flash-fiction story in week six. A chart of the classes and their lecture or discussion material can be seen in Table 2.1.

Table 2.1 Weekly schedule of lecture and discussion material

	Pre-Class:	Tuesday, 2:30–3:50 pm	Pre-Class	Thursday, 2:30–3:50 pm
Week 5:	Write: Dialogue writing exercise (prior week) Read: Toni Morrison's 'Recitatif' Gloria Anzaldua's 'How to Tame a Wild Tongue' Select story from *One World*, 'The Kettle on the Boat', by Vanessa Gebbie	Complete pre-exercise survey Lecture: Global Englishes – What are Global Englishes? – What role does dialect play in short stories? – Literacy narrative Introduction	Write: 2–3 page 'Creative Literacy Narrative' Watch: 'The Danger of a Single Story', by Chimamanda Adichie (TED Talk)	Group Workshop: Sharing literacy narratives; discuss in conjunction with 'The Danger of a Single Story'
Week 6:	Read: 'Translanguaging as part of the creative process', by Dr. Sara Wheeler (2020) 'Language Minority Stories' immigrant and language minority blog 'Language Barriers' travel experience blog post	Lecture: Translanguage Concept introduction – What is translanguage? – Why do you need to know this as a writer?	Write: Language Minority flash-fiction story, 750–1500 words (prompt in appendix)	Group Workshop: Language minority flash fiction Complete post-exercise survey

The culmination of this assignment was week six's aforementioned flash-fiction story (750–1500 words) and corresponding small-group workshop. The story prompt can be found in Appendix 2.1, but, in short, it asks students to 'write a story about a character placed in a situation where they do not understand the "language" of the setting they are in. How do they navigate/negotiate the language barriers? How do they feel during the process?' Further details encourage the use of psychological realism and other writing practices for consideration. They are guided to write a compelling and realistic story and encouraged to focus on the portrayal of the language negotiations and barriers rather than attempting to realistically portray a 'foreign' language. After writing this, they took part in a day of small-group workshopping. There was no restriction on what type of language minority to write about. Many of the students opted to write fantasy or science fiction settings rather than real-world examples: one student wrote about an alien prison, where inmate cellmates were constantly changed so no one could learn each other's languages, but the main character works out a system of 'language universals' through trial and error to coordinate a prison escape. What this ultimately allowed for was that they could put themselves into the perspective of a population to which they could not otherwise connect and begin to develop a sense of CLA and appreciation for radical inclusion's importance.

Discussion

Overall, I learned valuable lessons on how to apply creative writing as a tool for CLA and radical inclusion. I was correct in assuming that this would be a challenging topic for the student demographics at my institution, but we were able to navigate them fruitfully in the end. For instance, one student comment on the pre-survey stated:

> Immigrants entering a new country and intending to stay there permanently should learn the native language of that country, not expect the people of the new country to adapt to the immigrants. i.e: Signs in America should only be written in English, and not contain the italicized Spanish underneath.

This clearly indicates the general resistance to notions of CLA and radical inclusion. However, while resistance remained, the general shift after the lesson indicates that students on both sides of this spectrum came to better understand the rationality and empathy behind CLA. In general, I found this exercise a useful tool for introducing CLA to resistant populations and a good way for opening the door to further conversation. However, I found it to have a stronger effect on promoting concepts of radical inclusion, as all students (to varying amounts) displayed a greater sympathy to language barriers – and towards recognizing and reimaging the inequitable language barriers of society – after participating in this assignment.

Two students expressed strongly in the comments, both pre- and post-survey, their feelings against language diversity; one comment in particular in the post-survey was that 'The dominant language in America should always be English, and anyone coming to the country must adapt to that, not vice versa'. The other student was more concerned with the efficiency of a single language, stating 'Overall, understanding the dominant language of society is considered as much a courtesy as a convenience. Both formal and informal language, likewise, have their respective places and are equally important'. Towards this theme, in class, the discussion was derailed onto the topic of the importance of a single dominant language, primarily arguing along the lines of efficiency of communication – though some students who had been on study-abroad trips spoke of the importance of meeting halfway on this topic, as making people of all languages feel welcome is a key aspect of communication. These discussions, though at times somewhat heated, proved fruitful.

Students responded particularly well to 'The Danger of a Single Story', by Chimamanda Adichie, which we watched outside of class and then discussed. This particular video proved helpful towards expanding student perspectives and opened the path to discussing CLA; several students personally thanked me afterwards for sharing the video with them. Overall, there was a shift in the overall tone from before the beginning of the two-week sequence to after; while some students retained opposition to the idea of teaching multiple languages equally, they warmed up to the concept of CLA and indicated more signs of cooperation with the concept. In particular, one of the students who was most vocal in opposition to CLA eventually came to me after the class had ended. They personally expressed gratitude for these CLA lessons in regards to both research and creative writing alike, as they had since recognized the benefit it had both for their creative writing and research writing. Additionally, as mentioned previously, one student highlighted the empathy and humility of perspective this assignment builds, as it 'helped us, as writers, to put ourselves in the perspective of someone else'. Both cases illustrate the reflective potential of this assignment.

Limitations, however, are relatively obvious. There was only so much time for students to meaningfully engage with the idea. Additionally, given the resistance of some of the population to language diversity, there were strong reactions against their perceptions of me trying to forcefully steer their perspectives. In addition to the comments discussed, one student countered my statement regarding developments of dialects by stating that language varieties started as a punishment from God at the Tower of Babel. I had to carefully moderate the discussion and acknowledge perspectives from both sides of the political spectrum to cool the temperature of the room at certain points, especially in the face of sentiments like these. In particular, I found the writing exercise to be helpful on this front; by continuing to return to their role as writers in best representing a language minority from that individual's perspective, we were able to distance the conversation from the more political aspects and keep returning to the 'lived' aspects of people's actual lives. However, it must be noted again that, post assignment, student opposition softened; most of the students expressed positive interactions with this lesson and walked away with a heightened appreciation for both CLA and representation of diverse perspectives in creative writing. This was an introductory lesson, but several students have since begun incorporating aspects of it in their research projects for other classes – perhaps the most ideal result of all.

Given all of this, I argue that the data supports my claim that a creative writing assignment can indeed be used to open discussion for CLA and create groundwork for additional CLA work. Borrowing from translingual creative nonfiction exercises to develop CLA is a useful method for navigating CLA topics in SAE-dominant regions, especially at rural schools. This allows a soft way to bypass some of the resistance against diversity while exposing students to differing perspectives in less politically-charged avenues. If this assignment were paired with more extended lesson components, it could be expanded even further.

There are several different directions in which programs or instructors might take in carrying this forward. Creative writing programs in particular could utilize an assignment like this to start an entire segment on CLA or a more extended sequence on writing from different perspectives. In particular, given more time and resources, the preparatory readings and discussions could feature authors like Toni Morrison's 'Recitatif' and Gloria Anzaldua's 'How to Tame a Wild Tongue'. These were originally intended as part of my original lesson plan but had to be swapped to recommended readings due to time constraints. Other multicultural or global readings might also be incorporated to provide more space for discussion. Additionally, this could easily be modified for radical inclusion in multilingual classes, as demonstrated in resources from Canagarajah (*Literacy as Translingual Practice*, 2013).

First year composition courses, especially those focusing on applications of global Englishes, may use this as an introductory assignment to bridge the topic of CLA and set the stage for further groundwork. Reducing the prompt to a smaller scale would be beneficial towards this end, whether written in class or as an assignment to bring to class for discussion. Scholarship has somewhat explored the idea of tying creative writing to composition, but, as it has been demonstrated, it is often kept to nonfiction or poetry; this can help display the inherent truth that, in writing, all choices are a 'contingent selection' among many possibilities (Mays, 2018: 338). Both fields can learn from each other, in this instance, particularly in an age when authentic human writing is in demand post-advent of AI platforms. Further studies could continue to explore the history of scholarship of connections between the two fields.

Creative fiction is a powerful tool of expression and perfectly situated as an educational tool for CLA and radical inclusion. Research supports that creative fiction has value, or at least generates interest, for current student populations, and my survey data helps support that it can support radical inclusion. It is not a magic pill that immediately bypasses embedded and systemic issues in our society, but it does provide a platform to bypass some of the rhetorical defenses political forces have constructed and open the door to genuine discussion and thought. If nothing else, trying to personally imagine the experience of language minorities may at least expose some SAE-dominant students to the limits of their own perspective. Options for how to further incorporate this are numerous; more extensive segments and lessons are easily incorporated, or it could give voice to minority expressions in a way they may not have felt comfortable with prior. In any of these, creative writing fiction can serve as a powerful tool for inclusion, perspective shaping, and CLA, giving us one more chance to rewrite and redress the fictional 'truths' society tries to say about language.

References

Black, R.W. (2009) Online fan fiction, global identities, and imagination. *Research in the Teaching of English* 43 (4), 397–425.

Canagarajah, S. (2011) Codemeshing in academic writing: Identifying teachable strategies of translanguaging. *The Modern Language Journal* 95 (3), 401–417. http://www.jstor.org/stable/41262375

Canagarajah, S. (2013) Negotiating translingual literacy: An enactment. *Research in the Teaching of English* 48 (1), 40–67. http://www.jstor.org/stable/24398646

Canagarajah, S. (ed.) (2013) *Literacy as Translingual Practice: Between Communities and Classrooms*. Taylor & Francis. https://doi.org/10.4324/9780203120293

Cummins, J. (2019) The emergence of translanguaging pedagogy: A dialogue between theory and practice. *Journal of Multilingual Education Research* 9 (13). https://fordham.bepress.com/jmer/vol9/iss1/13

Heng Hartse, J., Lockett, M. and Ortabasi, M. (2018) Languaging about language in an interdisciplinary writing-intensive course. [Special issue on transdisciplinary and translingual challenges for WAC/WID.] *Across the Disciplines* 15 (3), 89–102. https://wac.colostate.edu/docs/atd/trans/henghartseetal2018.pdf

Johnson, L.P. (2017) Writing the self: Black queer youth challenge heteronormative ways of being in an after-school writing club. *Research in the Teaching of English* 52 (1), 13–33. https://doi.org/10.58680/rte201729198

Kubota, R. and Ward, L. (2000) Exploring linguistic diversity through world Englishes. *English Journal* 89 (6), 80–86.

Lee, E. and Canagarajah, S. (2019) Beyond native and nonnative: Translingual dispositions for more inclusive teacher identity in language and literacy education. *Journal of Language, Identity & Education* 18 (6), 352–363.

Matsuda, P.K. (2003) Second language writing in the twentieth century: A situated historical perspective. In B. Kroll (ed.) *Exploring the Dynamics of Second Language Writing* (pp. 15–34). Cambridge University Press.

Mays, C. (2018) 'You can't make this stuff up': Complexity, facts, and creative nonfiction. *College English* 80 (4), 319–341.

Nicolarakis, O. D. and Mitchell, T. (2023) Dynamic bilingualism to dynamic writing: Using translanguaging strategies and tools. *Languages*, 8 (2), 141. https://doi.org/10.3390/languages8020141

Park, G., Bogdan, S., Rosa, M. and Navarro, J. (eds) (2023) *Critical Pedagogy in the Language and Writing Classroom: Strategies, Examples, Activities from Teacher Scholars*. Routledge.

Sánchez-Martín, C. (2022) 'The power of many' (counter)stories: Materializing spaces of belonging for (im)migrants in rhetoric and composition. *College English* 85 (2), 167–184.

Sengeh, D. (2023) *Radical Inclusion: Seven Steps to Help You Create a More Just Workplace, Home, and World*. Flatiron Books.

Shapiro, S., Gere, A.R., Curzan, A., Hammond, J.W., Hughes, S., Li, R., Moos, A., Smith, K., Van Zanen, K., Wheeler, K.L. and Zanders, C.J. (2022) Interchanges: A Kairotic moment for CLA? Response to Anne Ruggles Gere et al.'s 'Communal Justicing: Writing Assessment, Disciplinary Infrastructure, and the Case for Critical Language Awareness'/Response. *College Composition and Communication* 74 (2), 373–387.

Sui, G. (2021) Short fiction writing in English by Chinese university students: An integrated F-A-I-T-H approach: How do Chinese university students use English in creative ways to 'write truly' while describing something fictional or 'untrue'? *English Today* 37 (2), 120–126. https://doi.org/10.1017/S0266078419000476

Sumpter, M. (2016) EMERGING VOICES: Shared frequency: Expressivism, social constructionism, and the linked creative writing-composition class. *College English* 78 (4), 340–361.

Syllabi – Materializing Translingualism. Department of English, University of Washington. (n.d.) https://english.washington.edu/syllabi-materializing-translingualism (accessed 18 July 2023).

US Census Data. (n.d.) https://data.census.gov/

Wheeler, D.S.L. (2020) Translanguaging as part of the creative process. *Medium*. https://serensiwenna.medium.com/translanguaging-as-part-of-the-creative-process-d549731013da

Zhang-Wu, Q. (2021) (Re)Imagining translingualism as a verb to tear down the English-only wall: 'Monolingual' students as multilingual writers. *College English* 84 (1), 121–137.

Appendix 2.1: Language Minority Flash-Fiction Story Prompt

Language Minority Story

Format: Flash Fiction
Length: 750–1500 words
The Assignment:
Write a story about a character placed in a situation where they do not understand the 'language' of the setting they are in. How do they navigate/negotiate the language barriers? How do they feel during the process?
Details:
Write a 'translanguage' themed story about negotiation of meaning in language. Ideally, you'll situate your character as a language minority in a situation where they are trying to convey meaning but don't have the words to do so. How do they navigate this situation? What other ways might they find to communicate? How might different cultural practices or assumptions play into the 'dialogue'? How can 'dialogue' happen without words?
Some common themes you might include:

- Code-meshing (combining phrases from one language to another; i.e. 'the three amigos over there')
- Negotiation of meaning between two groups who do not speak the same language (note: this can apply to what we might even call dialects or different 'standards' of the same language, or between entirely different language branches)
- Avoid 'dialectical typecasting'; how do you develop the accent of a 'character' as compared to a sterilized blanket 'accent' that isn't located to place or person?

Story Elements:
This short story should focus on the dynamics of communication when there's a language barrier. You do not need to know a second language to write this. Lean into your own monolingual status and embody the protagonist's complete bewilderment in the text. You are welcome to use Google Translate to help generate dialogue in another language, but please be aware that this is far from a perfect translation service. Your protagonist, however, *should not* understand the language of the situation they are in.

Use **sensory details and psychological realism** to convince your reader of the veracity of your story. Get inside the head of your character.

3 Toward Radical Inclusivity in First Year Composition: A Lesson for CLA, Translingual Writing and Metacognitive Development

Sophia Minnillo

Introduction

Critical pedagogies pave the way for radical inclusivity, in the classroom and world. Radical inclusivity describes 'a commitment to keep fighting for everyone to be included, no matter who they are, where they come from, and how they show up' (Sengeh, 2023: xii). Through this act of hope, we as educators can work to end legacies of oppression against historically marginalized populations, including BIPOC and multilingual students. Critical approaches to education – which guide us and our students to listen, question, and advocate for justice – provide the necessary tools for enacting radical inclusivity.

Three critical pedagogical approaches stand out as beneficial for promoting radical inclusivity in the writing classroom: (1) critical language awareness (CLA), (2) translanguaging, and (3) metacognitive practice. CLA pedagogy is 'an approach to language and literacy education that focuses on the intersections of language, identity, power, and privilege, with the goal of promoting self-reflection, social justice, and rhetorical agency among student writers' (Shapiro, 2022: 4). Translingual pedagogy valorizes language use that is not constrained to one linguistic code, but rather draws from and moves flexibly between codes and other semiotic resources to make meaning (Canagarajah, 2023). Metacognition-oriented pedagogy helps students develop the ability to recognize and reflect on one's ways of thinking and strategies for completing tasks (Lee & Mak,

2018). These pedagogies align well with contract-based grading assessment, which strives to promote equity and social justice by de-emphasizing grading based on the instructor's perception of student writing quality (Inoue, 2022).

Taken together, these approaches to teaching and assessment invite students to reconsider what they believe to be true about 'correct' writing and language. These reflections guide students toward celebrating language diversity and interrogating monolingual and standard language ideologies (Lippi-Green, 2012). The pedagogical approaches also build students' rhetorical skills by prompting students to explain their compositional choices and intended effects. What is perhaps most important is that these approaches encourage students to express pride in their linguistic and cultural backgrounds and share their funds of knowledge with classmates to foster collective, community-driven learning. In the subsequent sections, I describe concretely how I translated these approaches into the focal lesson.

Context

I taught the lesson in a first year composition course (FYC) at a public university in the Western US. This university is classified as an emerging Hispanic Serving Institution and has a relatively large international student population. Taught over the summer, the FYC course lasted six weeks and included two hour-long class meetings four days a week.

My course, taught in 2023, comprised of 18 students. All were majoring in STEM, and 17 of the 18 students were multilingual. Many reported communicating in Arabic, Korean, Mandarin, or Vietnamese with their family, in addition to communicating in English in other contexts. A majority also reported having transnational and multicultural experiences. I highlight my students' backgrounds because they served as an asset for honing CLA and metacognition through translingual practice.

The lesson in action

I taught this lesson at the end of week four, when students were revising their complete research paper. I chose to include the lesson on this day because students would soon switch from focusing on global concerns to local concerns while providing peer feedback and completing their final paper revisions. Before students decided to reenforce standard language ideologies through their feedback and revising practices, I wanted them to engage in reflection about language diversity. My goal was for students to become familiar with issues related to 'Standard English' and to practice translanguaging as a form of motivated deviation from the norm. In this way, students would reflect on the rhetorical power of language choices, better informing their next steps for language-level revision.

Table 3.1 Student learning outcomes

By the end of the lesson, students will be able to:
(1) define key terms related to CLA, multilingualism, and translanguaging (2) describe their existing multilingual and translingual practices (3) craft an argument about the importance of valuing language diversity (4) create a translingual text (5) practice metacognition by reflecting on their rhetorical choices during translingual composition

The lesson's student learning outcomes (SLOs) are reported in Table 3.1. The SLOs were aligned with the course's broader learning outcomes, in that they supported students' development of metacognition and knowledge of how conventions can differ across and within discourse communities.

Before class, students read the book chapter 'How to Tame a Wild Tongue' from *Borderlands/La Frontera* (Anzaldúa, 1987) and the article 'Beyond Language Difference in Writing' (Sánchez-Martín, 2021). In addition to serving as model texts for CLA and translanguaging, these readings contributed to inclusivity in the classroom, as the authors represent multilingual, female, Latinx, and LGBTQ+ identities. Furthermore, Sánchez-Martín's *Writing Spaces* text served as an accessible resource to students learning about these topics for the first time. Students were instructed to read Anzaldúa's text carefully, using it as the basis for their reading reflection, and to skim Sánchez-Martín's article, as we would read certain parts more carefully in class. The 200–250 word, low-stakes reading reflection guided students to connect Anzaldúa's arguments with the course language policy. The prompt was as follows:

> In the [course] syllabus, we have a statement on language diversity. Please comment on how this statement relates to Anzaldúa's points in 'How to Tame a Wild Tongue'. You might discuss the author's description of Chicano Spanish and her reflection on how others view this language variety.

This assignment led students to think critically about language-related policies and how they can support or hinder different groups, including Latinx and multilingual students.

While I had planned for the lesson to last 60 minutes, it took approximately 80 minutes of the two hour-long class because students needed more time to complete the activities. Table 3.2 represents the actual time distribution.

As a warm-up activity (10 minutes), students shared their homework responses with peers. I also highlighted two exemplary student responses. The group discussions and examples prompted students to think about the notion of 'correctness' related to language use and how this concept can foster injustice. Many students brought in personal examples of scenarios

Table 3.2 Lesson plan with time estimates

Pedagogical activity	Time (80 minutes total of class time)
Homework: read 'How to Tame a Wild Tongue' (Anzaldúa, 1987), skim 'Beyond Language Difference in Writing' (Sánchez-Martín, 2021), and write a reading reflection	90–135 minutes
Small-group discussion of homework, leading into full class discussion about language policies and their effects	10 minutes
Viewing of TED Talk (Leung, 2018), post-reflection in small groups leading to full class discussion about multilingualism, translingual practices, and norms of communication	20 minutes
Analysis of translingual writing in Sánchez-Martín (2021) and definition of key CLA terms in the text, leading into full class discussion about language and power	15 minutes
Presentation of translingual writing activity and my own model text	5 minutes
Individual translingual writing	15 minutes
Partner explanation about rhetorical choices in translingual text, leading into full group discussion and lesson conclusion	15 minutes

in which they felt lesser because of language difference, which led us to start unpacking these deficit ideologies.

In the subsequent activity (20 minutes), students watched and discussed the TED Talk, 'Embracing Multilingualism and Eradicating Linguistic Bias' (Leung, 2018). Leung, a Chinese-American and multilingual student, describes the difficulties that her parents faced due to linguistic prejudice. She argues in favor of celebrating multilingualism, which she supports through evidence of its cognitive benefits. Leung also provides an example of normal communication practices in her household that exist between Cantonese and English. My multilingual students, especially those with similar language backgrounds, resonated strongly with this example. My students followed Leung's video by sharing their own reflections about multilingualism and language diversity. Many students voiced arguments in support of communicating using multiple codes based on their own experiences with translanguaging in their homes and communities. Thus, Leung's video prompted students to reconsider norms enforced by educational institutions and articulate reasons for more inclusive approaches to language.

Next, we defined key terms for CLA and translanguaging through further engagement with the readings (15 minutes). I started by presenting examples of translanguaging that Sánchez-Martín (2021) cites, including excerpts from Young (2010) and Anzaldúa (1987). We compared and contrasted these two examples to understand variation within approaches to translingual writing. Then, I tasked students with finding the definitions of six terms in Sánchez-Martín's article: *language variety*, *dialect*, *sociolect, idiolect, multilingual,* and *translanguaging.* Students volunteered to share their definitions on the board. As a class, we workshopped their definitions and added examples for clarity. This activity gave students the vocabulary to express important ideas related to CLA and translingual practice, including that language variation is normal. This led to conversation about language and power – why are certain language varieties stigmatized while others are deemed prestigious?

The next activity (35 minutes total) provided an opportunity for students to practice translingual writing, comment in greater depth on the lesson's topic, and use their metacognitive skills to reflect on their writerly decisions. I introduced the writing task with the following directions:

- It's your turn to try incorporating multiple different languages, dialects/sociolects/idiolects, and/or registers in writing.
- The task: Spend 10 minutes freewriting about your reflections on what we've learned today. Be sure to include as much language diversity as possible.

I framed the task as a freewrite so students would feel open to taking risks in their writing and embracing the fluidity of translingual practice (Elbow, 2000). Before students began writing, I further scaffolded the task by showcasing an example translingual piece that I had written in response to the prompt.

Once students finished the task, they engaged in the metacognitive work of explaining their compositional choices to a partner. First, they presented their freewrite to their partner, reading it out loud if they were comfortable doing so. Reading these compositions out loud encourages students to negotiate meaning in real time with their audience, which is often necessary due to the hybrid nature of translingual texts. After the presentation, the students described how they engaged in translanguaging and provided a rationale for using certain language resources in various parts of their composition. As this was a partner dialogue, the partner had an opportunity to comment on the effectiveness of the author's translingual choices.

I evaluated students' accomplishment of the majority of the SLOs informally and formatively, through listening to their group discussions and responding to their comments in the large-group discussion. However, I did formally and formatively assess students' ability to create a translingual text. Following my labor-based grading contract, I evaluated students based on their labor dedicated toward completing the writing activity guidelines. Students received a 'complete' (full credit) if they followed the guidelines, along with encouraging comments in the margins of their pieces. The fact that students were not evaluated based on the 'quality' of their writing may have further incentivized them to break from the 'standard' language mold in this assignment.

Takeaways

What did my students learn?

This lesson's success is evidenced in the freewrite of one student, Aliya. Aliya was a strong writer and a multilingual student of color; I mention this as multilinguals and students of color have been historically marginalized by traditional approaches to literacy (Baker-Bell *et al.*, 2020; Carando *et al.*, 2023). Her composition demonstrates how the lesson's pedagogical approach gave students the terminology to express what many of them already knew from experience. Aliya (2023) writes, 'When I first learned about the concept of translanguaging, I did not think it was something new or something different. I think it is something that perfectly describes me, something that I was born with. اللسان العربي يجري في دمي'. In this opening, Aliya explains that once she learned the term 'translanguaging' in class, she found a new resource to express her lived experiences and heritage. She then practices translanguaging, changing codes to highlight her ancestral connection to the Arabic language.

She continues on to portray how Urdu, Fijian, Spanish, and English all figure into her language background, based on the places her family has lived and the communities in which she has participated. Aliya ties this plurality to her complex identity: 'I grew up like this, juggling languages. Thinking in one language and writing in another. It is hard for me to identify who I am… I am still understanding who I am, but over time, I have realized that I am simply me'. In this excerpt, Aliya celebrates her multilingual identity and highlights the normality of plurality, flipping the script on monolingual language ideologies.

Aliya further demonstrates CLA by elaborating on how translingual practices have served as her norm. She explains, 'Translanguaging is something that has shaped me. *Meri dill he*. I have realized that on paper, I live on both the right and left margins. My languages move in different directions and I find beauty in the red lines under words…' Here, Aliya shows that forces of standardization in language use, such as word processors, fail to account for her normal language practices. She views the signs of her departure from standardization as beautiful, based on their connection to her unique identity.

Aliya's classmates similarly crafted compelling arguments for the value of language diversity in the freewrite assignment. Many students supported their claims with evidence from their own and their family members' multilingual, multicultural, and often transnational experiences. One student valorized her mother's multilingual repertoire and connected it to Leung's (2018) point about bilingualism being an asset. Most students used translingual practices to convey their argument, moving fluidly between varieties of Mandarin, Japanese, Vietnamese, Spanish and English, as well as visual semiotics such as emojis. Overall, the freewrite activity gave students a space to expose and celebrate their translingual repertoires while practicing CLA and metacognition.

What did I learn?

This lesson allowed me to learn more about my students, especially in terms of their identities, motivations, and literacy practices. The in-class discussion and low-stakes freewrite encouraged students to tell their story, more than they had in the research paper-oriented assignments that constituted the class's focus. By asking students to reflect about linguistic justice, I gleaned a better sense of the social issues that my students care about. Students also shared with me more about their languaging practices during that lesson than they had before, perhaps because they may have assumed that I would reinforce standard language ideologies, as is often done in other classes. By sharing their stories and experiences languaging in unique ways, my students helped me to serve them more effectively as a teacher.

Challenges

Perhaps the most important challenge I encountered stemmed from not allocating enough time to the lesson, as my initial 60-minute lesson plan turned into 80 minutes of activity. The lesson could have benefitted from even more time so students could engage in a more in-depth discussion about language and power and dedicate more time to writing and reflecting.

Another challenge in implementing this lesson is that the content can run contrary to what some students believe. Standard language and raciolinguistic ideologies are often deeply entrenched (Lippi-Green, 2012). Thus, it is essential to establish a classroom environment of respectful and productive dialogue at the beginning of this lesson. Some students – in my experience, particularly those who come from privileged backgrounds – will be more resistant to translanguaging than others. The low-stakes freewriting task can assist these students in noticing the variety of codes in their repertoires. Once they better understand how they can translanguage, and how it can help them accomplish their rhetorical goals, these students will be better prepared to implement translingual practice in higher-stakes writing.

Adaptations and extensions to other contexts

The elements of this lesson could be expanded throughout the course. For example, my students write a positionality statement at the beginning of the course as part of their research paper project. To apply what they learned from this lesson, in the following week, students could revise their positionality statement to include translingual practice and to more critically address how their linguistic and cultural backgrounds influence them as scholar-authors. As students engage in peer response to the research paper, they could further reflect on the rhetorical impact of translanguaging in their peers' work.

The lesson can be adapted for FYC classes that focus on other topics, such as multimodal composition. In line with studies that recommend translingual remix projects (e.g. Sánchez-Martín *et al.*, 2019), the translingual freewrite could become a remix homework assignment, in which students have access to their entire multimodal communicative repertoire to reflect on what they learned in the lesson.

The lesson could also be tailored for a class that focuses on critical AI literacy. One important concern about AI tools is that they carry harmful biases found in their training data (Byrd, 2023). Students could develop critical AI literacy and CLA by assessing the extent to which AI tools display linguistic prejudice. This activity would follow naturally after the class discussion of language and power supported by the Sánchez-Martín (2021) reading. For example, students might prompt AI with a question such as 'Should I write "ain't" in academic papers?' I asked this to Microsoft's (2024) Copilot, and one portion of its response included, '"Ain't"…is best reserved for creating dialogue for uneducated or careless speakers'. Students would benefit from analyzing how Copilot's response reflects raciolinguistic and classist ideologies perpetuated through AI systems. CLA pedagogy thus offers a useful approach for honing students' understanding of AI's limitations, which may be of heightened importance as this technology becomes increasingly ubiquitous.

Conclusion

By facilitating students' development of CLA, translingual writing, and metacognition, and implementing contract grading as a critical assessment practice, this lesson contributes to making our classrooms and communities more inclusive. Aliya's translingual piece exemplifies how the lesson supported students' whole selves, encouraging them to share their insights from lived experiences and to celebrate the value of their language repertoires. The lesson also contributed to accomplishing key FYC learning outcomes related to developing metacognition and knowledge of how conventions can vary across and within discourse communities. Despite its advantages for student learning and inclusivity, this lesson's critical approach may be met with resistance from students or administrators. I encourage readers to *aguantar* ((not give up) give up), as dismantling long-standing language ideologies takes time. Listening to critiques and engaging in productive dialogue about these topics can make a considerable impact toward rendering our classrooms and communities radically inclusive.

References

Aliya. (2023) *The Identity of Someone Who is Multi-Racial*. [Unpublished manuscript].
Anzaldúa, G. (1987) *Borderlands/La Frontera: The New Mestiza*. Aunt Lute Books.
Baker-Bell, A., Williams-Farrier, B.J., Jackson, D., Johnson, L., Kynard, C. and McMurtry, T. (2020) This ain't another statement! This is a DEMAND for black linguistic justice! Conference on College Composition and Communication. https://cccc.ncte.org/cccc/demand-for-black-linguistic-justice

Byrd, A. (2023) Truth-telling: Critical inquiries on LLMs and the corpus texts that train them. *Composition Studies* 51 (1), 135–142.
Canagarajah, S. (2023) Decolonizing academic writing pedagogies for multilingual students. *TESOL Quarterly* 58 (1), 280–306. https://doi.org/10.1002/tesq.3231
Carando, A., Minnillo, S., Fernández-Mira, P., Davidson, S., Sagae, K. and Sánchez-Gutiérrez, C. (2023) Writing development in Spanish as a second and heritage language: A corpus study on complexity. *Journal of Spanish Language Teaching* 10 (1), 59–71. https://doi.org/10.1080/23247797.2023.2201989
Elbow, P. (2000) *Everyone Can Write: Essays Toward a Hopeful Theory of Writing and Teaching Writing.* Oxford University Press.
Inoue, A.B. (2022) *Labor-Based Grading Contracts: Building Equity and Inclusion in the Compassionate Writing Classroom.* The WAC Clearinghouse; University Press of Colorado. https://doi.org/10.37514/PER-B.2022.1824
Lee, I. and Mak, P. (2018) Metacognition and metacognitive instruction in second language writing classrooms. *TESOL Quarterly* 52 (4), 1085–1097. https://doi.org/10.1002/tesq.436
Leung, K. (2018) *Embracing Multilingualism and Eradicating Linguistic Bias.* TED Conferences. https://www.ted.com/talks/karen_leung_embracing_multilingualism_and_eradicating_linguistic_bias
Lippi-Green, R. (2012) *English with an Accent: Language, Ideology, and Discrimination in the United States.* Routledge.
Microsoft. (2024) Copilot (10 January version) [Large Language Model]. https://www.microsoft.com/en-us/bing/chat/enterprise/?form=MA13FV
Sánchez-Martín, C. (2021) Beyond language difference in writing: Investigating complex and equitable language practices. *Writing Spaces: Readings on Writing* 4, 269–280.
Sánchez-Martín, C., Hirsu, L., Gonzales, L. and Alvarez, S.P. (2019) Pedagogies of digital composing through a translingual approach. *Computers and Composition* 52, 142–157. https://doi.org/10.1016/j.compcom.2019.02.007
Sengeh, D.M. (2023) *Radical Inclusion: Seven Steps to Help You Create a More Just Workplace, Home, and World.* Flatiron Books.
Shapiro, S. (2022) *Cultivating Critical Language Awareness in the Writing Classroom.* Routledge.
Young, V.A. (2010) Should writers use they own English? *Iowa Journal of Cultural Studies* 12 (1), 110–117. https://doi.org/10.17077/2168-569X.1095

4 Radically Inclusive Teaching: A Lesson Utilizing the Learning about Written Languages (LaWL) Approach

Marie Webb

Introduction and Course Context

Being radically inclusive in my undergraduate pre-academic English courses often means that I involve myself and my international students in difficult conversations about our linguistic and racial backgrounds. My academic writing classes are predominantly filled with Chinese international students, and I often question whether they are truly supported by the institutional system. In other words, I must take on 'the shared responsibility to help Chinese international students succeed academically, and at the same time, make sure they do not drop into the complex racial milieu of the US without a meaningful support system' (Yu, 2025: 169). Radical inclusivity, for me, means creating a safe classroom support system as students learn how to discuss and explore their transnational and transcultural experiences. It also means educating my students with current and historical knowledge about educational inequities in America, so that they more fully understand the intersections of English language learning and society. American universities uphold a neoliberal discourse of diversity, which is a move that valorizes international students as having the power to benefit and provide value to the student body via their multilingual competence (Wang, 2022). While this neoliberal perspective of international student diversity on campus is encouraging for students and faculty, it can also essentialize students' experiences. When we embrace a neoliberal discourse of diversity, we can be blinded by our international students' 'bodily experiences of linguistic discrimination' (Wang, 2022: 43), and I also believe we can be blinded by their experiences of racial discrimination.

One of the first steps in practicing radical inclusion is identifying the exclusion (Sengeh, 2023). Many of my international students do not have the everyday language to enter conversations about racism and social inequalities; some also feel that they are not or will not ever be affected by issues of racial or linguistic discrimination. Many Chinese international students 'place themselves outside of the US racial system' (Yu, 2025), which leads them to believe that they may be unaffected by issues surrounding race and prejudice. For many international students in America, 'racism, segregation, and language discrimination were a reality of their campus lives', which contradicts the view of the American university as a diverse, global campus (Kang, 2015: 163).

The lesson I share in this chapter is informed by a recent approach to college writing courses theorized and named by Di Gennaro *et al.* (2023) as Learning about Written Language (LaWL). The chapter title says it all: 'Uniting CLA with WAW via SLA: Learning About Written Language as a Model for College Writing Courses'. As an applied linguist and writing studies instructor, I can't imagine *not* teaching my academic writing courses with the use of anti-oppressive pedagogies and critical language awareness (CLA) – or what I now know is in line with the LaWL approach.

Description of a Class Lesson

The academic writing course I highlight in this chapter shares one lesson from a 10-week course centered upon the class theme: 'Systemic Inequities, Racism, and Stereotypes: Confronting Bias in Education'. The focus of this flipped instruction and LaWL lesson is students learning about social justice vocabulary and collocations, and most importantly, how language changes over time. Students analyze a chapter from Jonathan Kozol's (1991) *Savage Inequalities* and discuss language that they might replace or adapt with the newer social justice vocabulary they have learned. They then turn to their drafts of their paper centered upon conversations about educational inequality in the US and the importance of diversity in today's colleges and workplaces. They analyze their writing to see how they might improve their language in a way that promotes equity and avoids perpetuating unconscious biases. They end with a reflection on editing their writing with a linguistic justice lens. Following the inquiry-based learning approach, students use this activity to help co-create their original thesis in a collaborative podcast script.

A brief description of the activity goals/learning outcomes

By the end of the lesson, students will be able to:

(1) Apply social justice vocabulary and collocations accurately in writing.
(2) Analyze source text vocabulary and rhetorical moves from a CLA perspective.

(3) Analyze their own writing and vocabulary use from a CLA perspective.
(4) Create new understandings about issues of justice about racism, diversity, and systemic educational inequalities.
(5) Develop critical and global self-awareness about their social positioning, identities, and cultural competencies.

Pre-lesson readings/flipped classroom materials

(1) Jonathan Kozol's 'Other People's Children' chapter excerpt from *Savage Inequalities*.
(2) YouTube video from 'Your Favorite English Teacher' titled 'English Vocabulary About Social Issues: 20 Words You Need to Know'.
(3) A handout titled 'Tips for Socially Just Writing' about outdated and current vocabulary from The Debby Ellis Writing Center at South Western University.
(4) A handout titled 'Inclusive Language Guide' by the University of South Carolina Aiken.
(5) A DEI glossary titled 'The Language of Inclusion' by Line 25 Consulting, Michelle Ngome.
(6) A 2022 *New York Times* article titled 'Why We're Capitalizing Black'.
(7) An instructor-led video lecture with nuanced perspectives of the vocabulary handouts.

The vocabulary from Joy (2021) 'Your Favorite English Teacher' is one of the key elements of fostering the LaWL approach in this lesson and it is one instrumental tool that can guide any instructor's application of anti-racist pedagogy. Your Favorite English Teacher notes the following in the description for her video on social justice vocabulary words and her lesson on collocations that go along with them: 'We have a lot of complex and controversial social issues in the US, and in this video, I will teach you 20 vocabulary words about social issues that will help you better understand and talk about them'.

(1) to discriminate against
(2) people of color
(3) social justice
(4) social construct
(5) socioeconomic status
(6) social/societal norms
(7) institutional/systemic racism
(8) privilege
(9) the gender pay gap
(10) gender roles
(11) gender identity
(12) equal rights
(13) racial/gender equality

(14) to treat (someone) equally
(15) to promote equality
(16) to advocate for something
(17) widespread support
(18) widespread acceptance
(19) widespread belief
(20) to become widespread

Pre-lesson flipped classroom activity

Students watch the video lecture to study appropriate collocations that go along with social justice language from 'Your Favorite English Teacher'. Next, they complete an online discussion by writing sentences with the vocabulary aimed at the ideas in their collaborative podcast writing project for the course. Second, students watch the video lecture from their instructor introducing the various social justice vocabulary handouts. After watching the video, they post a discussion response with the following:

(1) Students react to something the instructor shared in the video lecture regarding how language changes over time as they work to join the discussion about language variation.
(2) Students share any terminology that was new or surprising to them. They are invited to discuss their ideas or concerns about language they are questioning or may have misused.
(3) Students are invited to ask other questions they have about social justice vocabulary. I also remind students to be respectful and careful. If they have questions about racial slurs or 'bad' words I suggest they reserve those questions for me or their peers in private, or they may do some further research on them outside of the discussion forum space to further their knowledge and understanding. My students often have good intentions to learn more about applying social justice vocabulary; but, naturally, many students want to know more about racial slurs or other words that they should avoid or use with caution.
(4) Students respond back to a peer with encouragement and support in learning more about navigating language related to race, equity, and social inclusion/exclusion.

The key to the flipped classroom activities is that students complete an activity that shows their understanding of that content before coming to the next lesson. In my hybrid class, flipped activities are also graded as participation.

In the classroom activities

Warm-up: Students come into the class and begin writing a journal. We often start the class with a journal or low-stakes review quiz to help them recall new information. For this warm-up journal, students are connecting back to a chapter that they discussed in-person the class session prior and connecting it to the new reading they did for homework about Jonathan Kozol. They spend 10–15 minutes writing on the following question:

(1) How is Malcolm Gladwell's chapter on 'The Matthew Effect' illustrated in Jonathan Kozol's excerpt we read from 'Other People's Children'?

Vocabulary review: Students join a partner and begin working on a collaborative review quiz with a sample paragraph with gap fills to insert related collocations to be used with the social justice vocabulary they were introduced to in the flipped homework discussions and tasks and their corresponding video lectures. After 10–15 minutes, the instructor brings the class together to share answers and review.

Critical language awareness analysis: The instructor highlights some of the important takeaways from the flipped classroom discussions, and asks students if they have any further questions. They often may bring up language variation by sharing personal experiences and reactions while listening to the *Code Switch* podcast 'Is it time to say R.I.P. to POC?' (Meraji & Demby, 2020). The instructor explains that students will listen to the podcast along with a transcript for homework but that the current class activity prepares them to analyze source text vocabulary and rhetorical moves from a CLA perspective. The instructor reviews the lesson learning outcomes and asks the class if they have ever experienced analyzing language to examine and interrogate privilege and power. The instructor leaves room for open discussion and vulnerably shares their first encounters with doing so and the challenges they may have faced as they acknowledge their social positioning and background.

Students are directed toward a passage from Jonathan Kozol and are asked to begin circling or boxing vocabulary in the reading that they think meets the expectations of social justice vocabulary as in use today, or out-of-use. They are directed to leave a question mark in the margins if they are considering whether or not it is mainstream discourse that is acceptable for everyday use in the media and daily conversation.

After some time has passed and the instructor can see that students have begun pulling out some words in their analysis, the instructor allows students to get into their chosen groups and share findings. Conversations and questions start emerging about the acceptability of certain vocabulary words in the passage, and students also discuss reasons why they might supplement or replace that vocabulary with a newer social justice term that they learned in the flipped classroom discussions. The instructor may encourage whole class or small-group discussion to discuss their findings.

In-class collaborative writing via a synchronous chat: Students join a small group with 2–3 other students and begin working on collaborative writing. Instructors may find it useful to use live chat technology from their learning management systems for small groups, or even a group messaging app among the students. Before beginning, instructors may review and show examples of dialogic versus dialectical conversation. Then they can provide students with several questions to discuss including the following:

(1) Have you ever had the opportunity to learn about systemic racism in America before moving to the United States?
(2) How comfortable do you feel talking about issues of race, class, sexual orientation, social positioning, and cultural biases?
(3) Have you or anyone you know ever experienced racial or cultural biases that you want to share? Have you read or heard about any other racial or cultural biases or events in the United States among other social groups or racial groups that you identify with? Have any of these happened in schools?
(4) Do you feel that you are learning more about your own identity and role as a potential global ambassador and multilingual/multicultural or transnational/transcultural advocate through the readings and discussions in our class?
(5) What emotions and feelings, stories, and goals come up for you about the readings you have done on systemic educational racism thus far in our course?

While these are challenging questions, students are encouraged to naturally chat back and forth with one another to see what ideas and questions naturally emerge in their discussions. This activity helps to model the conversational style required in their podcast script writing for their first summative writing project of the course, a collaborative podcast project.

End of class debrief: The instructor may encourage students to share in a whole class debrief about anything interesting that came up in their silent chats. The instructor encourages students to save their writing and explains that they will continue engaging in the silent chat with their group in the next class. Continuing the silent chat as homework or in the next class can be useful for outlining conversations and narrowing down topics for their podcast script writing with their classmates. They will work to begin outlining their podcast scripts with their groups in the next class session drawing upon ideas that emerged in their silent chat.

Flipped classroom homework: After this class activity, students listen to a podcast from *Code Switch* and complete a listening gap-fill of a transcription of the podcast, and a few multiple-choice listening comprehension questions. The podcast hosts debate the terms BIPOC vs. POC by interviewing linguistic experts and laypersons during 2020 when the term BIPOC emerged. Using discussions and materials about important vocabulary related to anti-racism helps them become more critical of language that may be in use or out of use in the texts and media they encounter throughout the course. This flipped homework activity provides scaffolding for students to design and write a podcast script alongside their peers for their first collaborative writing project. They culminate the podcast project by recording their group, and individually writing a final metacognitive reflection paper about the creation of their podcast with their group members.

My class in action: A classroom portrait

There are 18 hardworking undergraduate international students in my hybrid (in-person and online) academic writing class housed in the Department of Linguistics at a public university in California. As my students trickle into the classroom, I reflect on the lesson before. I recall that most of my students know very little about the education system in America other than the names of a few well-known colleges and universities. They read and discussed questions from a classic chapter in a book on the fight against educational injustices in America; many of them reported how surprised or confused they were. They return to class today feeling uncertain about entering the conversations about systemic inequalities in America's education system.

The class begins with quiet journaling as students reflect upon their reading homework from Jonathan Kozol and its relationship to a prior class reading from Malcolm Gladwell about 'The Matthew Effect'. The next activity consists of a collaborative review quiz on collocations and definitions from the social justice vocabulary (flipped classroom homework) we have been studying. I observe one student who is struggling to write a verb that commonly comes before the word 'diversity'. I direct them to the freecollocation.com website activity in their book. They navigate to the online collocation dictionary, find the words 'promote' and 'foster', and then write those down on their review quiz. Another student quickly fills in the answer to the word 'resegregation' while referencing the landmark *Brown v. Board of Education* case they learned about in an article reporting about the embarrassingly segregated schools in our nation's capital. I can tell from their faces and our online discussion activities that some of my students feel empowered and happy to learn about this history while others appear caught off guard.

I collect the review quiz and guide students into their activity for the day. I begin by asking them how they liked the flipped classroom lectures and practice writing activity on social justice language. One of the students quickly raises their hand and says, 'I felt bad because I didn't know the difference between the words American and Native Americans. I didn't know African American and Black had different meanings too. I want to use this language better and not sound bad'. The class prior, they watched a lecture from me about social justice language and another from my colleague's popular YouTube channel about collocations and social justice vocabulary.

I use my students' comments as a starting point for the next activity and write on the board 'language changes over time'. I explain that we are studying social justice language, so that they can feel confident speaking and writing about society. I share with them that even I have had challenges using and learning about social justice and Diversity, Equity, Inclusion, and Belonging (DEIB) language. Turning to face my computer screen at the podium in front of the class, I type in NPR.com and navigate to the 2020 section of the podcast show 'Code: Switch'. I say to them, 'In 2020, I listened to this podcast, "Is it time to say R.I.P. to POC?" and I was so confused about the hosts' discussions about the terms BIPOC and POC as I didn't even know there was a debate about these terms going on'. I quickly write what each term stands for on the board. I transition to the big task of the lesson, which is to analyze some of the language from articles we previously read about educational segregation in the United States.

Post-activity thoughts, reflections, and/or discussion of challenges
Instructors may find numerous alternative ways for students to do similar critical language analysis activities. They could allow more time for students to find alternate source texts, podcasts, or clips of discussions and online media. After students find their sources to analyze, they may dive into the critical language analysis activity and synchronous silent chat discussions with their peers. Instructors may want to allow students time for a short presentation of their findings to foster more student agency and interest in exploring various source materials. Shapiro (2022) provides ample examples of her classroom writing projects; as such, she demonstrates that when students are provided with opportunities and support to design writing projects that are socially and personally relevant, they can respond to real-world problems in creative and engaging ways.

In scaffolding anti-racist pedagogy within a LaWL classroom, instructors should practice and prepare for discomfort. They should review some of the language for setting ground rules for class discussions and avoid language that seeks to normalize discomfort but haphazardly abandons ideas of classroom safety provided by Shapiro (2022) in her chapter on 'Infusing CLA into Classroom Instruction'. Finally, I encourage anyone engaging in LaWL and anti-racist pedagogy to keep a classroom journal (or a collaborative journal with a colleague) noting interesting teaching observations. Returning to my journals and screenshots of student writing and discussing challenges and observations with my colleague in our collaborative journal helps me to re-design and create more engaging activities for my students each time I teach a course.

References

Di Gennaro, K., Choong, K.-W.P. and Brewer, M. (2023) Uniting CLA with WAW via SLA: Learning about written language as a model for college writing courses. *Journal of Second Language Writing* 60. https://doi.org/10.1016/j.jslw.2023.100967

Joy, A. (2021) English vocabulary about social issues: 20 words you need to know. *YouTube*. https://www.youtube.com/watch?v=UqlRX03f1UM

Kang, Y.K. (2015) Tensions of local and global: South Korean students navigating and maximizing US college life. *Literacy in Composition Studies* 3 (3), 86–109. https://doi.org/10.21623/1.3.3.6

Kozol, J. (1991) *Savage Inequalities: Children in America's Schools*. Perenial.

Meraji, S.M. and Demby, G. (Hosts) (2020) Is it time to say R.I.P. to 'POC'? Code Switch [Audio podcast]. *NPR*. https://www.npr.org/podcasts/510312/codeswitch

Sengeh, D. (2023) *Radical Inclusion: Seven Steps to Help You Create a More Just Workplace, Home, and World*. Flatiron Books.

Shapiro, S. (2022) *Cultivating Critical Language Awareness in the Writing Classroom*. Routledge.

Wang, Z. (2022) Autoethnographic performance of difference as antiracist pedagogy. In B.R. Schrieber, E. Lee, J.T. Johnson and N. Fahim (eds) *Linguistic Justice on Campus: Pedagogy and Advocacy for Multilingual Students* (pp. 41–57). Multilingual Matters.

Yu, J. (2025) The racial learning of Chinese international students in the US: A transnational perspective. *Race Ethnicity and Education* 28 (1), 154–173. https://doi.org/10.1080/13613324.2022.2106878

Part 2

What Does Radical Inclusivity Look Like in the Preparation of Language and Writing Teachers?

Part 2

What Does Radical Inclusivity Look Like in the Preparation of Language Teachers?

5 Critical Language Awareness and Translingual Pedagogies in the Language Teacher Education Classroom: An Enactment

Havva Zorluel Ozer

Background

Ideologies of monolingualism and standardization have consistently been at the center of language education, no matter the context. I studied English as a foreign language in Türkiye, where English was part of school curricula as of grade 4. My own English learning experiences were shaped by the belief that there was one and only way of using English and this way was paved with standards, rules, and norms. Any departures from the prescribed ways of using English in my writing would be highlighted in red and result in losing grade points from the assignment. To illustrate, I remember how I was obsessed with English songs when I was in high school and one of my favorites was 'Shut Up' by Black Eyed Peas. Finding the lyrics on Google, I memorized the song which included vernacular expressions such as 'cause', 'ain't', 'gotta', etc. I had never been taught these expressions at school and using them somehow made me feel a more proficient English language user. With the finding of there being no place for such 'nonstandard' words in my English essays, however, I silenced myself in academic discourses to avoid 'inappropriate' language use.

Reflecting on these memories, I realize how language-based racism and discrimination operated within the discourses of language and literacy education that I attended. As Flores and Rosa (2015: 152) assert, 'notions such as "standard language" or "academic language" and the discourse of appropriateness in which they both are embedded must be conceptualized as racialized ideological positions'. I now see English education that I received as complicit in perpetuating standard language ideologies, privileging a standardized variety of the language and prescribing its norms for all language users to conform to, or otherwise be stigmatized.

Given that not much has changed in the educational landscape of Türkiye, which could be generalized to many ESL/EFL contexts beyond the local, it is urgent to take pedagogical steps toward deconstructing institutionalized racism in the teaching of English. The recent call for increased criticality in language teacher education (Kubota, 2023; Kubota & Miller, 2017; Tian & Zhang-Wu, 2022) as well as special issues dedicated to Critical Language Awareness (CLA) in the recent volumes of flagship journals in the field (e.g. *Journal of Language, Identity, and Education*, 2023; *Journal of Second Language Writing*, 2023) highlight the exigency of these pedagogical steps to advocate language teachers' agency in recognizing, understanding, and critiquing the norms and standards within the communicative expectations of discourse communities (Shapiro, 2022). These pedagogical steps must explicitly be radically inclusive to work within the framework of social linguistic justice toward an antiracist English education, 'enacting criticality for transformation' (Kubota, 2023: 7) in scholarly and instructional praxis.

Facilitating concrete actions for transforming the educational milieu, a critical language awareness pedagogy grounded in critical discourse analysis and the interconnected pedagogy of translingualism has the power to raise language teachers' consciousness of historical, political, and ideological aspects of language through antiracism-oriented class activities on linguistic diversity, inclusivity, and identity. While CLA pedagogy 'focuses on the intersections of language, identity, power, and privilege, with the goal of promoting self-reflection, social justice, and rhetorical agency among student writers' (Shapiro, 2022: 4), translingual pedagogy is an approach that 'sees difference in language not as a barrier to overcome or as a problem to manage, but as a resource for producing meaning in writing, speaking, reading, and listening' (Horner *et al.*, 2011: 303). Although CLA and translingual pedagogies are disparate in their philosophical origins, with the former born from attention to the study of language at schools to fortify students' 'knowledge about language' (Shapiro, 2022: 30) and the latter responding to the changing linguistic realities with the increased transnational contact in academic spheres, there are many philosophical tenets that intertwine, e.g. both pedagogies 'treat language difference as an asset' (Shapiro, 2022: 9). They complement each other in powerful ways, facilitating language teachers to think critically about and complicate the discrete and discriminatory views of language traditionally imposed in most educational settings globally.

Pedagogical explorations of how to open up discussions on racism, dismantle language-based discrimination, and support learners' understandings of language-power relationships have been documented largely by second language writing, composition, and writing center studies scholars (e.g. DeLong *et al.*, 2018; Greenfield & Rowan, 2011; Lotier *et al.*, 2023; Morrison & Garriott, 2023; Picower, 2021) in the context of Anglophone institutions or 'inner circle' (Kachru, 1996) countries where norms and standards are created in the first place. 'One reason you don't see translingualism outside the West', in the words of Atkinson and Tardy (2018: 87), 'is because it's inspired by top-down Western critical theory, which is closely connected to neo-Marxist, modernist critical pedagogy'. CLA and translingual pedagogies have indeed not entered much outside the American scholarly centers and in this chapter, I illustrate how these pedagogies could be picked up internationally drawing on my teaching experiences in a language teacher education program in Türkiye, an expanding circle country where English is not used as a primary means of communication in society, but as a foreign language to study at school.

Connecting theory and practice, I hereby report on a classroom activity informed by CLA and translingual approaches applied in two lesson hours of a sophomore-level college course to develop learners' self-reflexive and critical awareness of language, responding to Kubota's (2023: 13) call to 'integrate and promote decolonial thinking by questioning with students taken-for-granted beliefs and assumptions about language, race, gender, culture, and other kinds of human difference'. By creating learning environments that dismantle mainstream notions of language and facilitate difference-oriented dispositions, I aim to bring practical aspects of radical inclusivity into my teaching, in efforts to undo language teacher candidates' socialization into dominant ideologies that 'stigmatize particular linguistic practices perceived as deviating from prescriptive norms' (Rosa, 2016: 163). Based in Sengeh's (2021: 43) definition of radical inclusion, 'that every child – regardless of family origin, location, gender, or disability – is educated', radical inclusivity within the context of the current pedagogical action means that all differences in language are appreciated in all discourses of communication, including oral and written. It is crucial for prospective teachers of English to realize the possibilities for using language beyond the standardized limits in order to make informed pedagogical choices in their teaching and transform the future of literacy and language education.

Introduction and Context of the Course

This pedagogical enactment took place in the English Language Teaching (ELT) Program, a four-year undergraduate degree program housed in the Department of Foreign Languages Education within the Faculty of Education, at a public university in Northern Türkiye. While the university was relatively newly established in 2007, the ELT program was even newer, holding its first graduation ceremony in Spring 2023. Under ELT program policies, participation in the prep school is compulsory for all newcomer students who pass the university entrance exam and earn the right to enroll in the ELT program. In their freshman year, students take basic language skills classes – i.e. Writing Skills, Reading Skills, Listening Skills, and Oral Communication Skills – in addition to the required first-year curriculum, e.g. History, Turkish, Introduction to Education, etc. In their second year, students are required to take field-specific courses such as Approaches to English Language Teaching, English Literature, Second Language Acquisition, Linguistics, etc.

In the Fall semester of 2023, I taught two sections of the Introduction to Linguistics course to sophomore students who were all Turkish, but came from diverse geographical regions of Türkiye. Thirty-eight (38) students (11 male, 27 female) were enrolled in Section A, and 27 (7 male, 21 female) in Section B. All students were aged between 18–24 and they were all, except for five juniors and two seniors taking this course for the second time as they failed in the previous academic year, second-year students who would become English language teachers upon graduation from the program. The students transitioned into the ELT program after studying English in the preparatory school for an academic year and passing the proficiency exam. In this course opened in Fall 2023, the medium of instruction was English and students were introduced to linguistics as the scientific study of language. They explored the origin, nature, structure, and diversity of human language as they got to know about some of the major subfields of linguistics, i.e. phonetics, phonology, morphology, and syntax. They further delved into language and variation, regional and social, and explored implications of each for language and literacy education.

The Activity

Rationale

Scholarship has documented the benefits of implementing CLA for promoting rhetorical agency (Siczek, 2023), critical stance toward identity (McPherron & An, 2023), and interrogation of the link between language, identity, and power (Alim, 2010), while the translingual approach for cultivating openness to language differences (Lee & Jenks, 2016; Wang, 2017), decolonizing linguistic/cultural identities (De Costa *et al.*, 2017), and raising critical awareness of the negotiability of language standards, norms, and print-centric conventions (Ayash, 2020; Canagarajah, 2013;

Sánchez-Martín *et al.*, 2019). CLA and translingual pedagogies combine in effective development of learners' critical language awareness, helping them perceive the complexity of linguistic identities and power relations. Promoting learners' critical inquiry into language, transformative pedagogical practices informed by CLA and translingual perspectives can lead learners to radical ways of knowing and knowledge making, facilitating an opening for them to appreciate language and language differences in communication.

Within the pedagogical framework of this chapter, I enacted CLA and translingual approaches to stimulate critical inquiries among Turkish EFL teacher candidates concerning language standards, norms, and expectations. My objective was to cultivate an awareness of the standard language ideology – what it does to individuals and how it perpetuates systemic racism and linguistic discrimination. While doing this, I exposed teacher candidates to possibilities of differences, prompting them to reconsider their linguistic dispositions. Through this process, I endeavored to create an inclusive space where future generations of teachers could explore their choices in using, learning, and teaching language as they learn to navigate the varied linguistic practices they encounter in life.

Lesson outcomes

Students were introduced to standard language ideology and language subordination processes, engaging in dialogues around language, variation, and linguistic diversity in the discourses of oral and written communication. At the conclusion of lesson, students were able to:

- develop awareness of linguistic diversity, variation, and standard language ideology;
- recognize language and power relations through readings, discussion, and analysis;
- reflect on their own languaging practices in speaking and writing.

These outcomes could be observed in students' discussion notes that they took during lesson hours in class and their post-activity assignments.

Pre-activity task

Students had read Chapters 4 and 5 from Lippi-Green's (2012) *English with an Accent* prior to the first lesson, and Young's (2010) 'Should Writers Use They Own English?' in advance of the second lesson. To encourage completion of the readings before class, I assigned students to submit an online discussion post including their major take-aways from and questions about the readings on our course learning management system, Canvas Instructure, in preparation for effective in-class learning.

Procedure

First Lesson

(1) I started the lesson with a 5–10 minute warm-up discussion on the following questions:
- How would you describe the way you speak English?
- How would you describe the way you want to speak English?
- Do you use any of the following words in your speech? Why/why not? ain't, gonna, wanna, coz… etc.

Students first took notes, which I collected later, to prepare for discussion and then shared their answers with their peers in small groups. I then asked each group to report back to class a summary of their discussion and transitioned into the learning outcomes and a preview of the lesson. To present snapshots of discussion beyond anecdotal evidence, I analyzed the notes students took in class and found two main student wishes: fluency (e.g. 'I would like to speak English fluently without any stopping', or 'I want to speak fluently by not doing translate in my mind') and native-like usage (e.g. 'I want to pronounce the whole sentence like a native', or 'I want to be so good that people would mistake me as a foreign whose mother tongue is English'). Concerning the use of nonstandard varieties of English such as ain't, gonna, wanna, etc., most students noted that they avoid using them in academic settings (e.g. 'I speak English in class generally. So, the class environment is formal. It is not suitable to use them'.)

(2) As a class, we watched short video clips from three different movies, i.e. *My Fair Lady* (1964), *Akeelah and the Bee* (2006), and *Sorry to Bother You* (2018), on YouTube. I selected these movies purposefully to demonstrate media representations of language usage deviating from the monolithic standard.

(3) I shared the scripts to maintain students' comprehension of the video clips they had just seen (see Appendix 5.1). To make it more engaging, I invited volunteers to read the scripts out loud to the class, acting out the situation.

(4) To engage students with the materials and assigned readings, I implemented a discourse analysis activity and placed students in groups of three or four to discuss the following questions:
- How would you explain standard language ideology in the discourse of these scenes?
- With which of the eight language subordination processes below would you associate the scenes you have just watched?
Language is mystified.
> You can never hope to comprehend the difficulties and complexities of your mother tongue without expert guidance.

Authority is claimed.

> We are the experts. Talk like me/us. We know what we are doing because we have studied language, because we write well.
>
> Misinformation is generated.
>
> > That usage you are so attached to is inaccurate. The variant I prefer is superior on historical, aesthetic, or logical grounds.
>
> Targeted languages are trivialized.
>
> > Look how cute, how homey, how funny.
>
> Conformers are held up as positive examples.
>
> > See what you can accomplish if you only try, how far you can get if you see the light.
>
> Non-conformers are vilified or marginalized.
>
> > See how willfully, stupid, arrogant, unknowing, uninformed and/or deviant these speakers are.
>
> Explicit promises are made.
>
> > Employers will take you seriously; doors will open.
>
> Threats are made.
>
> > No one important will take you seriously; doors will close.
>
> (Lippi-Green, 2012: 70)

Following the small-group discussion, I handed out sticky post-it notes to students. I asked them to write their answers on the non-sticky side of post-it notes and stick them to the board.

(5) After all groups placed their post-its, we analyzed them as a class. I read each post-it out loud to class and led students to share their thoughts and comments on what was written.

(6) I ended the post-it discussion by outlining the standard language ideology and language subordination processes associated with the movie clips under scope. For example, I demonstrated how 'explicit promises are made' (Lippi-Green, 2012: 70) by presenting the following excerpts from the movies:

> 'If you are good and do what you are told, you'll sleep in a proper bedroom, have lots to eat, money to buy chocolates, and take rides in taxis' (*My Fair Lady*, 1964).
>
> 'You wanna make some money here? Then read the script with a white voice!' (*Sorry to Bother You*, 2018).

(7) Once completing the discourse analysis and discussions, I ended the lesson asking students to summarize the key concepts they learnt today and reminding them of the reading assignments for the next lesson.

Second Lesson

(1) I started the lesson with a 5–10 minute warm-up discussion on the following questions:
- How would you describe the way you write in English?
- How do you feel about writing in English?

- Do you use any of the following words, or etc., in your writing? Why/why not? ain't, gonna, wanna, coz... etc.
- Do you ever use your mother tongue in your English writing? Why/why not?

Students once again drafted their answers on a small piece of paper prior to sharing them with their group members. In their responses, most students reported that they attended to using a Standard variety of English to their best capacity in composing texts. Maintaining their views of formality and appropriacy as in oral discourses of communication, students avoided using nonstandard varieties of English in their writing (e.g. 'I don't use these words in writing because writing is an academic space. It should be formal'.). After each group reported back to class a summary of their discussion, I introduced the learning outcomes and plan of the lesson.

(2) I instructed students to quickly review Young (2010), which they were supposed to read before class, with the task of crafting in groups of three or four a one-sentence statement about how the text is related to our discussions in the previous lesson.

(3) I then projected statements on the board and invited students to talk about the content and engage in meaningful dialogue in connecting the reading to previous class discussions.

(4) In further engagement with the reading, I asked: What do you think about the author's language in the text? Do you agree or disagree with the author in the following excerpts?
- 'We all should know everybody's dialect, at least as many as we can, and be open to the mix of them in oral and written communication' (2010: 111).
- 'Everybody mix the dialect they learn at home with whateva other dialect or language they learn afterwards. That's how we understand accents; that's how we can hear that some people are from a Polish, Spanish, or French language background... We hear that background in they speech, and it's often expressed in they writin too. It's natural' (2010: 111).

As students progressed, they reflected on how the text was related to their personal lives, what their experiences writing in English were like, whether their writing represented who they were, and what the text could do for them. While these questions led students into translingual realizations about their own languaging and writing practices, I projected on the board snippets from Canagarajah's (2011) work demonstrating a multilingual student's incorporation of multiple languages in the same text to facilitate students' imagination to be critical with owning their linguistic repertoires.

(5) Following up, I briefly introduced CCCC's resolution on 'Students' Right to Their Own Language' (National Council of Teachers of English, 1974) to students, highlighting its implications for language and literacy education.

(6) I asked students to reflect on how they were feeling about using nonstandard varieties and dialects of English or languages other than English in their writing after all class discussions and readings. Students first gathered their thoughts on a piece of paper and then shared them with their peers. Students' notes demonstrated diverse opinions including appreciation of language differences (e.g. 'I feel reasonable about using these words in English writing. Cuz it's natural to have different cultures and specific words for specific cultures') and critical awareness of language (e.g. 'After all of this, I realized that using these words is not problematic or something wrong') as well as cautiousness of the writing situation (e.g. 'I'll continue to use them in my daily writings. I wouldn't dare to use them in my assignments unless I'm allowed').
(7) I concluded the lesson with a quick recap of linguistic facts of life, with reference to Lippi-Green's (2012) Chapter 1 which had been covered earlier in the semester, addressing variation and linguistic diversity in the discourses of spoken and written communication.

Post-activity task

To assess students' understanding of linguistic diversity in the discourse(s) of oral and/or written communication, I assigned them a linguistic diversity cartoon project (see Appendix 5.2). The intention of this assignment was to support students' development of critical language awareness and antiracist dispositions toward nonstandard varieties and dialects of English through readings, discussion, research, and writing. Instead of asking students to report on their understanding of linguistic diversity in a traditional essay, I required them to work with multimedia in the sense that Wang (2017: 64) observed how 'struggling writers flourish when they used…cartoon drawings'. Creating a space of learning through critical and creative uses of multimodalities, the cartoon assignment facilitated opportunities for students to demonstrate their theories about language through visual representations.

Reflections

What have I learned?

I enacted CLA and translingual pedagogies in the context of Turkish higher education for the first time and the major lesson I learnt from my teaching experience was that it is possible! When I was first introduced to CLA and translingual perspectives on teaching English during my doctoral studies, I always contemplated how I could bring these radical approaches to literacy and language education to my home country where language teaching happens within standard language frameworks, just as in many other EFL contexts. Reiterating Park *et al.*'s (2023) nuanced attention to the accessibility of criticality in diverse educational contexts across the globe, putting the theories of criticality and translingualism in the language teacher education classroom taught me that transformation could start in this very classroom with these very people who would become language teachers in the future in educational institutions complicit in racist practices. Although it is not very likely for them to encounter diverse varieties of English in Türkiye, prospective teachers of English can benefit from radically inclusive pedagogies as they prepare for teaching English to language learners that come to class with languaging experiences beyond the standard as a result of their increased contact with the world around them with the affordances of advanced digital technologies, broadcast and social media.

What have my students learned?

At the end of our lesson on the various ways in which people may use language in oral and written discourses of communication, my students learned that variation in language was natural. While assessing their works on the linguistic diversity cartoon assignment, I could gather that they developed a critical stance toward ideologies of standardization, gained awareness and appreciation of linguistic diversity, and could critique standard language cultures. They came to understand that 'Standard English' was a social, political, and ideological construct and it represented one style of using English, among others. To demonstrate students' critical engagement with language, I analyze two sample student assignments, which are shown in Figures 5.1 and 5.2.[1]

The first cartoon (Figure 5.1), which originally included 12 panels, demonstrates the student writer's critical view of nonstandard varieties of English through a creative story that takes place in the college classroom setting. The teacher seems to be oriented toward the ideologies of monolingualism and standardization, calling students' attention to the importance of conforming to norms in assignments, and the student, a vernacular English speaker, takes a critical stance toward the teacher's imposition of a particular style of writing. By challenging the teacher's singularity approach to language difference in both oral and written discourses of communication, the developer of this cartoon demonstrates active engagement with antiracist language perspectives on teaching literacy and language.

In the cartoon 'Wild Wild West' (Figure 5.2), the student portrays three cats in the roles of a sheriff and two cowboys. When the sheriff cat says: 'I'm the law here, ye hear?', one of the other cats responds: 'Law? You can't even speak English properly! We shall not be intimidated by the likes of you!' As in the previous sample, this cartoon demonstrates the student's understanding of power and language relations, how nonstandard varieties of English are denigrated and disempowered, too deficient to represent the 'law'.

What challenges came up while implementing the lesson/activity?

The main challenge while implementing the lesson was managing the tension-filled radical class discussions as students engaged with hard

Figure 5.1 Linguistic diversity cartoon assignment, Sample 1

questions and critical dialogues about language, identity, and power. Just as some language and literacy scholars argued for the need to conform to the norms of 'Standard English' and others advocated differences in the use of language, students differed in their views of variations. For instance, a student brought to attention the news programs on TV during in-class discussion and emphasized the need for anchormen/anchorwomen to use a 'standard' language to appeal to a broad audience. While some of the student's peers agreed with them, others disagreed to the point of starting a loud argument. However, with critical and translingual pedagogies' intention to teach learners to respect difference, handling the difficult dialogues around language and discrimination turned from challenge to affordance.

What is my advice for adapting or implementing the lesson/activity in various contexts?
- Cooperate with students to develop a contract at the beginning of the lesson, or semester, to consult during class discussions. Co-construct rules democratically with students and communicate that rules have

Figure 5.2 Linguistic diversity cartoon assignment, Sample 2

consequences. Functioning as a toolkit for instructors to facilitate discussions, the contract must represent the classroom language of democracy and help navigate critical dialogues in lessons.
- I strongly recommend adding an artist's statement to the required elements for the linguistic diversity cartoon assignment, asking students to explain their intentions and choices in their composing processes. I had to ask students to write one after completion of their cartoon assignments as I had difficulty understanding some works – their purpose, message, implications, etc. during assessment. Not only did I make the artist's statement part of the assessment criteria for which students received credit, but I also referred to it while grading the cartoons to understand the thought processes behind them. Furthermore, given the significance of the 'cyclical process of reflection and action' (Kubota & Miller, 2017: 142) in the praxis of critical approaches to teaching, students can reflect back and forth on their learning experiences in class and their composing processes of the cartoons in their artist's statements.
- Consider organizing a class exhibition event upon students' submission of their linguistic diversity cartoon assignments. It did not take place in the context of my teaching due to time constraints in our class schedule; however, I suggest creating a space for students to showcase their works to build a sense of community and make their learning meaningful by sharing their compositions with a larger audience.

Note

(1) All student texts including in-class discussion notes and assignments were collected under the supervision of Sinop University's IRB Board.

References

Alim, H.S. (2010) Critical language awareness. In N.H. Hornberger and S.L. McKay (eds) *Sociolinguistics and Language Education* (pp. 205–231). Multilingual Matters.

Atchison, D. (2006) *Akeelah and the Bee* [Film]. Lionsgate.

Atkinson, D. and Tardy, C.M. (2018) SLW at the crossroads: Finding a way in the field. *Journal of Second Language Writing* 42, 86–93. https://doi.org/10.1016/j.jslw.2018.10.011

Ayash, N.B. (2020) Critical translation and paratextuality: Translingual and anti-racist pedagogical possibilities for multilingual writers. *Composition Forum* 44.

Canagarajah, S. (2011) Translanguaging in the classroom: Emerging issues for research and pedagogy. *Applied Linguistics Review* 2, 1–28.

Canagarajah, A.S. (2013) Negotiating translingual literacy: An enactment. *Research in the Teaching of English* 48 (1), 40–67.

Cukor, G. (1964) *My Fair Lady* [Film]. Warner Bros.

De Costa, P.I., Singh, J.G., Milu, E., Wang, X., Fraiberg, S. and Canagarajah, S. (2017) Pedagogizing translingual practice: Prospects and possibilities. *Research in the Teaching of English* 51 (4), 464–472.

DeLong, R., Coleman, T.J., DeVore, K.S., Gibney, S., Kuhne, M. and Deus, V. (2018) *Working toward Racial Equity in First-year Composition: Six Perspectives*. Routledge.

Flores, N. and Rosa, J. (2015) Undoing appropriateness: Raciolinguistic ideologies and language diversity in education. *Harvard Educational Review* 85 (2), 149–171.

Greenfield, L. and Rowan, K. (2011) *Writing Centers and the New Racism: A Call for Sustainable Dialogue and Change*. Utah State University Press.

Horner, B., Lu, M., Royster, J.J. and Trimbur, J. (2011) Language difference in writing: Toward a translingual approach. *College English* 73 (3), 303–321.

Kachru, B. (1996) World Englishes: Agony and ecstasy. *Journal of Aesthetic Education* 30 (2), 135–155.

Kubota, R. (2023) Linking research to transforming the real world: Critical language studies for the next 20 years. *Critical Inquiry in Language Studies* 20 (1), 4–19. https://doi.org/10.1080/15427587.2022.2159826

Kubota, R. and Miller, E. (2017) Re-examining and re-envisioning criticality in language studies: Theories and praxis. *Critical Inquiry in Language Studies* 14 (2–3), 129–157. https://doi.org/10.1080/15427587.2017.1290500

Lee, J.W. and Jenks, C. (2016) Doing translingual dispositions. *College Composition and Communication* 68 (2), 317–344.

Lippi-Green, R. (2012) *English with an Accent: Language, Ideology, and Discrimination in the United States*. Routledge.

Lotier, K.M., Perez, X.T., Pierre, A. and Shah, P.V. (2023) Antiracist protest pedagogy: Writing about writing, 'Standard English,' and systemic change. *Pedagogy: Critical Approaches to Teaching Literature, Language, Composition, and Culture* 23 (2), 213–224. https://doi.org/10.1215/15314200-10295887

McPherron, P. and An, L. (2023) Supporting Asian American multilingual college students through critical language awareness programming. *Journal of Language, Identity, and Education* 22 (4), 340–358.

Morrison, T.H. and Garriott, D.A.E. (2023) *Writing Centers and Racial Justice: A Guidebook for Critical Praxis*. Utah State University Press.

National Council of Teachers of English. (1974) Students' right to their own language. *College Composition and Communication*.

Park, G., Bogdan, S., Rosa, M. and Navarro, J. (eds) (2023) *Critical Pedagogy in the Language and Writing Classroom: Strategies, Examples, Activities from Teacher Scholars*. Routledge.

Picower, B. (2021) *Reading, Writing, and Racism: Disrupting Whiteness in Teacher Education and in the Classroom*. Beacon Press.

Riley, B. (2018) *Sorry to Bother You* [Film]. Annapurna Pictures.

Rosa, J.D. (2016) Standardization, racialization, languagelessness: Raciolinguistic ideologies across communicative contexts. *Journal of Linguistic Anthropology* 26 (2), 162–183.

Sánchez-Martín, C., Hirsu, L., Gonzales, L. and Alvarez, S.P. (2019) Pedagogies of digital composing through a translingual approach. *Computers and Composition* 52, 142–157.

Sengeh, D. (2021) In the trenches: Radical inclusion. *Finance & Development* 58 (001), 42–43.

Shapiro, S. (2022) *Cultivating Critical Language Awareness in the Writing Classroom*. Routledge.

Siczek, M.M. (2023) Promoting critical language awareness at the graduate level: A discovery oriented approach. *Journal of Second Language Writing* 60 (4).

Tian, Z. and Zhang-Wu, Q. (2022) Preparing pre-service content area teachers through translanguaging. *Journal of Language, Identity & Education* 21 (3), 144–159. https://doi.org/10.1080/15348458.2022.2058512

Wang, X. (2017) Developing translingual disposition through a writing theory cartoon assignment. *Journal of Basic Writing* 36 (1), 56–86. https://doi.org/10.37514/jbw-j.2017.36.1.04

Young, V.A. (2010) Should writers use they own English? *Iowa Journal of Cultural Studies* 12 (1), 110–118.

Appendices

Appendix 5.1: Movie Scripts

(1) *My Fair Lady* (1964)

Dr. Higgins:

'Eliza... you are to stay here for the next six months learning how to speak beautifully like a lady in a florist shop.

If you are good and do what you're told, you'll sleep in a proper bedroom, have lots to eat, money to buy chocolates and take rides in taxis.

But if you are naughty and idle, you will sleep in the kitchen amongst the black beetles and be walloped by Mrs. Pearce with a broomstick.

If you refuse this offer, you will be the most ungrateful wicked girl and the angels will weep for you.'

(2) *Akeelah and the Bee* (2006)

Akeelah:	So why are you home during the day? Ain't you got no job?
Professor:	Do me a favor, leave the ghetto talk outside, all right?
Akeelah:	Ghetto talk? I don't talk ghetto.
Professor:	'Ain't you got no job?' You use that language to fit in with your friends. Here you will speak properly or you won't speak at all. Understood?
Akeelah:	Yeah. Whatever.
Professor:	You can leave now.
Akeelah:	Excuse me?
Professor:	I said you can leave.
Akeelah:	How come?
Professor:	Because I don't have time to waste on insolent little girls.
Akeelah:	Insolent? I ain't insol – I mean I am not insolent. It's just the first thing you do is start doggin' on – criticizing the way I speak.

(3) *Sorry to Bother You* (2018)

Coworker: Hey, youngblood!
Cash: What up?
Coworker: Lemme give you a tip. Use your white voice.
Cash: My white voice? Man, I ain't got no white voice.
Coworker: Oh, c'mon, you know what I mean, youngblood. You have a white voice in there, you can use it. It's like, when you get pulled over by the police.
Cash: Oh no. I just use my regular voice when that happens. I just say, 'back the f.ck up off the car and don't nobody get hurt!'
Coworker: All right man, I'm just trying to give you some game. You wanna make some money here? Then read the script with a white voice.
Cash: Well people say I talk with a white voice anyway, so why it ain't helping me out?
Coworker: Well, you don't talk white enough. I'm not talkin' bout Will Smith white. I'm talkin' bout the real deal. Like this youngblood 'Hello Mr. Cramer. This is Langston from Regalview. I didn't catch you the wrong time, did I?'

Appendix 5.2: Linguistic Diversity Cartoon Assignment Guideline

Assignment Description

We'll begin the semester with a fun writing assignment. Your task is to develop a cartoon that demonstrates your understanding of linguistic diversity in the discourse(s) of oral and/or written communication. You will communicate your understanding through text, images, and drawings.

You have two options to create your cartoon:

a. Draw your own cartoon. Sketch out the panels using a ruler and pencil before you begin drawing. You need to make decisions about the style, shape, and size of boxes, balloons, and other word-framing devices.
b. Use an online cartoon maker. Here is a list of helpful tools:
https://www.canva.com/create/cartoons/
https://www.animaker.com/cartoon-maker
https://www.toonytool.com

Collaboration Statement
You can work in a team of 2–3 students to collaboratively produce your cartoon. Teamwork is common in business world and the workplace. It is important that you learn how to work together to develop and deliver content. However, collaboration is not easy and not all people are enthusiastic about group work. For this reason, the decision is yours to make whether to collaborate or to work independently. If you choose to collaborate on this assignment, I will ask you to develop an action plan in which you reflect on the roles and responsibilities of each group member, identifying processes and action steps for successful collaboration. I will assess collaborative works in the same way I assess individual works. I will assign grades based on your product and the group members will receive the same grade, regardless of individual contribution.

Length and Format
Your cartoon will be worded and contain 1 to 8 panels fitting on one or two pages. It can be in color or black and white, or anything in between. The top of your paper must include a title and your name. The potential audience of this assignment includes your instructor and peers.

Required Elements
- Consistent Narrative
  Establishing a clear and consistent narrative about linguistic diversity
- Literary Devices
  Using literary devices such as character, dialogue, and an accurate setting
- Design
  Employing effective design choices (fonts, visuals, word choice, diction, etc.)
- Author's Statement
  Explaining the 'what, why, how' of your composition
  – What was your purpose in composing this cartoon? What message did you aim to communicate?
  – Why did you employ the chosen design features?
  – How did you compose your cartoon? How did you find the process?
  Please note that these questions are to stimulate your thinking, not an outline for your statement.

6 Linguistic Landscapes, Discussion Forums and *Conscientização*: A Pedagogical Ensemble to Address Linguistic Glottonormativity in Language Teacher Education

Sílvia Melo-Pfeifer and Vander Tavares

Introduction

Classrooms in many parts of the world serve as microcosms of the broader linguistic diversity present in society. Our responsibility as educators is thus to foster an inclusive environment that celebrates, acknowledges, and also builds on the richness of every language and culture.

We understand glottonormativity as the ideologically constructed societal norms that privilege certain languages (and their speakers) while marginalizing others, thereby often leading to the invisibility of languages in the latter group. Our standpoint is that one powerful way to engage with the concept of glottonormativity is through a critical exploration of linguistic landscapes (LLs), which can promote discovery and awareness of ideologies that sustain the inclusion and exclusion of languages in the public spheres (Shohamy & Ben-Rafael, 2015; Shohamy & Pennycook, 2021). Briefly, LLs encompass the various languages and semiotic cues that surround us in our everyday lives, from street signs and advertisements to public spaces and institutions. By incorporating LLs into language classrooms, we can actively dismantle glottonormative biases and foster more inclusive linguistic environments.

In this contribution, we engage in reflection and discussion of the pedagogical potential of LLs in developing student teachers' *conscientização* of social, political, and ideological aspects of languages in society and education. We describe an interactional activity developed online during the pandemic within the framework of the internationalization of teacher education. For a semester, soon-to-be language teachers in Hamburg (Germany) and Sydney (Australia) collaborated in a writing activity in discussion forums related to migratory movements and their impact on teaching and learning, but particularly for the inclusion of linguistic and cultural diversity in the classroom. We draw on the Freirean concept of *conscientização* – which as both a process and a product is meant to awaken the critical consciousness of learners and therefore confront dehumanization (Tavares, 2023) – to highlight future, yet real possibilities for and engagements with criticality and radical inclusivity, which we conceive of as inclusive practices that push ideological boundaries in a transformative act of inclusion of the self and the other(ed).

We aim to discuss some of the ways in which working with LLs in discussion forums might support language student teachers to develop and enhance their (critical) understanding of processes of (re)production of power and inequalities in public spaces through the unequal representation of languages. In the next section, we will discuss the conceptual background of LLs and highlight its ethical potential in education.

Theor*ethical* Background

Insights into glottonormativity through linguistic landscapes

LLs traditionally refer to the presence of languages in public spaces (Gorter & Cenoz, 2024). Recent evolutions of the concept transcend sense-making through reading and the written word to include multi-sensorial and multi-semiotic stimuli (Prada, 2023). By challenging mainstream definitions of multilingualism and inclusion in multilingual research, we can open up spaces for underrepresented languages, such as braille and sign languages, and decenter multilingualism from ocularcentrism (Melo-Pfeifer, 2024).

Studies on LLs shed light on the presence and absence – or the hierarchy – of languages in public spaces more generally. LLs also shed light on which public spaces, contexts, and supports different languages are allocated, along with the reasons for such sociopolitical configurations, thereby evoking cognizance of relations of power and of social (in)justice (Shohamy & Pennycook, 2021).

For these reasons, LLs can serve as a basis to develop critical and inclusive approaches to research and (language) education grounded in praxis, potentially leading to committed reflection and action for positive transformation within the local contexts (Chan, 2023; Sengeh, 2023). In philosophical terms, 'normativity' entails that 'some action, attitude or mental state of some other kind is justified, an action one ought to do or a state one ought to be in' (Darwall, 2001). Based on this starting point and for the sake of this contribution, we define glottonormativity as the mainstream or the commonly unquestioned and shared ways of thinking about norms associated with languages, language contact and, concomitantly, with their users and the functioning of multilingual societies. Our exploration sheds light on the often-implicit norms and benchmarks that govern LLs and the sociocultural dynamics of language use.

A theor*ethical* stance: *Conscientização* of glottonormativity through linguistic landscapes

In public spaces, it is easier to perceive which languages are included and why (e.g. as a commodity, status symbol, sign of political influence), but more difficult to understand why others are excluded. Cases in which exclusion is visible are reported in regions where a minority language is used by the population, but not present in public signage. Exclusion and erasure of languages from the LL can occur, for example, due to the perceived minority status of a language, stereotypes attached to their speakers, or tensions between linguistic communities.

Nevertheless, the inclusion of certain languages in a given LL can also denote stereotypes, prejudice, and linguistic racism. In other words, giving visibility to some languages is not always a proxy for respect and inclusion (see Melo-Pfeifer, 2024). The photo in Figure 6.1 was taken in Jena, a city in eastern Germany, in 2022, and illustrates how some languages, despite being included, are systematically associated with a negative representation of their speakers (in this case, Romanian and Russian). According to the 2021 census, Jena has a population that includes 95,020 German and 13,837 foreign citizens, the latter comprising 14.5% of the population. The largest groups of migrants in the city are Russians, Chinese, and Ukrainians.

The photo was taken at the entrance to a bank. It shows the wording 'WARNING! Our ATMs are safe guarded [sic]' in six languages: German, English, French, Romanian, Russian, and Bulgarian. The word 'warning' is in uppercase and followed by the second part of the message one row below (except for French, which takes two rows). The image is intended to be catchy, as the background is red and includes a visual presentation of a bomb exploding. The bomb is placed next to an open hand showing a preventive/prohibitive gesture (with a rather redundant inscription 'STOP', also in uppercase).

This example illustrates that certain languages and their speakers are systematically represented in some typologies of signs, such as prohibitions or warnings, that present the speakers as potential criminals or outlaws.

Figure 6.1 A warning to potential criminals on the door of a bank in Jena.

If we consider the demographic constitution of the population in that particular city, we could ask ourselves why some languages are included/excluded from both signs. We would conclude that they are targeting specific linguistic groups.

Figure 6.1 demonstrates how the glottonormative (in)visibility of languages may be constructed in public spaces. This glottonormativity constructs and mainstreams ideas of moral wrongness, virtue, and well-being associated with linguistic populations. Understanding the making of linguistic (in)visibility is important for at least two reasons. First, to understand how public spaces reproduce ideas of normality and control, by permanently exposing the audience to 'official' signs that create a language-focused imagination, and constructimg ideas of acceptance or rejection of different languages and their speakers. Second, to challenge and disrupt the seen but not noticed manipulation present in public spaces. Both objectives are concerned with not only describing phenomena, but also understanding their consequences, which is why they have an ethical and social intervention dimension. In this sense, the glottonormative (in)visibility of languages can be addressed in educational contexts through activities of *conscientização*, which we consider an act of radical inclusivity, by ensuring that multiple languages and dialects are visible and valued and creating spaces where students feel empowered to celebrate, use, and capitalize on their linguistic repertoires.

Paulo Freire argued that 'education, as a practice of freedom, is an act of knowledge, a critical approach to reality' (Freire, 1979: 15, our translation) and that education is always political. We adopt the position that *conscientização* is necessary for agency and emancipation from structures and ideologies of oppression. Freire defended that 'conscientização is obviously linked to utopia. The more aware we become, the more capable we are of being heralds and denouncers, thanks to the commitment to transformation we have taken on. But this position must be permanent...' (Freire, 1979: 16; our translation).

Conscientização has to do with consciousness in the sense of restoring students' critical consciousness or awareness that has been suppressed by authoritarian governments, particularly through an education that is indoctrinating. Freire conceptualized such an approach to education as banking education because students are made to passively receive irrelevant information deposited by the teachers (Tavares, 2023). A key feature of banking education is the removal of students' life experiences from the curriculum, including experiences of language. *Conscientização* may be understood as:

> a pedagogical process that seeks to develop a critical awareness in students in relation to their place in the world. *Conscientização* is about humanization: it is a process of self-reflection through which students discover their potential for agency. Indeed, what distinguishes this process from others is that *conscientização* leads the individual to action.

Conscientização develops in the students the ability to think and propose real, rather than mythical, explanations for why the social experiences of people are the way they are. (Tavares, 2023: 153)

Pedagogical activities anchored in *conscientização* promote a critical awareness of inequalities, discrimination, and struggles in society. As such, our aim is that students come to understand that the presence of languages in the LL is not (always) a sign of inclusion of their populations (but possibly quite the opposite), and that, by inverse analogy, their absence does not necessarily mean intolerance or exclusion. The dynamics of glottonormativity are complex and interact with patterns of creating linguistic inequality that go beyond purely linguistic issues. The glottonormativity that leads to the (in)visibility of languages in public spaces is the product of the intersection of linguistic ideologies, stereotypes of languages and their speakers, and social imaginaries at the local, regional, and national levels.

From the above, we consider that the domain of language education, while still drawing on sound theoretical and empirical approaches, needs a 'theor*ethical* approach' (Melo-Pfeifer & Chik, 2022: 504). Melo-Pfeifer and Chik (2022) coined 'theor*ethical*' to imply a positive, affirming, empowering, and celebratory attitude towards linguistic and cultural repertoires and experiences. Theor*ethical* merges 'theoretical' and 'ethical' concerns, revisiting models, theories, and materials to be better suited to respond to the complex needs of language education nowadays. By extension, these concerns position political issues related to linguistic and cultural diversity as issues permeating across the curriculum in diverse educational settings. In other words, they are not of relevance only for the language classroom.

Context of the Activities

The experience we report on in this chapter transpired online, during the pandemic, in an effort to internationalize language teacher education in Hamburg and Sydney. 'In Others' Shoes: But How?', the project framing this chapter, aimed to enhance the critical-reflexive capabilities of pre-service teachers so as to enable them to understand and analyze the diverse contexts in which they will be expected to teach. As reported on the website of the project, 'through their involvement in the planned activities, student teachers at both institutions will be able to: i) compare patterns of migration in both cities/countries, reflecting on the contextual and historical conditions underlying them; and ii) reflect on the composition of linguistic repertoires in both groups, thereby enabling them to identify commonalities and differences across them'.[1] These project aims were shared with the participants in both sites, on the platform for the joint activities. The two cities are interesting from a comparative standpoint as both are considered linguistically superdiverse, while at the same time being influenced by a strong monolingual mindset in education (see Ollerhead *et al.*, 2023).

The target audience was student teachers at both universities. The group whose data will be presented in this chapter was composed of student teachers of French, in their last year before leaving the University of Hamburg. All the activities took place online on the learning platform of the University of Hamburg[2] asynchronously (due to extreme differences in time zones) and in discussion forums. Twenty-nine student teachers took part in the project: 23 from the German university, working as tandems randomly assigned by the university, and six from the Australian university. The discussions took place in English, as a shared linguistic resource, all the German students having studied English as their first foreign language in school (alongside French and/or Spanish and several heritage languages).

The first step consisted of participants presenting themselves in the forum 'Breaking the Ice'. The second consisted of student teachers presenting and discussing their linguistic biographies by means of production of a visual linguistic autobiography (see Melo-Pfeifer & Chik, 2022, for an explanation on the use of this methodology). The activities then unfolded around three thematic areas, articulating a place-based education principle (Chan, 2023) with an international and comparative design:

- comparisons of school systems and of the degree of multilingual pedagogies in Hamburg and Sydney;
- comparisons of multilingualism in both cities, by means of researching and explaining LLs in both cities; and
- collaborations to produce a lesson plan that would include the societal or individual plurilingualism[3] of potential future students.

It was expected that the collaborative production of the lesson plan, including the rationale and the theoretical background, would reflect lessons learned from the preceding phases of the work online. This lesson plan constituted the object to be evaluated at the end of the semester. By the end of the project 'In Others' Shoes: But How?', moderators of the discussion forum (i.e. a postdoctoral researcher and two graduate students) addressed the group for a qualitative evaluation of the project, conducting individual interviews. The aim was to analyze the impact of the project on the professional development of the participants. Six student teachers agreed to be interviewed individually, through a semi-structured interview, for a qualitative assessment of the project. In this chapter, we focus on the written activities in the discussion forum.

The Activity in Action: 'Multilingualism in *your* city/ Mehrsprachigkeit in *deiner* Stadt'

Rationale

In the literature, LLs have been exploited methodologically by two means (Brinkmann *et al.*, 2022): first, through *in sito* LL analysis (following Malinowski *et al.*, 2020), meaning that students and educators observed the constitution of the LL in place; and second, through the inclusion of LLs in (and as) multilingual resources, meaning that videos or photos of LL were brought to the school/classroom to serve as the basis of pedagogical work. Activities of the first case tend to involve field trips and ethnographic exploration, photo documentation, and discussions about the various languages present in public spaces, *in situ* or back in the classroom. In the second case, photos and videos displaying LLs can become sites of analysis in the classroom, leading to the co-construction of an environment that values linguistic diversity. The activity analyzed in this chapter merges both cases. In the discussion forum of the activity 'Multilingualism in *your* city/ Mehrsprachigkeit in *deiner* Stadt' (which was open for several weeks, between 29 March 2021 and 23 August 2021), participants were given a bilingual instruction: 'Upload a photo here depicting multilingualism in your city/neighborhood! You just need to look around and snap! and explain why that photo is important and/or representative for you :)'.

The aims of the activity, which have to be understood in relationship to the rest of the tasks and the profile of the group, were (even if we did not use the term glottonormativity at the time) to identify glottonormative patterns in public spaces, to analyze possible ways in which glottonormativity operates within LLs, and to envisage pedagogical approaches to challenge glottonormative biases. As a preparation for the activity, student teachers were provided with the following freely available online resources, which covered both the LLs of Hamburg and Sydney, and provided information for a comparative understanding of the two urban and superdiverse LLs:

- Gogolin, I., Duarte, J., Hansen, A. and McMonagle, S. (2015) *Multilingualism in Hamburg. LUCIDE City Report*.[4]
- A video titled 'Multilingual Sydney' recorded as a lesson for the students by Alice Chik (with a duration of 13 minutes).
- Chik, A., King, L. and Moloney, R. (2019) Sydney: A multilingual city in a multilingual world. In A. Chik, P. Benson and R. Moloney (eds) *Multilingual Sydney* (pp. 3–12). Routledge.
- Benson, P., Clarke, N., Hisamuddin, H.F. and McIntyre, A. (2019) Linguistic landscapes 2: The linguistic landscapes of suburban Sydney. *Multilingual Sydney Working Papers 3*. Macquarie University.[5]

In the first phase of this activity, student teachers took pictures of their neighborhoods. In the second phase, they uploaded, presented, and discussed those pictures online, focusing on description of the (un)seen. Twelve messages were written in this forum and 16 pictures were uploaded. As the duration of the activity was flexible and spanned over five months, the participants could return to the forum at any point in the semester. Also, they could take as long as they wanted to write their posts in the forum and to read those of their peers. Nevertheless, no specific requirements in terms of how often student teachers needed to view and post were given.

The instructors and the moderators of the forum provided comments on participants' posts, pushing particularly towards reflection and towards the maintenance of the social-affective human feel (a challenge common to online teaching and learning). These reactions by the instructor and moderators were meant to guide the student teachers while at the same time constituting a form of informal and informative assessment of the work.

A snapshot of the activity in action

In this section we offer a vignette of what the student teachers' written work were about and how they reflected on the urban linguistic diversity. One first observation is that despite the potential for *conscientização* that the task presented, most of the participants related to LLs only as signs of linguistic and intercultural diversity, conviviality, and conflict-free zones (e.g. 'Everyone is welcome there, languages, [we] meet languages without stereotypes and prejudices'). The following quote[6] illustrates this descriptive utopian (and even exoticizing) tendency:

> When I read this task, I immediately thought of 'Schanze', a part right in the center of Hamburg that I think is one of the most multicultural and multilinguistic. Everyone is welcome there, languages, meet languages without stereotypes and prejudices. In my opinion, the picture I took shows somehow this spirit of Schanze and you can even read quite a few different languages there (I like the 'C'est la vie – Sankt Pauli' the most :D). (Student S)

Just as in the discussion presented previously in the theoretical section, in this reflection, French is present and its presence is naturalized as part of the glottonormativity of the urban landscape. As participants are writing in a discussion forum, signs of dialogism are visible. The next excerpt demonstrates Student B's reaction to Student S's post ('Your photo reminded me…'), but with an added sociolinguistic perspective, reflecting on the linguistic support offered to migrants in a specific neighborhood in the city:

> Your photo reminded me of the picture that I took in my neighborhood with the similar multilingual style. It is a door of the intercultural advice

center for migrants that offers German and integration classes. The center gives advice on every topic regarding education, family, social benefits [...]. Besides, it organizes workshops and intercultural events for everybody [...]. The employees can interact in 10 languages (German, English, French, Spanish, Turkish, Polish, Éwé, Mina (Gen), Farsi and Dari) - how impressive is it? (Student B)

In terms of inclusivity, Student B underscores that the establishment where the photo was taken gives support 'for everybody' and that this inclusive nature is visible in the LL and in the multilingualism of the establishment through the employees. Nevertheless, she does not go further than identifying the languages, without reflecting on the choices to include them that lead to the exclusion of other languages. The reflection on the sociolinguistic realities, inequalities, and discrimination triggered by the analysis of LL is more visible in the next excerpt, from Student T, where she reflects on the temporality and timing ('Just yesterday, they put a sign in front of their door') of some signs and connects them to a neoliberal agenda:

In the picture, you can see a Spanish tapas and wine bar right next to a travel shop, called 'Bon Voyage!' They not only advertise Turkish airlines, but also Western Union, which is a company, who provides easy money exchange around the world. Just yesterday, they [travel agency] put a sign in front of their door, advertising this specific service in Romanian. I think that has to do with the harvesting season. Normally, there are a lot of Romanians (and also Polish people) coming to Germany for the summer, working in the fields, since they earn 'a lot of money' in comparison to Romanian field works. [...] For them in Romania, it might be a lot of money, but I personally think, they are not paid enough here in Germany! Do you [the other German students] have any thoughts on that topic concerning the 'Gastarbeiter:innen' in Germany? (Student T)

The recent addition of Romanian signage by the travel agency sparks Student T's reflection on the possible connection to the harvesting season, suggesting a targeted effort to attract seasonal workers ('Gastarbeiter:innen'). The participant raises concerns about the wages earned by Romanians and Polish workers in German fields during the summer, questioning whether the compensation truly reflects the value of their labor. This prompts T to seek input from fellow German students. The student teacher's commentary reflects a thoughtful examination of the intersection between the presence of languages in the LL, economic migration, labor conditions, and the lived experiences of those contributing to Germany's workforce. This is an instance in which the participant was engaged in the process of *conscientização*, most simply illustrated by her questioning of social structures that disadvantage the 'foreigner' as *the other*. It is worthwhile to return to our theor*ethical* discussion and compare this reflection to the construction of Romanian and Polish speakers as potentially dangerous in the images.

Another instance of the value of critically exploring LLs is noticeable in the comment by Student J. Based on his own account, he had already been paying attention to LLs as public discourse ('I took this picture last year in November') prior to enrolling in the course. The participant connects the photo of LL he uploaded onto the platform to a local social protest, where the *status quo* around restrictions for and violence against women were challenged:

> I took this picture last year in November, when there were several protests by parts of the Polish community in Hamburg because of the intensification of the restrictive abortion laws in Poland. A friend of mine who had just moved from Warsaw to Hamburg was really touched by seeing the picture because for her it meant on the one hand that she felt encouraged to use her native language in Hamburg and felt less homesick. On the other hand she appreciated the visibility of political struggles outside of Germany. (Student J)

Student J provides a poignant reflection on a picture taken during the protests by the Polish community in Hamburg against Poland's restrictive abortion laws (Figure 6.2).

Student J's narrative encapsulates some of the profound impacts that LLs can have in connecting individuals to their roots and broader societal concerns. He reports understanding that the presence of languages and social struggles in the LL can give the speakers of those languages a sense of connection and solidarity, namely when they are newly arrived.

The last excerpt chosen for this activity shows that working with LL has the potential to impact other people around the participants. Student Ph was unsure about finding a suitable photo, opting instead for one taken by a friend, meaning that they discussed the content and the activity assigned in the course.

> I had first thought about where I could find a suitable photo. But when my friend wanted to go to her work, she took a photo for me of a poster about the access restrictions during the Corona pandemic at Asklepios. I was very surprised when I asked if there was a version in German next to it and she told me there was not. Maybe such a poster already existed or the people in charge already know about it. (Student Ph)

Student Ph's surprise arises when questioning the existence of a version of the sign in German, only to learn that German, the majority language, is absent from the sign. The participant then hypothesizes that perhaps an equivalent poster in German already existed, as the glottonormative situation implies that German cannot be invisible. This account raises critical questions about the inclusivity of information dissemination across different language groups, but is interesting because it raises the question of the inexistence of that information in the majority language.

Figure 6.2 Photo uploaded by Student J.

Post-Activity Thoughts and Discussion of Challenges

LL serves as a dynamic and multimodal (re)source of inspiration and material for writing and makes the act of writing an (inter)culturally embedded experience. By searching for, observing, and (collaboratively) analyzing LLs in their own environment, language student teachers, as writers in the discussion forum, draw from the authenticity of these materialities to support their opinions, discoveries, and problematizations. In the same vein, embedding the writing task into the participation in a discussion forum to enhance professional development with peers serves the important purpose of stressing the value of writing for a genuine audience. Even if not always denoting enhanced criticality or going beyond ocularcentrism, using LLs as a springboard for writing encouraged reflection on the role of language in contemporaneity: it prompted writers and readers alike to dialogically contemplate the societal, cultural, political, and economic dimensions, as well as the struggles and tensions embedded in the LL, even if an answer was not immediately available to address them (Sengeh, 2023). Student teachers learned to recognize and appreciate the cultural, societal, and political dimensions embedded in language use. Furthermore, by analyzing the role of language in contemporary society and reflecting on the entanglements of language with societal, cultural, political, and economic factors, they potentially developed a habit of critical inquiry and reflection: an enactment of *conscientização*.

In terms of lessons learned as teachers-researchers, we acknowledge that student teachers possess an initial level of critical awareness when it comes to observing linguistic diversity in the LL. However, the presentation of student teachers' work made it evident that the languages present/absent and the reasons behind such choices often went unnoticed and unquestioned, despite the act of writing requiring some level of planning and reflection on the part of the writer, which could have supported a (re)examination of one's own understanding of the subject matter. Such missed opportunities emphasize the importance of guiding student teachers towards a deeper, more critical engagement with the linguistic elements they encounter, which could have been achieved if we had introduced the concepts of 'glottonormativity' and '*conscientização*' from the very beginning and addressed ocularcentrism as a bias limiting our perception of what counts as languages. These are aspects to consider in similar interventions.

Another lesson learned was that when participants are left to complete the task with minimal guidance, unstructured peer interaction may not be sufficient to raise the desired level of *conscientização* among them. While we consider that peer interaction is valuable, it became clear that there is a need for additional content and critical interactional scaffolding. Such scaffolding involves incorporating carefully designed content that not only leads student teachers to explore linguistic diversity, but also guides them through critical reflections on the glottonormativity they uncover, its symbolic and ideological implications, and the underlying reasons. Dialogue is essential for the development of *conscientização* (Tavares, 2023); however, the asynchronous nature of the activity poses challenges to the maintenance of dialogue from a pedagogical perspective.

In terms of challenges in the implementation of the activity, because of the different time zones, we had to opt for an asynchronous modality. This apparently caused the task to extend too much in time (several months), perhaps because no synchronous interaction was possible. During the interviews with the student teachers, the design of the platform was also criticized: the participants could not receive notifications and often forgot to visit the platform to build on the discussions. This technical issue probably contributed to the lack of engagement and interaction during the commentary phase.

The limitations in the development of the activity are evident in the asymmetry of the number of students from Sydney (fewer) and Hamburg (more). This numerical imbalance left the German participants feeling more 'at home' among their peers. Coupled with the sense of shared cultural familiarity from being in the German context, they might have felt as though they did not need to engage very deeply with the subject matter. Although nearly all student teachers uploaded pictures, few proceeded to comment on the pictures, and even fewer actively sought peer input.

Based on these reflections, we put forth the following recommendations for future activities:

- Implementing structured activities and discussions that specifically target aspects of linguistic (in)visibility: this involves focusing more on questions of why and how linguistic (in)visibility is created and reproduced in the LL than on purely seeing languages in the LL; it also implies providing participants with a critical theor*ethical* overview of concepts such as 'glottonormativity', '*conscientização*' and 'ocularcentrism', for example.
- Combining compiled material by the teacher with the ones discovered and uploaded by the student teachers in order to generate sufficient visual basis for the discussions in writing so that in-depth peer engagement may be promoted.
- Creating moment-by-moment structured scaffolding, through moderators, tutors or peer questioning, which lead participants to discover, become (critically) aware of, and challenge glottonormativity in the LL. This involves making *conscientização* an explicit and intentional learning outcome, suggesting that aims of the online course should be more transparent from the outset.
- Ensuring there is a balanced number of participants from each country when implementing transnational projects, so that the written interaction encompasses a more diverse audience and stimulates more participation and *conscientização* through an exchange of international perspectives. This might mean a more thorough preparation of the virtual written exchange, considering time zones, profiles of the groups, and teacher education programs' design (such as duration, start and end dates, etc.). Opening up the exchange to more than two institutions can also be considered. Integrating students from closer time zones could allow for the inclusion of synchronous communication modalities in the project design.
- While the tasks were designed to enhance written telecollaboration between two different geopolitical and linguistic contexts, they can be transposed to hybrid scenarios: students can collect and upload their data into an online platform and then discuss them in the face-to-face sessions.

Conclusion

This chapter argued that LLs are a source of glottonormativity and a proxy to understand practical reasoning about languages and societal multilingualism in a given context. It is necessary to view research and local impact through a single lens, or in the words of Kubota (2022: 4), 'to amplify a synergy between producing scholarly knowledge within academe and making efforts to put the knowledge into practice through concrete actions for transformation in the real world'. This chapter illustrated how the scholarly knowledge on LL can be transposed to teacher education programs and, eventually to language classrooms, thus having an impact in the real world. Because student teachers become potential multipliers of academic knowledge, it is important that they come into contact with contemporary theories and practices of education that challenge normativity, the monolingual mindset, or the merely exoticizing and romanticizing vision of societal multilingualism.

The discussed activity 'Multilingualism in *your* city/Mehrsprachigkeit in *deiner* Stadt', implemented through language student teachers' participation in a transnational discussion forum, was designed and implemented to promote *conscientização*. We considered how *conscientização* is a means to stimulate the awakening to social (in)justices backed by glottonormativity in the LL, a bias that exposes (or even overexposes) some languages, under either a positive or negative veil, and impacts individuals and communities. Finally, we consider that the proposed activity, developed specifically with student teachers, has the potential to promote their *conscientização* and therefore to produce positive change in society and education through the implementation of critical (language) pedagogies in their own future classrooms.

Acknowledgements

The project 'In Others' Shoes: But How?' was part of the program IVAC – International Virtual Academic Collaboration, from DAAD. It obtained the Project grant 57563713 and was developed from September 2020 to October 2021.

Notes

(1) See here for information: https://www.ew.uni-hamburg.de/einrichtungen/ew4/didaktik-romanische-sprachen/projekte/in-others-shoes.html
(2) https://www.openolat.uni-hamburg.de
(3) We use plurilingualism to denote multilingualism at the individual level.
(4) https://www.researchgate.net/publication/349640412_Multilingualism_in_Hamburg_LUCIDE_City_Report
(5) www.multilingualsydney.org
(6) All excerpts are reproduced in their original form, maintaining the original orthography and syntax. Some examples were shortened (signaled in the excerpts).

References

Brinkmann, L.M., Duarte, J. and Melo-Pfeifer, S. (2022) Promoting plurilingualism through linguistic landscapes: A multi-method and multisite study in Germany and the Netherlands. *TESL Canada Journal* 38 (2), 88–112. https://doi.org/10.18806/tesl.v38i2.1358

Chan, A. (2023) Localizing the practice of critical pedagogy through place-based, problem-posing education. In G. Park, S. Bogdan, M. Rosa and J. Navarro (eds) *Critical Pedagogy in the Language and Writing Classroom: Strategies, Examples, Activities from Teacher Scholars* (pp. 106–118). Routledge.

Darwall, S. (2001) Normativity. In *Routledge Encyclopedia of Philosophy*. Routledge. https://doi.org/10.4324/9780415249126-L135-1

Freire, P. (1979) *Conscientização. Teoria e Prática da Libertação. Uma Introdução ao Pensamento de Paulo Freire*. Cortez & Moraes.

Gorter, D. and Cenoz, J. (2024) *A Panorama of Linguistic Landscape Studies*. Multilingual Matters.

Kubota, R. (2022) Linking research to transforming the real world: Critical language studies for the next 20 years. *Critical Inquiry in Language Studies*. https://doi.org/10.1080/15427587.2022.2159826

Malinowski, D., Maxim, H. and Dubreil, S. (eds) (2020) *Language Teaching in the Linguistic Landscape: Mobilizing Pedagogy in Public Space*. Springer.

Melo-Pfeifer, S. (2024) Challenging mainstream perspectives on multilingual pedagogies. An analysis of teachers' online discussions on linguistic landscapes. In R. Zaidi, U. Boz and E. Moreau (eds) *Transcultural Pedagogies for Multilingual Classrooms* (pp. 167–184). Multilingual Matters.

Melo-Pfeifer, S. and Chik, A. (2022) Multimodal linguistic biographies of prospective foreign language teachers in Germany. *International Journal of Multilingualism* 19 (4), 499–522. https://doi.org/10.1080/14790718.2020.1753748

Ollerhead, S., Chick, A. and Melo-Pfeifer, S. (2023) Building a virtual transnational space for initial teacher education: Visual language biographies as mediation instruments between Australian and German higher education students. *Journal of Multilingual and Multicultural Development (special issue)*. https://doi.org/10.1080/01434632.2023.2179579.

Prada, J. (2023) Sensescapes and what it means for language education. In S. Melo-Pfeifer (ed.) *Linguistic Landscapes in Language and Teacher Education: Multilingual Teaching and Learning Inside and Beyond the Classroom* (pp. 243–258). Springer.

Sengeh, D. (2023) *Radical Inclusion: Seven Steps to Help You Create a More Just Workplace, Home, and World*. Flatiron Books.

Shohamy, E. and Ben-Rafael, E. (2015) Introduction: Linguistic landscape, a new journal. *Linguistic Landscapes* 1 (1/2), 1–5.

Shohamy, E. and Pennycook, A. (2021) Language, pedagogy, and active participant engagement: Gaze in the multilingual landscape. In R. Blackwood and U. Røyneland (eds) *Spaces of Multilingualism* (pp. 31–47). Routledge.

Tavares, V. (2023) A century of Paulo Freire: Problem-solving education, *conscientização*, dialogue and TESL from a Freirean perspective. In V. Tavares (ed.) *Social Justice, Decoloniality, and Southern Epistemologies within Language Education: Theories, Knowledges, and Practices on TESOL from Brazil* (pp. 145–162). Routledge.

7 Critical Language Awareness in Language Teacher Education: How Can Critical Autoethnographic Narrative Help?

Bedrettin Yazan, Ceren Kocaman and Kristen Lindahl

Background: Anchor in Scholarship

Educational institutions are sites of identity construction and, as such, include and legitimize certain identities, while excluding or marginalizing others (Sarangi & Baynham, 1996). At the intersection of privilege and marginalization, nobody is immune to exclusion (Sengeh, 2023). The language classroom, especially, is full of stories of exclusion in the form of being discriminated against because of accent (Lippi-Green, 2012), not being recognized because of sexual orientation/gender identity (Güney, 2024), not having access to opportunities because of ethnoracial background (Valenzuela, 1999), or not being hired due to non-native English speaker status (Selvi *et al.*, 2024), as well as other realities, ideologies, and practices in which power imbalances among groups are used to learners' and teachers' (dis)advantage, which is almost invariably indexed by language.

As discriminating and exclusive as the language classroom can be (or perhaps because of this), it also offers language teachers and teacher educators a productive space to critically examine exclusion, discrimination, and marginalization and open up a space for inclusivity and belonging. Critical Language Teacher Education (CLTE) situates language (and its learning and teaching as an extension of that) within inclusive/exclusive sociopolitical discourses of race, gender, sexuality, and class among others (Hawkins & Norton, 2009). As critical language educators, in this chapter we operate within the premise that classrooms are not neutral, apolitical, or ahistorical places (Freire, 1996). Instead, they are sites where identities are constructed, negotiated, and enacted, mainly through our use of language (Canagarajah, 1993; Norton, 1997). Language classrooms as well as language teacher education programs harbor discourses that determine who should be seen as 'legitimate' language users and teachers (Bartolomé, 2004; Lindahl & Henderson, 2019; Varghese *et al.*, 2016; Yazan & Rudolph, 2018). A way for us, the authors of this chapter, to practice inclusivity and to create community and a sense of belonging lies at the intersection of recognizing diverse identities that are represented in the classroom and a critical examination of these identities through language use, specifically how language indexes power and can be used to include/exclude.

Our understanding of *radical inclusivity* draws from two lines of research. First, we see CLTE as an opportunity to interact with Teacher Candidates (TCs) to identify and denaturalize uneven power relations, and the ways in which language is a venue, activity, and subject in the creation and maintenance of those relations (Park *et al.*, 2023), thus demystifying language learning and teaching. Within this context, critical language awareness of how language and institutional discourses both include and exclude through language ideologies can lead to the development of TCs' 'political and ideological clarity' (Bartolomé, 2004; see also Lindahl *et al.*, 2021), which should guide their instructional decisions and practices. Second, we use an identity approach to teacher education, which draws from over two decades of research on language teacher identity (LTI) (Yazan & Lindahl, 2022), and use LTI as an 'organizing principle' (Varghese *et al.*, 2016) to make clearer and more visible the relationship between personal, professional, and political dimensions of language education (see Park, 2017). Such an identity lens helps teachers and teacher educators recognize the diverse identities, life experiences, emotions, hopes and desires that both learners and TCs bring to the classroom context, and leverages the language of exclusion and discourses of marginalization and othering to include, resist, and ultimately create belonging to language communities and facilitate a sense of ownership of languages.

Our exercise in radical inclusivity in our respective teacher education contexts is Critical Autoethnographic Narrative (CAN; Yazan, 2019) as a critical, identity-oriented teacher learning activity. Drawing from the implications of LTI research and in response to oppressive language ideologies that frame difference as deficit instead of an organic component of glocalizing communities (Menard-Warwick, 2013; Motha, 2014; Sayer, 2012), CAN offers a semester-long scaffolded writing activity which relies on critical autoethnography's methodological affordances to pedagogize LTI. In CAN, TCs narrate and analyze past experiences as language learners, users, and teachers to better understand the intricate interplay between 'the self', 'the other', and 'the sociocultural/political discourses' (Yazan, 2019) to identify ideologies which influence our approach to language and its learning and teaching. Breaking down the term 'autoethnography' is a clear way to understand the purposes of the approach: by attending to their own experiences critically ('auto') in relation to others and surrounding discourses, teacher candidates can gain a critical understanding of the cultural aspects ('ethno') of their teaching context through writing ('graph'). In doing so, they start to conceptualize language classrooms as sites of power that are not apolitical, ahistorical or neutral. Hopefully, such an identity lens can contribute to the transformation of language classrooms in the long run.

Finally, our contribution in this chapter is an attempt at and a documentation of our ongoing *praxis* (Freire, 1996), or how we, as critical teacher educators, use our critical consciousness to take action in the real world (Kubota, 2023). Critical, identity-oriented teacher education not only allows us to uncover and demystify language use that marginalizes and excludes, but also to imagine ways to 'be', 'think', and 'act' differently in teacher education as well as other classroom contexts. CAN operationalizes *praxis* on two levels: (1) as teacher educators bring up issues of power, exclusion and inclusion through the study of language ideologies in their respective teacher education contexts, and (2) as TCs reflect on their imagined identities (in connection with their past teaching practices) and how they can transform their own understanding of language, power, inclusion and exclusion by engaging in narrative writing.

Against this backdrop, we understand radical inclusivity to be teacher educators' intentional attention to power relations, the situatedness and fluidity of identities within sociopolitical contexts, as well as their ongoing efforts to attend to, raise awareness of, disrupt, and transform unjust, unequal, marginalizing and othering (language, teaching, social, educational) practices. In our respective contexts, CAN helps us be radically inclusive by making clear the unequal power dynamics in relation to TCs' linguistic practices and by helping them gain agency over their sense-making processes by externalizing their experiences of language learning, teaching, and use through (re)storying.

Introduction and Context of the Course

Bedrettin designed and used CAN in his graduate-level teacher education courses in MA in TESOL programs housed in large research universities in Alabama and Texas, where he works as a professor. Those courses included mostly ESL TCs, in addition to world language and content area TCs, along with occasional doctoral students. Since 2018, he has used CAN four times with student groups ranging in size from three to twelve, one of which was a synchronous online course.

In search of an identity-oriented teacher education activity, Ceren, a doctoral student and teacher educator, adapted Bedrettin's initial conceptualization of CAN for her teacher education courses with pre-service teachers enrolled in an MEd program in Germany. The courses in which she used CAN focused on cultural learning; course sizes ranged between 12 to 18. One difference in the German context is that TCs prepare to teach two subjects (e.g. English and German, English and Maths, Politics and History), which means that the focus is not only on LTI but also how TCs experience their professional identities (differently and simultaneously) in the two subjects they study.

Kristen, also a professor and teacher educator, incorporated CAN in an advanced PhD seminar in applied linguistics, with a specific focus on Language Teacher Education (LTE). The seminar explored LTE topics, and encouraged reflection on those topics and connections to students' own lives via a CAN assignment sequence. The course, held at a large public US-based university with a Hispanic-Serving Institution (HSI) designation, consisted of between 7–10 students, all of whom had diverse linguistic repertoires, ethnoracial and transnational identities. The use of CAN in this class allowed for the centering not only of teacher identity but also of teacher *educator* identity among the group of future scholars and potential teacher educators (see Dao *et al.*, 2025).

Description of the Activity in Action

Background and rationale of the activity or lesson

CAN extends the use of language learning or literacy autobiographies (Park, 2013) that are already commonly used in teacher education courses. CAN positions language teaching as a political act with teachers and learners as political actors. This positioning highlights the ideologies and discourses circulating within the sociopolitical context in which language, learners, and teachers are situated. The rationale of CAN as an activity in language teacher education is to include identity as an explicit pedagogical frame and goal that guides teacher-learning.

Brief description of lesson outcomes, goals and/or student learning objectives

The goals of CAN include to (a) engage in a critical cultural examination in the context of language teaching by 'mak[ing] the personal political' (Holman Jones, 2005: 765), (b) analyze ideologies in the stories TCs tell as well as corresponding identities, agency, and emotions of the individuals involved, (c) become politically and ideologically clearer, and (d) develop a critically-oriented identity lens to apprehend TCs' learning and practice in the sociopolitical context. Below, we describe the process(es) we used when implementing CAN as an example for colleagues to begin or reflect on their own implementation of CAN or similar identity-oriented activities.

Preparation

We used CAN as an assignment that TCs work on throughout a 15-week course. The activities as well as the issues covered in the course were selected to prepare TCs to write their CANs by familiarizing them with the genre, helping them brainstorm stories, and supporting them in critically analyzing and structuring their CANs in line with the course content (e.g. language ideologies). The preparation stage of CAN included (a) a reading sample of published (e.g. Solano-Campos, 2014) and unpublished (e.g. Donnelly, 2015) autoethnographic writing to familiarize teachers with autoethnography as a writing and research genre, (b) discussing the interconnection between teacher identity and teacher learning and practice (e.g. Olsen, 2016), and (c) introducing teachers to the critical applied linguistics research literature around concepts of discourse and language ideologies in education (e.g. Pavlenko & Blackledge, 2004). We did these preparatory activities within the first few weeks of the course before we asked teachers to narrate their past and recent experiences with language use, learning, and teaching in their first CAN installment.

Procedural step-by-step description of the assignment

We asked teachers to submit their CAN in three or four installments, depending on the number of students in the class (see Table 7.1 for an

Table 7.1 An outline of CAN-related activities

Time	CAN-related activity	Purpose
Beginning of the course (the first 2–3 weeks)	- reading published and unpublished autoethnographies - brainstorming stories of language learning, teaching, and use - drafting the first CAN installment	preparation, getting to know autoethnographic writing
Mid-course	- written feedback - individual feedback session / peer feedback - exploring language ideologies in class through readings and discussions - drafting the second CAN installment	generating stories, finding an analytic lens
Second half of the course	- written feedback - individual feedback session / peer feedback - (collaborative) analysis with guiding questions - drawing up a concept map	critically analyzing the stories, structuring the text
End of the course	- co-creating the assessment rubric - drafting and submitting the final installment	supporting the inclusion of teachers' voices in the academic knowledge generation

outline of CAN activities). We asked them to narrate any experiences they could re-remember in initial installments, and then begin analyzing those experiences in later installments. Following the submission of each installment, we provided written feedback or asked them to engage in peer feedback in the case of doctoral students (i.e. the emerging language teacher educators). We also had individual feedback sessions to clarify our written feedback and scaffolded the analysis later in the process. Additionally, we engaged in general feedback conversations and addressed students' questions about CAN in class sessions. Around mid-semester, we conducted collaborative analysis activities in class and practiced with some guiding questions: 'Who is involved in this story? What has happened? What decisions are made? Who is the decision maker? What identity positions are assumed or enacted?' Towards the end of the semester, in some instances we had students draw a concept map of their CAN up until that point and had them co-construct a rubric in groups or pairs which we used to create an overarching rubric to evaluate their CAN engagement throughout the semester.

Assessment

We conducted formative informal assessment through written comments on each installment, individual and peer feedback sessions, and classroom activities (e.g. collaborative data analysis, concept maps). Through the formative assessment, we aimed to help TCs better structure their texts, generate more stories, and reflect on underlying ideologies. We provided formal and summative assessment at the end with the above-mentioned rubric they contributed to create.

Post-Activity Thoughts, Reflections, and Discussion of Challenges

What have we learned about radical inclusivity and critical language awareness in/through CAN writing?

Bedrettin: From my experience, the use of CAN in my teacher education classes taught me that the intersectionality of language teacher identity can only be addressed through extended engagement with identity work. Most of the time, we as teacher educators focus on the language/linguistic dimension of identity in relation to language teacher identity, which is definitely crucial. However, helping teachers make connections or see the connections between their professional identity and all other pertinent social identities needs more time and focused self-examination. I think CAN affords the space for such self-examination, not only for teachers but also for teacher educators. In my use of CAN four times so far, language teachers analyzed their stories to surface and examine their language and teacher identities in relation to racial, ethnic, cultural, religious, national, sexual, political, and familial identities at variable degrees. I think critical language awareness requires understanding language use, learning, and teaching within the sociopolitical discourses and CAN, with intersectional identity work, offers the learning activity to develop such awareness.

Ceren: One affordance of CAN for my own professional development has been the recognition that marginalization and privilege co-exist (Park, 2017; Varghese *et al.*, 2016) and all our stories are marked by inclusion and exclusion. Although I work in a context and with TCs that I do not necessarily share a cultural background with, there are striking similarities in our stories of language learning, teaching, and use, which creates a sense of community. This, in turn, creates a renewed sense of commitment in investing my time and energy in identity work as part of TCs' professional development as well as mine.

Kristen: In my specific context, perhaps the greatest affordance of CAN has been the inclusion of stories, experiences and perspectives that have been mostly missing or grossly underrepresented in the 'scholarly' literature on teacher education and teacher educator preparation and mentoring. In the US, this body of work has historically been based largely on the experiences of monolingual English-speaking teachers who may or may not work with multilingual children, and teacher educators of a similar profile, to the exclusion of research and tertiary practices that account for the lived experiences of diverse ethnoracial linguistic communities. In highlighting the transnational, translingual identities of the scholars via CAN implementation, I believe space was created to re-story their experiences in such ways that allowed for recognition of how they continued to grapple with tensions resulting from the ways that all of them had experienced marginalization related to their social identities, including language background, country of origin, gender, sexual orientation, and ethnoracial identity. Their critical analysis of various incidents throughout their lives related specifically to their experiences as language users, and later, language teachers, created a larger sense of empathy for the language learners they themselves educated or the imagined language teachers they would one day educate.

What have our students learned about radical inclusivity and critical language awareness in/through CAN writing?

Bedrettin: Teacher candidates learn more about teaching through their observations of teacher educators' modeling than reading about 'best' ways of teaching. Therefore, when engaging in CAN writing, which involves in-depth critical reflection, I think language teachers learn to frame their professional learning and their future students' language learning from an intersectional identity lens. Situating language (and themselves as language teachers) within sociopolitical discourses, teachers also develop their critical language awareness as part of that lens. When approaching their teaching with an identity lens, teachers would be more likely to engage in inclusive practices to help language learners see language and language learning as part of their whole person, inseparable from all different dimensions of their identity. Regarding radical inclusivity and critical language awareness, teachers also learn how to navigate professional identity tensions that are an organic, formative, and transformative part of becoming teachers (Britzman, 2012).

Here's an example from Sara's (pseudonym) last individual feedback session whose CAN I analyzed a few years ago (Yazan, 2019):

> I always thought native speaker was the language you speak at home. … My godfather is from Canton Province and his wife is from Taiwan and they have two kids and at home they only speak Chinese. It's the rule of the household. … Whenever I go to visit, that's the only time the kids are allowed to speak English at home. And so, they are native speakers of English and Chinese, but at home they only speak Chinese. So, that wouldn't really work in that case. … Yeah, so [nativeness] is too slippery. There's not really a fixed way to define it. … I think if you feel like you can control the language, you're a native speaker. So, all the people in Dr. [Mendoza]'s class, they're native speakers if they feel like they can control the language. … The term has to evolve with the times or just has to go away.

Ceren: In analyzing and reinterpreting their stories of language learning, teaching, and use, TCs can learn to see themselves and talk about themselves as language users in alternative ways. They may question what it means to be a (non-)native speaker and explore who is or is not allowed to be bi/multilingual. CAN opens up alternative identity options for teacher candidates so that they can gain a sense of legitimacy as professionals (Pavlenko, 2003). I find this to be inclusive in two ways. First, by critically discussing our past experiences through the lens of language ideologies, we get to imagine a professional community in which there is space for those who have been traditionally marginalized due to their racial, ethnic, gender, or linguistic identities, among others. We make *all* identities relevant for the teaching-learning process and for our profession. Second, TCs are often able to start thinking about their (future) learners beyond their roles as learners. For instance, when TCs reflect on what it means to create language materials that have 'real-life relevance', they are often able to include the various identities that learners bring with them. An analysis of language ideologies creates opportunities for a more compassionate approach to language learning, in which learners are recognized for who they are and their language use is understood within the sociopolitical processes that (re-)produce their identities.

Kristen: My impression as an observer and facilitator was that for my students, they knew on an intuitive, personal level that certain incidents in their lives centered around power dynamics and cycles of privilege and marginalization. Many had already engaged in other reflective genres of writing, such as poetry, *testimonio*, and journaling. However, CAN – with the analytical component and connection to extant scholarship – provided avenues to develop the metalanguage necessary to analyze these events and their implications on the authors' lives and ultimately, their scholarly and pedagogical practices as well. Thus, the writing of CAN and the analysis of the events therein further legitimized the marginalization that the authors expressed, nominalizing these experiences in what was perceived as a 'scholarly' writing activity. Not to say that 'scholarly' writing is the only way to legitimize experiences and critical perspectives on them, but it is one avenue for contributing to the larger sociopolitical discourses that shape how we as a field view language teacher education. Because CAN is unique to each individual, as a method it is not constrained to historical conventions of genre and knowledge construction, and remains more flexible to various sociocultural ways of knowing, learning, and expression.

What challenges came up while implementing the lesson/activity in the classroom?

Bedrettin: I can share three challenges on which I've been reflecting for a while. First, teachers do not always accept autoethnographic writing as a legitimate way of research. I did not frame CAN as action research when introducing it to teachers, but I provided autoethnography as a research methodology which we adapted as an identity-oriented teacher learning. Their preconceived notions about what research is took me some time to convince them that collecting and analyzing data from own experience is also research. I am not surprised though, since autoethnography is still a highly contested methodology in our field of language education and broader educational research. Second, it was challenging for teachers to share their emotionally-charged and often traumatic experiences in their CAN. It was also challenging for me to navigate the scaffolding they needed to narrate and analyze those experiences. I never forced them to narrate any stories they did not feel comfortable with, but after they shared some of those difficult stories, I was not entirely sure if I should encourage them to keep reflecting on them or leave them in our feedback meetings. Third, I was having tensions regarding my own identities as a language teacher educator and researcher of language teacher education who is interested in autoethnography. I discuss this tension elsewhere at length (Yazan, 2022), but briefly, I was having difficulty foregrounding my teacher educator identity when having feedback meetings with teachers. My identity as a researcher would become dominant every now and then and I was afraid of being the researcher in those meetings and trying to analyze teachers' stories for them instead of facilitating their reflective storytelling and self-analysis. I wanted to serve, and I did mostly, as a language teacher educator who is committed to pedagogizing identity in my practice, rather than implementing CAN for the sake of collecting data for research purposes. I had the research component for sure, but in the implementation, I wanted to foreground my pedagogical purpose.

Ceren: One challenge that I've observed is that it can take a while for TCs to switch from a more academic, impersonal style of writing to writing narrative texts. As TCs get into the flow of narrating and analyzing, however, they usually appreciate writing in a new genre. Another recurring experience has been the emotions and tensions that naturally come up during the reflection process, which is an inseparable part of TCs' identity work (Tajeddin & Yazan, 2024). It is not possible to talk about identity without also attending to ideological tensions and emotions that come up in reflecting on, expressing or performing identities. This emotionally-engaging aspect of CAN opens up space for community building. Collaboration and guidance in dealing with tensions and various emotions help bring TCs closer to ideological and political clarity (Bartolomé, 2004) and an attention to emotions can promote agency (Benesch, 2018).

Kristen: Interestingly, the 'awareness' piece of critical autoethnographic narrative, and therefore critical language awareness, was one of the more challenging aspects in my context. While the student-authors were eager about the genre and the narrative aspect of the implementation, it required a few to several iterations of re-visiting their manuscripts to delve more deeply into the underlying language ideologies that engendered the incidents they unpacked via the CAN assignment. For instance, they may have reflected on others' comments about their language varieties, perceived accentedness, or bilingual identities, but in their analyses, they were also perpetuating ideologies of standardization or language separation without realizing it. These tensions provided ample opportunities to develop ideological clarity (Lindahl *et al.*, 2021) through peer feedback, wherein a colleague talked with the author through how their incident, analysis and subsequent interpretation could reflect more critical perspectives on language and language teaching.

What is your advice for adapting or implementing the lesson/activity in various contexts?

Bedrettin: I understand that implementing CAN in a class bigger than 15 students might be challenging or it also depends on what other assignments and activities are included in the course. I wanted to preface with that comment, because my advice will require teacher educators' extra time and commitment. What I really found helpful in opening up and maintaining a dialogue with my students is the one-on-one feedback meetings which, at times, felt like therapy sessions, but I think students needed to process some of the emotionally-charged past and recent experiences with somebody who would understand their challenges, contradictions, and tensions. I also found those meetings helpful in establishing rapport with students by telling them my own stories, opening myself up to humanize teacher education, and making myself vulnerable so that they feel comfortable to share their stories with me. I am not offering that as a strategy. I think it is a requirement for any honest and sincere dialogue that we would like to be productive and educative as part of identity work.

Ceren: For contexts in which teacher educators cannot commit to integrating an assignment with multiple installments and feedback rounds, they can make use of shorter, critical incident-like writing exercises of a critical autoethnographic nature. These incidents can still be analyzed from a language ideology perspective and commented on either by the teacher educator or in conversation with other course participants.

Kristen: Due to time constraints of class topic coverage but also wanting to incorporate CAN, I substituted the one-on-one feedback sessions with peer feedback sessions. Because of the advanced level of the doctoral students, I felt this better reflected their positionality as already-established writers with their own developing expertise who would serve as critical thought partners for each other during the writing process. Providing mentor texts of existing autoethnographies, as well as including other types of narrative-based research practices, situated our class practice so that they were not only learning about the topic of language teacher education but also engaging in a research approach simultaneously via CAN. As could (and should) be expected, each author had varying degrees of comfort with disclosing events and emotions, and different interpretations of those events. Formative activities during class time, such as mapping, peer feedback, and writer's workshops supported the CAN assignment and integrated it with the course materials so that the more summative CAN did not feel like a separate task from the rest of the course content.

In conclusion, this chapter has connected CAN to the notion of *radical inclusivity*, noting how critical language awareness can be actionably operationalized in teacher education (and teacher educator education). In sharing examples of our own praxis around CAN and the resulting identity negotiation among teacher candidates and future teacher educators, we hope this mapping proves useful in the ongoing support of teachers and teacher candidates to develop critical language awareness, consequently interrogating and disrupting ideologies and discourses of exclusion, in favor of those that perpetuate asset-based perspectives of inclusion.

References

Bartolomé, L.I. (2004) Critical pedagogy and teacher education: Radicalizing prospective teachers. *Teacher Education Quarterly* 31 (1), 97–122.

Benesch, S. (2018) Emotions as agency: Feeling rules, emotion labor, and English language teachers' decision-making. *System* 79, 60–69. https://doi.org/10.1016/j.system.2018.03.015

Britzman, D.P. (2012) *Practice Makes Practice: A Critical Study of Learning to Teach*. SUNY Press.

Canagarajah, A.S. (1993) Critical ethnography of a Sri Lankan classroom: Ambiguities in student opposition to reproduction through ESOL. *TESOL Quarterly* 27 (4), 601–626.

Dao, N., Lindahl, K. and Yazan, B. (2025) A transnational doctoral student becoming a TESOL teacher educator: Identities, emotions, agency and ideologies in critical autoethnographic narrative. *TESOL Journal*. https://doi.org/10.1002/tesj.70048.

Donnelly, H. (2015) Becoming an ESL teacher: An autoethnography. Unpublished master's thesis, Lakehead University, Thunder Bay, Ontario, Canada.

Freire, P. (1996) *Pedagogy of the Oppressed* (rev. edn). Continuum.

Güney, Ö. (2024) In pursuit of queer inquiry with Turkish EFL preservice teachers. *TESOL Quarterly* 58 (4), 1269–1292. https://doi.org/10.1002/tesq.3262

Hawkins, M. and Norton, B. (2009) Critical language teacher education. In A. Burns and J.C. Richards (eds) *The Cambridge Guide to Second Language Teacher Education* (pp. 30–39). Cambridge University Press.

Holman Jones, S. (2005) Autoethnography: Making the personal political. In N.K. Denzin and Y.S. Lincoln (eds) *The SAGE Handbook of Qualitative Research* (pp. 763–791). SAGE.

Kubota, R. (2023) Linking research to transforming the real world: Critical language studies for the next 20 years. *Critical Inquiry in Language Studies* 20 (1), 4–19. https://doi.org/10.1080/15427587.2022.2159826

Lindahl, K. and Henderson, K.I. (2019) The intersection of language ideologies and language awareness among in-service teachers of emergent bilinguals. *Journal of Immersion and Content-Based Language Education* 7 (1), 61–87.

Lindahl, K., Fallas-Escobar, C. and Henderson, K.I. (2021) Linguistically responsive instruction for Latinx teacher candidates: Surfacing language ideological dilemmas. *TESOL Quarterly* 55 (4), 1190–1220. https://doi.org/10.1002/tesq.3079

Lippi-Green, R. (2012) *English with an Accent: Language, Ideology and Discrimination in the United States*. Routledge.

Menard-Warwick, J. (2013) *English Language Teachers on the Discursive Faultlines: Identities, Ideologies and Pedagogies*. Multilingual Matters.

Motha, S. (2014) *Race, Empire, and English Language Teaching: Creating Responsible and Ethical Anti-Racist Practice*. Teachers College Press.

Norton, B. (1997) Language, identity, and the ownership of English. *TESOL Quarterly* 31 (3), 409–429.

Olsen, B. (2016) *Teaching for Success: Developing Your Teacher Identity in Today's Classroom* (2nd edn). Routledge, Taylor & Francis Group.

Park, G. (2013) 'Writing is a way of knowing': Writing and identity. *ELT Journal* 67 (3), 336–345.

Park, G. (2017) *Narratives of East Asian Women Teachers of English: Where Privilege Meets Marginalization*. Multilingual Matters.

Park, G., Bogdan, S., Rosa, M. and Navarro, J. (eds) (2023) *Critical Pedagogy in the Language and Writing Classroom: Strategies, Examples, Activities from Teacher Scholars*. Routledge.

Pavlenko, A. (2003) 'I never knew I was bilingual': Reimagining teacher identities in TESOL. *Journal of Language Identity and Education* 2 (4), 251–268. https://doi.org/10.1207/S15327701JLIE0204_2

Pavlenko, A. and Blackledge, A. (eds) (2004) *Negotiation of Identities in Multilingual Contexts*. Multilingual Matters.

Sarangi, S. and Baynham, M. (1996) Discursive construction of educational identities: Alternative readings. *Language and Education* 10 (2–3), 77–81.

Sayer, P. (2012) *Ambiguities and Tensions in English Language Teaching: Portraits of EFL Teachers as Legitimate Speakers*. Routledge.

Selvi, A.F., Yazan, B. and Mahboob, A. (2024) Research on 'native' and 'non-native' English-speaking teachers: Past developments, current status, and future directions. *Language Teaching* 57 (1), 1–41.

Sengeh, D. (2023) *Radical Inclusion: Seven Steps to Help You Create a More Just Workplace, Home, and World*. Flatiron Books.

Solano-Campos, A. (2014) The making of an international educator: Transnationalism and nonnativeness in English teaching and learning. *TESOL Journal* 5, 412–443.

Tajeddin, Z. and Yazan, B. (2024) *Language Teacher Identity Tensions: Nexus of Agency, Emotion, and Investment*. Routledge. https://doi.org/10.4324/9781003402411

Valenzuela, A. (1999) *Subtractive Schooling: US-Mexican Youth and the Politics of Caring*. State University of New York Press.

Varghese, M., Motha, S., Trent, J., Park, G. and Reeves, J. (2016) Language teacher identity in multilingual settings. *TESOL Quarterly* 50 (3), 545–571.

Yazan, B. (2019) Identities and ideologies in a language teacher candidate's autoethnography: Making meaning of storied experience. *TESOL Journal* 10 (4), e500. https://doi.org/10.1002/tesj.500

Yazan, B. (2022) Reflective practice as identity work: A teacher educator's reflections on identity tensions. In Z. Tajeddin and A. Watanabe (eds) *Teacher Reflection: Policies, Practices and Impacts: Studies in Honor of Thomas S.C. Farrell* (pp. 164–178). Multilingual Matters.

Yazan, B. and Rudolph, N. (eds) (2018) *Criticality, Teacher Identity, and (In)Equity in English Language Teaching: Issues and Implications*. Springer.

Yazan, B. and Lindahl, K. (2022) An identity approach to teacher education. In J. Liontas (ed.) *TESOL Encyclopedia of English Language Teaching*. Wiley-Blackwell. https://doi.org/10.1002/9781118784235.eelt1030

8 Increasing Pre-Service ESOL Teachers' Critical Language Awareness through Dialectical Variation

Brian Hibbs

Introduction

This section outlines four frameworks that undergirded both the class activities and the research investigation explored in this chapter: inclusivity, radicality, critical language awareness, and heteroglossia; each theory will be respectively examined in turn.

Inclusivity

M.S. and Siddiqui (2022: 155) define inclusivity as 'ensuring equal access to resources as well as opportunities to everyone, especially those who are at the risk of getting marginalized'. Johnson (2023: 237) concurs by suggesting that inclusivity involves 'the policy or practice of providing all people with equal access to opportunities and resources, especially those who might otherwise be marginalized or excluded'. More specifically, within the realm of education, the Branch Alliance for Educator Diversity (2021: 6) explains that inclusive instruction 'minimizes or removes barriers to learning or assessment and supports the success of all students' and 'is situated within a classroom climate that is conductive to learning and fosters a sense of belonging'. These definitions highlight that efforts should be made to include those who have typically been 'othered' or marginalized by traditional policies and procedures in various political and social realms. Hence, inclusivity should be an essential hallmark of education so that students' multicultural and multilingual backgrounds may be acknowledged, understood, and valued; it is also critical that educator preparation programs equip future teachers with the strategies and techniques needed to successfully integrate all learners into the classroom and school communities.

Radicality

In terms of the concept of radicality, Alaverdov *et al.* (2022: 17) contend that radicalism is 'the position of a person or group (party), which consists in the desire to…uncompromisingly change the existing social, political, and cultural state of affairs'. Again, within the context of education, Wang and Cranton (2013: 147) explain that radical or critical education 'is connected with social, political, and economic understanding of cultures, and with the development of methods to bring people to an awareness of responsible social action [which] is used to combat social, political, and economic oppression within society'. These observations point out that radicality typically involves questioning and challenging the status quo in specific environments with the ultimate goal of working towards equity and equality for all. As with inclusivity, educators must embrace at least some level of radicality in their instruction so that all students are provided with the opportunity to simultaneously learn about the world and themselves, particularly for learners that have not generally been served by traditional education paradigms. This chapter reviews one viable area in which educator preparation can support pre-service teachers to become radically inclusive educators in their future instructional practice: critical language awareness. Learning about possible applications of this approach to language and literacy education can help prospective teachers better understand the role language plays in not only shaping the ways we perceive others and the world but also understanding, respecting, and appreciating the linguistic strengths and assets that learners possess.

Critical language awareness

Fairclough (1992: 1) defines language awareness as 'conscious attention to properties of language and language use as an element of language education'. Hammersley-Fletcher and Hanley (2016: 979) argue that criticality centers around the notion that 'the nature of reasoning, the self and our relations with others, are open to challenge and debate'. Fairclough (1992: 7) then merges these notions by specifying that critical language awareness 'highlights how language conventions and language practices are invested with power relations and ideological processes which people are often unaware of'. Thus, one of the fundamental goals of critical language awareness is to better understand the political and social nature of language in order to challenge the monolingual norms and expectations that permeate many aspects of current society by inverting this paradigm and centering instruction on multilingual learners' linguistic (and cultural) funds of knowledge (González *et al.*, 2005) while also advancing educators' perceptions about viewing these students' funds of knowledge from an asset-based perspective (Bartlett & García, 2011). As a result, recognizing and promoting these stances is especially important in the realm of educator preparation which should not only prepare future teachers for the linguistic and cultural diversity they will encounter in their future classrooms but also, with particular respect to multilingual learners, guide them in seeing themselves as catalysts for changing the predominant monolingual narrative currently existing in society by helping them acknowledge and value the linguistic powers these students hold.

Several scholars have extended and applied the concept of critical language awareness to the area of multilingualism. For example, García (2017: 270) asserts that one of the fundamental objectives of critical multilingual language awareness is to 'focus [on] the potential of language education to change the linguistic hierarchies that have been socially established and thus change the world and advance social justice' to not only capitalize on the multilingual assets possessed by these learners but also dispute the favored and authoritatively-sanctioned position that (standard) English has customarily enjoyed. Such a curriculum would not only equip future educators with the skills and dispositions necessary to tap into the multilingual resources these students have but also help them understand the social nature of language and the ways in which language is often co-opted by others to achieve specific aims and objectives. Additionally, certain scholars have merged the concepts of critical language awareness and translanguaging into the concept of critical translingual awareness, which is predicated on the intentional and purposeful integration of learners' multilingual assets and strengths as a central component of educational programming and curricula. Seltzer (2022) conceptualizes an approach to critical translingual awareness that encompasses three crucial yet interdependent factors. First, such a program should provide opportunities for teacher candidates to reflect on and consider their own subjectivities regarding language along with their individual views and perspectives regarding students' language use in the classroom. Second, the program should introduce them to the procedures used by others to exert power, authority, and dominion in society through language and how non-dominant languages have traditionally been marginalized and excluded. Third, the program should guide and support them in designing and implementing lessons that capitalize on students' linguistic proficiencies and conscientiously integrate this knowledge into their instruction. Cinaglia and De Costa (2022) assert that this approach should be a crucial and critical component of educator preparation and that 'creating spaces for teachers to engage in…reflection, develop critical multilingual awareness, and hone their translingual stances is of the highest priority for teacher educators working in the service of educational equity' (2022: 457). García (2017: 277) concurs with this observation and notes that 'teacher education programs must engage teachers in challenging the sociolinguistic order and the ways in which languages have been constructed and hierarchized'. The course unit outlined in this chapter attempts to accomplish these lofty yet worthwhile goals in the realm of language variation by striving to assist pre-service teachers in viewing their current/future students' multidialectical competencies and abilities from an asset-based perspective.

Heteroglossia

Another theoretical construct which framed the course unit reviewed in this chapter is the concept of heteroglossia. Francis (2012: 3–4) posits that monoglossia refers to 'dominant forms of language, representing the world-view/interests of dominant social groups, which are positioned or imposed as unitary and total'. Fuller (2014: 322) states that monoglossia 'works within a narrow framework and muffles alternatives serving to centralise language and discourse'. Additionally, Fuller claims that 'the monoglossic discourse is also hegemonic' (2014: 322), meaning that the legitimization and promotion of one language (variety) over others is often employed to advance specific political and social agendas. Thus, heteroglossia involves 'specific points of view on the world, forms for conceptualizing the world in words, specific world views, each characterized by its own objects, meanings, and values' (Bakhtin, 1981: 291–292). Heteroglossia tends to view language as 'fundamentally socially constructed, with meaning created between the speaker/author and the listener/reader, who are themselves steeped in historic understandings and socio-political language conventions' (Francis, 2012: 4). Kershner (2010: 156) points out that heteroglossia consists of 'the simultaneous presence of competing languages and their social, historical, psychological, and physical conditions of utterance'. These scholars contend that language is not inherently an objective phenomenon but is in fact a social construction that is often co-opted for the achievement of political and social leaders' targets. This observation not only holds true for language in a general sense but also for dialects in a more specific sense, which are 'variet[ies] of a language associated with a particular regional or social group' (Wolfram & Schilling, 2016: 357). Dialects are commonly used for a wide array of purposes and objectives and, similar to the previous discussion concerning multilingualism, non-standard varieties of a given language have typically been marginalized from a linguistic perspective. Consequently, the intention of the course unit was to challenge this stance by familiarizing pre-service teachers with the issues surrounding language variation in order to facilitate the examination of their assumptions and beliefs concerning language variation and also support them in viewing their multidialectical students from a strengths-based position.

The Course Unit

Modules

The purpose of this chapter is to summarize the components of a course unit on dialectical variation designed for primary-education teacher candidates enrolled in an ESOL culture and education course offered at a four-year institution of higher education in the American Southeast.

The overall aim of the course unit was to encourage teacher candidates to embrace radicality by (1) challenging the traditional notion that promotes viewing culturally and linguistically-diverse students from a deficit perspective and instead conceptualizing these learners from an asset-based/strength-based perspective in which all linguistic/cultural identities are acknowledged, understood, and valued, and by (2) establishing and maintaining a safe and supportive environment in which everyone feels included and integrated into the class/school community. The unit was also designed to familiarize pre-service teachers with the nature of language variation with the ultimate intention of advancing their awareness of the underlying issues of diversity, equity, and power that frequently occupy a fundamental role in discussion concerning language. Additionally, the point of departure for the unit was to expose prospective teachers to the phenomenon of dialects in order to help them understand the linguistic features of different varieties of American English along with various cultural and social factors that come into play when considering such variation. The course unit consisted of five modules that include a series of readings and corresponding activities along with a culminating assignment devised to familiarize participants with the nature of dialectical variation in the United States and equip them with specific strategies for teaching English learners standard American English while also valuing these students' home languages/dialects. Table 8.1 reviews the modules and module themes that constituted the course unit.

The first module in the course unit is designed to acquaint teacher candidates with two predominant views concerning language variation (prescriptivism and descriptivism); during the module, students read Hinkel (2018) which provides a concise yet thorough synopsis of these two positions. Those who align with prescriptivism typically believe that the standard variety of a given language is the language system which must be emulated and utilized by all and that any variation from the standard is commonly perceived as deficient, inadequate, incorrect, ungrammatical, etc. In essence, prescriptivists tend to visualize language as a static and unchanging entity, and they generally make value judgments about others' language use. In contrast, those who subscribe to descriptivism (which is the position adopted by most linguists) consider that, since language is a

Table 8.1 Course unit on dialectical variation

Day	Description of the Module
1	Prescriptive versus Descriptive Views of Language
2	An Overview of Dialects of American English
3	Practical Analysis of Dialectical Variation
4	A Balanced Approach to Teaching Dialectical Variation
5	Critical Essay

living, breathing organism that adapts to evolving societal conditions, it is naturally altered and modified by speakers of a given language to achieve and fulfill communicative purposes. Thus, language varieties are frequently seen from a judgment-free stance, are perceived as natural and normal occurrences, and are not regarded as inherently superior or inferior to any other varieties. In the module, participants are familiarized with both theories and are encouraged to consider not only their own attitudes concerning language variation but also possible implications and ramifications of these views for their current/future students. During this module, teacher candidates become familiar with certain institutions in other languages that commonly view language from a prescriptive stance, which are contrasted with the United States, which does not currently have such a governing body (Wiley, 2005); they are then asked to visualize these two perspectives not as a dichotomy but instead as a continuum in which people may subscribe to both perspectives to some extent (depending on the context) and consider where they believe they personally fit on this continuum and why. The purpose of this activity is to invite them to become aware of their own stance on language variation along with the potential implications of their views for their current/future classrooms.

The second module is intended to deepen teacher candidates' initial exploration into language variation by providing them with multiple opportunities to become familiar with important linguistic features of various aspects of American English dialects while also examining the cultural biases often held and stereotypes commonly associated with speakers of these dialects; to that end, students watch two documentaries, *American Tongues* (CNAM, 1988) and *Do You Speak American?* (Thirteen/WNET, 2005). Although somewhat dated, the hour-long *American Tongues* film effectively presents predominant aspects of various dialects of American English and analyzes opinions that are frequently held concerning users of these varieties in an amusing and entertaining way. *Do You Speak American?* consists of three hour-long episodes in which Robert MacNeil travels across the United States, interviews people concerning their use of various dialects of American English and their perceptions of these dialects, and comments on important information concerning the historical evolution of the dialects as well as their place within the local/regional community. These documentaries provide students with a panoramic view of the major dialects of American English, common stereotypes associated with speakers of these dialects, and the extent to which reality does (not) correspond to these assumptions.

The third module invites teacher candidates to analyze and study various linguistic and grammatical features of various dialects of American English. The module is largely based on the six major dialects of American English identified by Jacewicz and Fox (2016) (Mid Atlantic, New England, The Midland, The North, The South, and the West). For the central activity of the module, students are randomly assembled into six groups (one for each dialect); they then watch a video clip containing one or more speakers of the respective dialect, identify any phonological, morphological, syntactic, semantic, and/or pragmatic characteristics they note as they listen to the clip, and share their findings with other classmates. Thus, the activity provides participants with an opportunity to explore a specific dialect of American English in depth while also learning about various attributes of other dialects in order to better understand particular ways in which American English specifically and languages more generally can differ. This activity is especially crucial given that many students have not traveled extensively and hence have had little to no previous exposure to other languages, let alone other varieties of (American) English.

The fourth module acquaints teacher candidates with a wide array of strategies and techniques to familiarize their current/future students with the phenomenon of language variation in a larger sense along with various aspects of dialects of American English more specifically. Throughout the course of the module, students read a series of articles (Christian, 1997; Delpit, 2006; Hazen, 2001; Wolfram, 2013) which are designed to support them as they consider the educational and pedagogical consequences and implications of linguistic/dialectical variation for the classroom and to equip them with numerous activities they may potentially utilize in their current/future classrooms to advance learners' understanding and appreciation of such variation in their own lives and communities. These readings were specifically included because they address various aspects of teaching students about the nature of dialectical variation from multiple perspectives. Christian (1997: 3) highlights the distinction between deficit and difference by affirming that 'language differences do not represent linguistic [or] cognitive deficiencies', thus clarifying that those who communicate via non-standard varieties of a language are not inherently inferior or lacking in any way. Christian (1997) also encourages teachers to strategically incorporate the study of dialects in the classroom in order to support students' understanding of the speech patterns of their communities and thus encourage them to adopt a pluralistic view of multilingualism. Delpit (2006: 95) contends that 'the linguistic form a student brings to school is intimately connected with loved ones, community, and personal identity', illustrating that denying one's ability to utilize a specific variety of a language is tantamount to erasing their cultural/linguistic background. Moreover, as did Christian (1997), Delpit (2006: 95) encourages teachers to see their students as 'language detectives' by providing them with opportunities to investigate the language varieties existing in their community and publicizing their learning through a variety of formats, including bilingual dictionaries, news shows, puppet shows, recordings, and role plays. Hazen (2001) asserts that people often hold misconceptions about language diversity because they have not had an opportunity to study the logistics of dialectical variation and that, consequently, 'if people had a better understanding of how language works, they would probably be less inclined to make negative judgments about speakers of different dialects' (2001: 2), one of the overarching aims of the course unit. Hazen (2001) then proposes a variety of activities that educators could integrate into their own instruction to familiarize students with different aspects of linguistic variation. Additionally, Wolfram (2013) concurs with the perspective adopted by Hazen (2001) that, children are continually surrounded by language ideologies from birth and that, if they do not become acquainted with the organic nature of language variation, the stereotypes commonly held about certain dialects will continue to circulate. Wolfram (2013: 29) argues that 'educating students about language diversity should be an essential component of…all disciplines' and reviews the logistics and findings of a research study designed to familiarize middle school students in North Carolina with various aspects of dialectical differences.

The fifth and final module asks teacher candidates to individually complete a critical essay in which they reflect upon the learning gained during the course unit and consider ways in which they could potentially implement such learning in their current/future instruction. The goal of this assignment is to assist them in consolidating the knowledge acquired during the previous four modules and supporting them in examining their views on linguistic/dialectical variation and contemplating possible avenues for teaching their students features of standard English while also respecting and valuing the language(s) (variety/ies) of the current/future learners with whom they (will) work (see Appendix 8.1 for directions for the critical essay).

Exploratory study

In the summer semester of 2023, a research project was formulated to collect and review information concerning teacher candidates' perspectives regarding the strengths and weaknesses of the course unit along with suggestions for improving the unit moving forward. Participants in the study included thirty-three pre-service elementary-education teachers enrolled in one of two sections of the ESOL culture and education course offered that semester that were taught by the author. A post-course questionnaire was administered at the conclusion of the course unit which consisted of ten Likert-scale statements concerning various aspects of the course unit and five open-ended questions which invited participants to comment on those facets of the unit that they believed were of most/least value to them and offer recommendations for strengthening the unit in the future. The qualitative data obtained during the study were analyzed using descriptive statistics (mean, median, mode, range), while the qualitative data were studied via content analysis.

Preliminary findings from the study demonstrated that, in general, teacher candidates in both sections believed that the course unit was effective in familiarizing them with fundamental issues and perspectives regarding language variation and was successful in building their awareness and understanding of linguistic features of various dialects of American English, and acquainting them with a variety of activities they might conceivably use in their current/future classrooms. (For example, a mean score of 4.68 out of 5 was obtained across all 10 Likert-scale statements from the responses of the participants in the first section, while a mean score of 4.74 out of 5 was obtained across all 10 Likert-scale statements from the responses of the participants in the second section). Several parallels emerged from the data across both sections of the course. For instance, with respect to statement #2 ('I understand the importance of understanding and valuing students' home dialects/languages'), participants' ratings were identical in regard to the statement (a mean score of 4.88 was obtained across both sections and was the highest-rated statement in both sections, indicating that students felt that the course unit assisted them in learning to acknowledge and appreciate the linguistic strengths and assets possessed by students. Another statement which was rated fairly equally across participants in both sections was statement #8 ('The articles helped me understand how to teach students about dialectical/linguistic variation'), with the statement receiving a mean score of 4.63 out of 5 by participants in the first section and 4.65 out of 5 by participants in the second section. This result shows that, according to teacher candidates, the readings included in the fourth module were reasonably effective in supplying them with the skills and dispositions needed to implement similar activities in their current/future instruction.

However, within these overall trends, variations in the data can be found. For example, there was some level of disagreement among participants in both sections regarding statement #1 ('I understand what dialectical variation is'), with participants in the first section rating that statement at a mean score of 4.44 out of 5 and participants in the second section rating that statement at a mean score of 4.77 out of 5. This finding seems to imply that teacher candidates enrolled in the first section were less inclined to believe that the course unit successfully promoted the development of their understanding of the phenomenon of dialectical variation in comparison with those enrolled in the second section. Among other possibilities, it is conceivable that participants in the first section may have not fully understood the meaning of the term since it is admittedly rather complex and technical; this in turn suggests that, moving forward, the author could more clearly explain what the expression means and utilize the term more regularly and intentionally during the course unit. Statement #5 ('The dialect activity helped me understand how to appreciate the variety of students' home dialects/languages') received a mean score of 4.81 out of 5 from participants in the first section and a mean score of 4.51 from participants in the second section. This finding appears to insinuate that, while the activity in the third module did support teacher candidates' emerging understanding of essential features of the major dialects of American English, the logistics of the activity may have prevented them from more successfully discerning and identifying such features in the video clips. Additionally, the activity presumes that course participants have a certain level of background knowledge regarding the field of linguistics more generally and the five subareas of linguistics examined in the activity more specifically; thus, future iterations of the course should include more exploratory and foundational work to provide students with the expertise they will need when completing the dialect activity. With respect to statement #7 ('The articles helped me understand how to appreciate the variety of students' home dialects/languages'), participants in the first section rated the statement more highly (a mean score of 4.88 out of 5) than participants in the second section (a mean score of 4.53 out of 5), suggesting that, similar to the discussion of the previous statement, the information contained in the readings may have been too complicated and difficult for students and assumed a higher level of familiarity with language variation and linguistics; moving forward, then, more class time could be spent on building students' awareness and understanding of linguistics more broadly and of linguistic/dialectical variation more precisely. In addition, statement #10 ('The critical essay helped me understand how to appreciate the variety of students' home dialects/languages'), received a lower rating from participants in the first section (a mean score of 4.56 out of 5) than from participants in the second section (4.82 out of 5), hinting that perhaps certain teacher candidates viewed the assignment more as busywork and less as an effective means for expressing and conveying their learning; more data should consequently be collected to solicit participants' views concerning positive and negative aspects of the critical essay and also regarding other possible ways for them to demonstrate the knowledge gained during the course unit. Consult Hibbs (2023) for more information about the context and findings of the study.

Reflection

Implementing the course unit yielded several benefits for these pre-service teachers. First, the unit was successful in familiarizing them with various matters and debates surrounding language variation, acquainted them with different perspectives on dialectical variation, and provided them with multiple opportunities to consider their own perspectives regarding linguistic variation. Second, the documentaries supplied the prospective teachers with important information concerning American English dialects along with common stereotypical images often associated with speakers of these varieties, and the dialect activity advanced their knowledge concerning various linguistic features of these dialects. Third, the readings included in the fourth module clarified their thinking about the nature of language variation and introduced them to specific activities about dialects that they could potentially integrate into their instruction.

However, the course unit may not necessarily have gone far enough in preparing these teacher candidates to challenge and confront the systemic injustices that culturally and linguistically-diverse learners still face. For instance, issues of equality, equity, or power were not specifically addressed in the unit. While the modules did inform them about the phenomenon of linguistic variation and the means by which languages can vary, they did not explore the attitudes or prejudices that are frequently held about speakers of non-standard varieties, nor did they expressly discuss methods or strategies for valuing their home varieties while also developing their competencies in standard English. Thus, moving forward, the author plans to include more information about possible approaches and techniques for supporting these students in linguistically and culturally affirming, relevant, responsive, and sustaining ways.

Concluding Thoughts

This chapter reviewed the logistics of a course unit on dialectical variation for pre-service elementary-education teachers pursuing the ESOL endorsement. The chapter began with a presentation of the concepts of inclusivity and radicality along with a description of the importance of these phenomena for educator preparation. The chapter then summarized the two theories that undergirded the course unit (critical language awareness and heteroglossia) and explained the contributions and relevancy of these theories to the unit. Next, the chapter highlighted the readings, activities, and culminating assignment that constituted the five modules of the course unit and discussed preliminary findings from an exploratory study conducted in the summer semester of 2023 designed to document and analyze teacher candidates' perspectives regarding the unit and their judgments with respect to improving the unit in future iterations of the course. It is hoped that the chapter will inspire other teacher educators to consider critical language awareness as one possible avenue for developing a strong cadre of radical and inclusive teachers interested in questioning and challenging the status quo in relation to hegemonic ideologies currently permeating the ESOL landscape while also acknowledging, understanding, and valuing the cultural and linguistic funds of knowledge that multilingual learners possess.

References

Alaverdov, E., Ilik, G. and Ugulava, M. (2022) Social radicalization in modern Russia and its impact on human security. In E. Alaverdov and M.W. Bari (eds) *Regulating*

Human Rights, Social Security, and Socio-economic Structures in a Global Perspective (pp. 1–17). IGI Global.

Bakhtin, M.M. (1981) *The Dialogic Imagination: Four Essays*. University of Texas Press.

Bartlett, L. and García, O. (2011) *Additive Schooling in Subtractive Times: Bilingual Education and Dominican Immigrant Youth in the Heights*. Vanderbilt University Press.

Branch Alliance for Educator Diversity. (2021) *A Primer on Inclusive Instruction*. M.E.B. Alliance for Educator Diversity, Inc.

Center for New American Media (CNAM) (Producer); Alvarez, L. and Kolker, A. (Directors) (1988) *American Tongues* [Video file].

Christian, D. (1997) *Vernacular Dialects in US Schools*. ERIC Document Reproduction Services No. ED406846. Retrieved from https://files.eric.ed.gov/fulltext/ED406846.pdf

Cinaglia, C. and De Costa, P.I. (2022) Cultivating critical translingual awareness: Challenges and possibilities for teachers and teacher educators. *RELC Journal* 53 (2), 452–459.

Delpit, L. (2006) What should teachers do? Ebonics and culturally responsive instruction. In S.J. Nero (ed.) *Dialects, Englishes, Creoles, and Education* (pp. 93–101). Routledge.

Fairclough, N. (1992) *Critical Language Awareness*. Routledge.

Francis, B. (2012) Gender monoglossia, gender heteroglossia: The potential of Bakhtin's work for re-conceptualising gender. *Journal of Gender Studies* 21 (1), 1–15.

Fuller, K. (2014) Gendered educational leadership: Beneath the monoglossic façade. *Gender and Education* 26 (4), 321–337.

García, O. (2017) Critical multilingual language awareness and teacher education. In J. Cenoz, D. Gorter and S. May (eds) *Language Awareness and Multilingualism* (pp. 263–280). Springer.

González, N., Moll. L.C. and Amanti, C. (2005) *Funds of Knowledge: Theorizing Practices in Households, Communities, and Classrooms*. Routledge.

Hammersley-Fletcher, L. and Hanley, C. (2016) The use of critical thinking in higher education in relation to the international student: Shifting policy and practice. *British Education Research Journal* 42 (6), 978–992.

Hazen, K. (2001) *Teaching about Dialects*. ERIC Document Reproduction Services No. ED456674. Retrieved from https://files.eric.ed.gov/fulltext/ED456674.pdf

Hibbs, B. (2023) Supporting pre-service ESOL teachers' critical language awareness through dialectical variation. In S.M. Curle and M.T. Hebebci (eds) *Proceedings of the International Conference on Academic Studies in Technology and Education (ICASTE)* (pp. 267–281). International Society for Academic Research in Science, Technology, and Education (ARSTE) Organization.

Hinkel, E. (2018) Descriptive versus prescriptive grammar. In H. Nassaji (ed.) *TESOL Encyclopedia of English Language Teaching*. Wiley. Retrieved from http://www.elihinkel.org/downloads/Descriptive%20v%20Prescriptive.pdf

Jacewicz, E. and Fox, R.A. (2016) Acoustics of regionally accented speech. *Acoustics Today* 12 (2), 31–38.

Johnson, N.N. (2023) Intersectionality in leadership: Spotlighting the experiences of Black women DEI leaders in historically White academic institutions. In T.B. Johnson (ed.) *The Experiences of Black Women Diversity Practitioners in Historically White Institutions* (pp. 213–238). IGI Global.

Kershner, R.B. (2010) Dialogism and heteroglossia. In G. Castle (ed.) *Literary and Cultural Theory* (Vol. 1, pp. 156–159). Wiley-Blackwell.

M.S., N. and Siddiqui, I. (2022) How inclusive is online education in India: Lessons from the pandemic. In M. Garcia (ed.) *Socioeconomic Inclusion during an Era of Online Education* (pp. 135–155). IGI Global.

Seltzer, K. (2022) Enacting a critical translingual approach in teacher preparation: Disrupting oppressive language ideologies and fostering the personal, political, and pedagogical stances of preservice teachers of English. *TESOL Journal* 13 (2), e649.

Thirteen/WNET and MacNeil-Lehrer Productions (Producers) and Cran, W. (Director) (2005) *Do You Speak American?* [Video file].

Wang, V. and Cranton, P. (2013) Adapting adult educators' teaching philosophies to foster adult learners' transformation and emancipation. In V. Wang (ed.) *Handbook of Research on Teaching and Learning* (pp. 134–147). IGI Global.

Wiley, T.G. (2005) Ebonics: Background to the current policy debate. In J.D. Ramirez, T.G. Wiley, G. de Klerk, E. Lee and W.E. Wright (eds) *Ebonics: The Urban Education Debate* (2nd edn, pp. 3–17). Multilingual Matters.

Wolfram, W. (2013) Sounds effects: Challenging language prejudice in the classroom. *The Education Digest* 79 (1), 27–30.

Wolfram, W. and Schilling, N. (2015) Why dialects? In W. Wolfram and N. Schilling (eds) *American English: Dialects and Variation* (3rd edn, pp. 27–58). Blackwell.

Wolfram, W. and Schilling, N. (2016) *American English: Dialects and Variation* (3rd edn). Blackwell.

Appendix 8.1: Critical Essay Directions

A. Purpose

For this assignment, you will explore various concepts, ideas and theories you have learned in this course concerning language variation and linguistic features of several dialects of American English along with activities, strategies, and techniques for teaching minority students standard English while also appreciating their home dialects/languages.

B. Task

The final product for this assignment is up to you (i.e. essay, PowerPoint, poster, video), so be as creative as possible! You should ensure that, regardless of the form of your assignment, the final product incorporates all of the requirements listed below.

Your essay should include the following components:

- an overview of dialectical variation
    - a definition of the word 'dialect'
    - a description of why dialects exist
    - an outline of various linguistic features of certain linguistic varieties of American English
    - an overview of cultural stereotypes people have regarding certain dialects, why these stereotypes exist, and why these stereotypes are (in)accurate
- a summary of prescriptive and descriptive linguistics
    - a definition and summary of prescriptivism
    - a definition and summary of descriptivism
    - a synopsis of how each perspective views dialects and why
    - a statement outlining which perspective you subscribe to and why
- an analysis of the pedagogical implications of dialectical variation
    - a rationale for why teachers should help minority students learn standard English while also valuing their home dialects/languages
    - an explanation of specific strategies and techniques you will use in your future classroom to help minority students learn standard English while also valuing their home dialects/languages

9 Radical Inclusivity in Language Teacher Education: Addressing Linguistic Bias and Linguistic Discrimination

Shannon Tanghe

Introduction

> …many more institutions of higher learning need to ensure that language bias, one of the most significant and overlooked dimensions of inequality, is substantively confronted, and interdisciplinary solutions must be programmatically incorporated into programs of diversity in our institutions of higher learning. (Wolfram, 2023: 48)

Linguicism refers to the ideologies and structures that justify and perpetuate unequal power divisions between groups based on language (Skutnabb-Kangas, 2000). It is said to be replacing racism as a more subtle way of hierarchizing social groups in today's world (Phillipson, 1992) because many people remain unaware of their language biases and attitudes (Wolfram, 2023). Building on Freire's (1970) critical pedagogy, which recognizes the need for critical consciousness in learners to dismantle power hierarchies and foster social justice, it is necessary for language teachers to explore how power dynamics are negotiated and constructed through language. Critical Language Awareness (CLA) pedagogy 'focuses on the intersections of language, identity, power, and privilege, with the goal of promoting self-reflection, social justice and rhetorical agency…[that]…aims to promote a more just future while also preparing students for the (often unjust) present' (Shapiro, 2022: 14). By embracing CLA, educators can foster radically inclusive learning environments where all learners feel valued, respected and empowered to engage in meaningful dialogue and action. Radical inclusivity involves purposeful recognition of the unique assets of each learner, while simultaneously acknowledging the impact of inequities and unearned privilege embedded in educational systems. For change to occur, this concept must be embraced both collectively and individually. For 'radical changes in EFL pedagogy to occur, they must be considered and reflected upon in the mindsets of individual teachers' (Bayyurt & Sifakis, 2015: 119). Radical inclusivity involves challenging societal norms and structures that perpetuate marginalization while appreciating and respecting diversity in all its forms. There is an urgent need to merge CLA with radical inclusivity to better prepare language teachers to counter linguicist realities. This chapter describes pedagogical activities that embed CLA and radical inclusivity into language teacher preparation, highlighting their impact on language teachers, their identities and practices.

Intersections of CLA and Radical Inclusivity

Positioning radical inclusivity as a key component of CLA emphasizes the power of language to inform and shape social realities. While language can be used to marginalize, it can also be a powerful tool for challenging oppression and advancing social justice in a radically inclusive way. Radical inclusivity and CLA intersect in their shared commitment to challenging power structures, promoting equity, and promoting social justice. Together, they are both committed to celebrating diverse strengths and creating spaces where all feel a sense of belonging.

The two intersect in many ways, including the following:

- Interrogating language norms: Both recognize the power embedded in language and how that can challenge existing language norms. Radical inclusivity seeks to challenge conventional norms and practices more broadly, and CLA narrows this focus more specifically to language. CLA highlights power dynamics embedded in language, and seeks to stop the perpetuation of stereotypes, language-based marginalization and the reinforcing of dominant ideologies.
- Challenge language practices: Radical inclusiveness includes critiquing and questioning marginalizing language practices and promoting linguistic diversity and inclusivity. CLA expands to incorporate a broader range, such as investigating language practices in everyday conversations, schools, in society and in the media.
- Advocating for linguistic justice: Both advocate for ensuring that all individuals have access to resources and opportunities regardless of linguistic proficiency.

Though there are many similarities, radical inclusivity and CLA need to merge to prepare educators to move from awareness to action. This chapter describes a CLA-informed radically inclusive lesson designed to address marginalization and privileges in the language teacher educator classroom.

The Curricular Context and the Course

This specific lesson occurs in an ESL teacher preparation program, specifically within a 'Immigrants and Refugees in Urban Schools' course, offered within a School of Urban Education at an urban Midwestern US university. This course is a required course for ESL licensure and can also be taken as an elective course at undergraduate or graduate levels. Overall, the course is designed to familiarize pre-teacher candidates with the experiences of immigrant-origin and refugee students in the local urban community and strategies for meeting their unique needs. This course is taught as a semester-long hybrid course, and the particular class session being described is a face-fo-face session.

Course learning outcomes

Among other standards, the course is designed to reinforce the following state initial teacher licensure standard requirements:

- The teacher understands how prejudice, discrimination, and racism operate at the interpersonal, intergroup, and institutional levels.
- The teacher explores their own intersecting social identities and how they impact daily experience as an educator.
- The teacher assesses how their biases, perceptions, and academic training may affect their teaching practice and perpetuate oppressive systems, and utilizes tools to mitigate their own behavior to disrupt oppressive systems.
- The teacher creates opportunities for students to learn about power, privilege, intersectionality, and systemic oppression in the context of various communities and empowers learners to be agents of social change to promote equity.

Background and rationale

This lesson is designed to facilitate opportunities for teacher candidates to first reflect on their own privileges, consider how these impact their teaching practices, and then to identify action steps to support multilingual language users. This lesson was originally created for and taught in a three-hour class session in a language teacher education program. Educators may also choose to select particular activities to integrate in courses, or to modify to teach at other levels, depending on one's particular teaching context. The following section provides an overview of the full lesson.

Step-by-step

Preparation: Focal Readings and Class Commitment:

Teacher candidates have completed the following readings and reflexivity discussions:

- Sarina Molina's (2022) 'Reducing Colonial Harm in Language Teaching: A Guide to Critical Self-Reflexive Practices for Language Teachers'
- Peggy McIntosh's (1989) 'White Privilege: Unpacking the Invisible Knapsack'
- Stephanie Vandrick's (2015) 'No "Knapsack of Invisible Privilege" for ESL University Students'
- Pre-class discussion board post:
    - What are some examples of linguistic discrimination that occur in schools?
- Learners have read Singleton's (2015) guidelines for Courageous Conversations and agreed to use these as our class discussion guidelines so we can have honest, vulnerable, and private dialogues.
    - Review four tenets:
        - Stay engaged
        - Speak your truth
        - Experience discomfort
        - Expect and accept non-closure

Full lesson overview:

- Tic Tac Toe warm-up activity (10 minutes)
    - Each class begins with a quick warm-up. In the long term, this is helpful in creating a strong, supportive classroom community where all know each other as individual colleagues/classmates. In the short term this helps to introduce the topic and results in a much deeper, richer discussion.
    - Students are shown a Tic Tac Toe board (see Figure 9.1) that reviews previous classes, previews today's class, and connects to ongoing class projects. Students ask and answer questions with a partner.
- Co-construct a definition of privilege (10 minutes)
    - Individually, write down your definition of 'privilege'.
    - Turn and talk to share definition with partner. Through discussion, try to merge the two definitions into one definition you are both comfortable with.
    - Join another dyad (four people total) and try to merge these definitions. Continue until there is one large group.
    - Write that definition of 'privilege' on the screen.
    - Whole group: Share their process of co-constructing this definition. Possible whole group discussion questions:
        - What are the most important concepts of privilege?
        - Is there anything missing from the current definition?

TicTacToe: With a partner, try to make a line of three consecutive by answering each question (rotate turns with partner)		
What is one example of a privilege that you enjoy, that you do not often question?	Describe ideas for your final paper topic in this class (or brainstorm if you don't know)!	What does intersectionality mean?
What are two examples of privilege that someone with English as a dominant language living in the US may experience?	Which book did you/will you read for your book review?	If you have arranged your personal interview for class, who will you speak with?
What is a contrastive analysis and how is it useful in the EL classroom?	How would you cite an academic journal article in APA style?	What is linguicism?

Figure 9.1 Tic Tac Toe warm up

- How did you come to an agreement (if you did)?
- Did everyone have a chance to share perspectives?
- Did everyone feel included in the process?
  - This co-construction of the definition helps to introduce the topic. The main point is not necessarily to agree upon the definition, but to hear classmates' thoughts on what 'privilege' means to them and how they understand it.
- Discussion of privilege and marginalization as it relates to language (30 minutes)
  - Instructor-led portion of the class where I introduce key components related to the topics of privilege, language discrimination, and linguicism practices, including the following topics:
    - Historical overview
    - Privilege and marginalization continuum (Park, 2015)
    - Linguicism
      - Historical overview: Skutnabb-Kangas, 2000; Phillipson, 1992
      - Historical examples: Shibboleth 1370–1070 BCE, 1937 The Parsley Massacre (*perejil*), 1282 Sicilian Vespers *ciciri* (chickpeas). How about today?
      - Examples of discriminatory practices
        - Discussion board posts, individual attitudes, media, movies, English-only policies, schools – job hiring, assessments, textbooks, classroom practices
      - Familiarity
        - McGurk effect and audio illusions

- Invisibility of privilege discussion (20 minutes)
  - Discussion of McIntosh (1989) 'White Privilege: Unpacking the Invisible Knapsack'
  - Whole group discussion: What were your general impressions of the article? What surprised you? Any specific quotes that caught your attention? Any personal connections you made with the article? What questions did this article raise for you? Have you read this article before?
  - Depending on discussion, possibility of asking questions relating to more unseen, silent invisible aspects of privilege
- Reflection on intersectionalities of privilege (10 minutes)
  - How do these connect with various personal intersectionalities?
  - Create a list of aspects of your identity that are privileged in your current context (while recognizing the ever shifting fluidity). [May select specific context to consider, for example, as a pre-service ESL teacher].
- Reflecting on one privilege (20 minutes)
  - Select from one of five areas of privilege, either that you hold yourself, or are interested in exploring more. Choices: ability privilege, Christian privilege in the US, cisgender privilege, socioeconomic privilege, or US citizenship privilege.
    - Learners select groups based on identified privilege. They are given a handout of a list of privileges that members of each group often experience (adapted from LSA Equitable Teaching website: https://sites.lsa.umich.edu/equitable-teaching/).
    - Read and discuss list in small groups. Possible topics: things you find surprising, had not considered, have experienced, questions raised, etc.
      - Where/how might this privilege show up in my teaching?
      - Here's how I might be able to apply my understanding in my work…
    - Each group can share out topics that emerged in their discussion.
  - *An Instructor's Guide to Understanding Privilege* is an excellent resource, created by the University of Michigan's LSA Equitable Teaching website, from which this activity was adapted.
- Discussion of Vandrick (2015) 'No "Knapsack of Invisible Privilege" for ESL University Students' (15 minutes)
  - Partner discussion: What were your general impressions of the article? What surprised you? Any specific quotes that caught your attention? Any personal connections you made with the article? What questions did this article raise for you? Have you read this article before?
  - While discussing, a digital padlet board is open and students input phrases highlighting key discussion points.

- Co-create own list (15 minutes)
  ○ Building on McIntosh's ('White Privilege') and Vandrick's ('University ESL Students') lists of privileges, work in small groups to create own lists of 'No "knapsack of invisible privilege" for K-12 immigrant-origin and refugee learners in (community)'. The list includes privileges that an immigrant-origin or refugee learner do not often have.
    - Each group shares examples and posts full lists to the course discussion board.
    - As they share out (and using the discussion board), I merge the lists together and re-post one complete class list.
    - Discussion: Looking at this list, what implications does this have for EL education?
- Global Thinking Routines: Circles of Action (20 minutes)
  ○ The Global Thinking Routine's 'Circles of Action' invite learners to go beyond raising awareness and moving into action by reflecting on their various spheres of influence, considering what they can do to facilitate impact in (1) their own inner circle (friends, family), (2) within their community (school, neighborhood), and (3) in the world.
  ○ A paper Circle of Action model (three concentric circles with each identified) is given to each student for them to fill in 1–2 responsible actions they can take in each of these spheres.
  ○ Learners first complete individually and then share with a partner or small group.
  ○ Whole group: For each circle, students share out an action they can do to facilitate positive change in that sphere.
  ○ Adapted from Harvard's Project Zero, *Routine for Global Thinking Routines*: pz.harvard.edu).
- Linguistic Discrimination Simulation (done simultaneously throughout class) and follow-up debriefing (20 minutes)
  ○ Brief overview: Explain purpose, and describe the two-phase simulation experience.
  ○ Divide class into two groups
    - For approximately forty minutes each, students in one-half of the class are intentionally privileged, with their language usage validated, while the other half is systematically excluded. Specific actions performed are drawn from students' pre-class discussion board postings.
      - Examples of classroom privileges:
        ○ Class materials (textbooks, videos, etc.) including only specific varieties of English
        ○ Calling on certain students more
        ○ Asking certain students to re-state peers' answers
        ○ Hiring preferences in teachers

- Examples of classroom exclusions:
  - Requiring English only, or specific varieties of English
  - Ignoring students, insufficient wait time
  - Expressing frustration or lack of understanding
  - Mimicking speech
  - Stating assumptions about intellect based on speech
  - Grouping students together e.g. 'hard to understand you all'
  - Expressing surprise when student does well
- Reflective debrief simulation experience and classroom implications. The following questions can be good starting points:
  - How did you feel when you were in each of the groups?
  - What other implications, possibly classroom related, can you draw from this simulation in addition to linguistic discrimination?
  - Do you think it is important to talk about discrimination-related issues in the classroom?
  - To what extent do you feel linguicism exists in the world? Local area? Your school?

Assessment

Informal assessment occurs throughout the lesson, based primarily on active engagement with the content and classmates. Several informal assessments are conducted at multiple points in the lesson (for example, interactions with students in small and large groups). Each learner was also asked to individually post examples of linguistic discrimination on the course discussion board.

Reflections

Though there is time to reflect, discuss and share throughout this lesson, in the last twenty minutes of class, there is an additional formal debriefing when learners have time to intentionally process, reflect on and share their experiences. Structured discussion questions are used to explore personal experiences within the simulation while reflecting on implications for students' own current/future classrooms. These debriefing sessions provide additional insights from the learners' experiences, and also offer a chance for me to reflect on the process.

Educator reflections

I have implemented different variations of this lesson in several formats and contexts over the past years. Prior to each lesson, I ask learners to first share their ideas of language discrimination, and then I intentionally integrate those into the simulation. Though I call it a simulation, I strive to provide ways for all students to connect with the content. The language usage is real and does not necessarily call out specific languages or varieties, but all participating students' language uses are challenged. For example, a student speaking with a midwestern USA accent may be challenged for not pronouncing the hard t's in Queen's English. This is done so that any students, from monolingual English speaking students to multilingual learners, all recognize and reflect on the power of language, with discriminatory actions included for many different varieties of Englishes, languages, and speech patterns. The main focus is recognizing the impact and developing strategies to respond to the linguicist inequities in classrooms.

One of the most powerful personal reflections for me has been reflecting on the impact of my positionality and role as a white female instructor who speaks English as a first (and dominant) language. I strive to center the course in diverse perspectives, readings, experiences, and contributions. The last time I taught this lesson, all students identified as a person of color and most students had grown up mutlilingual, with several sharing negative personal experiences with linguicism. Recognizing that while everyone has an accent, some are more often discriminated against, in this lesson described, one of my goals was to facilitate a conversation on intersectionalities of privileges held. On this topic, I realized that in attempting to provide an angle I felt needed consideration (white privilege), I had in fact grounded the lesson in a white perspective, shown by my using white privilege and the McIntosh article as a starting point. In spite of efforts to work toward creating a radically inclusive learning environment, it was still based on my own prior lived experiences. I am continuing to reflect on my own positionality and privileges in teaching this course, recognizing each day that being and becoming radically inclusive is an ongoing process.

Student reflections

Though students recognized and experienced this as a simulation, several students shared that it brought back memories of when they were younger and their experiences in school, sometimes decades ago. Other students made connections to the experiences of their parents or particular students in classes they teach.

One student shared that she felt like she was reliving her middle school experiences, but through a different lens. She recounted that though she had experienced many of these practices before, she had never felt comfortable standing up to what she was experiencing. Several students also disclosed experiences of language discrimination, as well as reflecting on ways they had also inadvertently performed some of these practices (specifically, allowing more talk time/calling on students who spoke varieties of English that were more comprehensible to many learners). These open reflections helped advance the discussion on how language teachers can actively confront linguicist practices in schools. Learners also reflected on how, once they became the school's EL teacher, other teachers viewed them as the 'EL expert'. They discussed the need to not only educate students, but also to be prepared to support their colleagues.

Advice for adapting or implementing in various contexts

Based on teaching this lesson, I share the following pieces of advice for educators interested in implementing some or all of this lesson.

(1) Build trust first.
   This lesson is done only after relationships and rapport have been established and there is adequate trust. The discussions and simulation can be outside of a learners' comfort zone, so making sure there is support to process and talk the experience through is important, as well as reminding students it is always ok to pause or step away if they need to.
(2) Acknowledge that the experience offers only a glimpse.
   While everyone has an accent, some accents are more privileged than others. Because this lesson is only a brief glimpse, the brief simulation cannot replicate actual lived experiences, but rather offers a brief starting point for further reflection and consideration of how to challenge these unjust practices.
(3) Reflect on one's own privilege.
   It is important to consider the impact of this lesson on both learners and oneself as instructor. This lesson offers opportunities to think deeply about one's own privilege and how that shows up in classrooms.
(4) Consider age appropriateness.
   Some aspects of this lesson can be done at any age level. For example, the Circles of Action thinking routine and recognizing individual privileges work well with all ages as they invite learners to consider their own personal communities. The linguistic discrimination simulation, however, may work better at older age levels when learners can more fully process the experience and implications.
(5) Maintain hope.
   This can be a challenging lesson, especially if learners feel unsure of what to do with the information that comes from the experience. It is critical to include time to reflect on possibilities for taking action to move toward positive change. The Circles of Action routine, for example, encourages movement from theory into concrete practice with action steps.

(6) Promote radical inclusivity in one's own way.
Radical inclusivity involves making both personal and collective efforts to challenge inequities and support all learners in fostering senses of belonging. Educators can determine what works best in their specific contexts as they explore how to integrate principles of radical inclusion into personal teaching practices. After reviewing the strategies in this chapter and book, I encourage all educators to adapt, experiment, and reflect on how to be radically inclusive in their own teaching.

References

Bayyurt, Y. and Sifakis, N. (2015) ELF-aware in-service teacher education: A transformative perspective. In H. Bowles and A. Cogo (eds) *International Perspectives on Teaching English as a Lingua Franca* (pp. 117–135). Palgrave Macmillan.

Freire, P. (1970) *Pedagogy of the Oppressed*. Continuum.

McIntosh, P. (1988) White privilege: Unpacking the invisible knapsack. https://admin.artsci.washington.edu/sites/adming/files/unpacking-invisible-knapsack.pdf

Molina, S. (2022) Reducing colonial harm in language teaching: A guide to critical self-reflexive practices for language teachers. *The CATESOL Journal* 33 (1), 1–10.

Park, G. (2015) Situating the discourses of privilege and marginalization in the lives of two East Asian women teachers of English. *Race, Ethnicity and Education* 18 (1), 108–133.

Phillipson, R. (1992) *Linguistic Imperialism*. Oxford University Press.

Shapiro, S. (2022) *Cultivating Critical Language Awareness in the Writing Classroom*. Routledge.

Skutnabb-Kangas, T. (2000) *Linguistic Genocide in Education–or Worldwide Diversity and Human Rights?* Routledge. https://doi.org/10.4324/9781410605191

Singleton, G. (2015) *Courageous Conversations About Race: A Field Guide for Achieving Equity in Schools*. Corwin Press.

Vandrick, S. (2015) No 'knapsack of invisible privilege' for ESL university students. *Journal of Language, Identity, and Education* 14 (1), 54–59.

Wolfram, W. (2023) Addressing linguistic inequality in higher education: A proactive model. *Language and Social Justice in the United States* 152 (3), 36–51.

Part 3

What Does Radical Inclusivity Look Like in Community Engagement?

Part 3
What Does Radical Inclusivity Look Like in Community Engagement?

10 Metrolingual Maps: Exploring Multilingual Practices in the Community

Nils Olov Fors

Introduction

Radical inclusivity requires fair and accurate counting and accountability. As Huzar (2014) points out, who or what gets counted determines the efficacy of equity practices. Making one out of many is inherently problematic since both the one and the many, the whole(s) and the parts, are being constructed and must be discursively visible in order to count and be counted. Being inclusive means empowering by increasing access and adding more of the many to the one; radical inclusivity employs a different math to challenge the discursive framework and the very notions of inclusivity, empowerment, and the one and the many. Radical inclusivity also questions who does the counting and what the consequences might be – even an inclusive 'us' creates a 'them', and the act of including presumes the power to exclude and to choose who could and should be included. A simple recount of discrete parts of a centered and orderly whole is a miscount that fails to account for the decentered, unstable, fragmented, multiple, and liminal.

In the field of applied linguistics, some of the loudest calls for inclusivity come from proponents of critical language awareness and critical applied linguistics. One of the commonplace assumptions about language and language use they challenge is that one language fits and does all in a community (e.g. Pennycook, 2001; Kumaravadivelu, 2003). Influenced by cultural and political interests and narratives of unity and cohesion, traditional descriptions frequently ascribe the work done by language in the community to the monolingual use of a privileged variety (e.g. Adler-Kassner & Harrington, 2002; Cummins, 2008). Such descriptions discount or overlook the paradoxical linguistic reality that highly valued and popular varieties may be less frequently used, and that less valued and popular varieties may be more commonly used and more functional.

More inclusive descriptions, such as linguistic landscapes, translanguaging, and metrolingualism, provide ways to include language use that would otherwise go unnoticed or be marginalized. Linguistic landscape research (e.g. Ben-Rafael & Ben-Rafael, 2015; Shohamy & Gorter, 2009; Wangdi & Savski, 2023) inventories and analyzes all the written language of an area, literally including all language use ranging from the official, privileged, and powerful to the unofficial, marginal, and even illegal. The inclusions raise awareness of the presence of and interaction among languages and varieties in an area, thus empowering the languages and their use. Linguistic landscape research is also inclusive in that it uses an accessible research methodology that allows virtually anyone to participate as a researcher. Translanguaging (e.g. Canagarajah, 2011; García & Li, 2014) further increases inclusivity by demonstrating how effective communication draws on all available linguistic resources and by counting language use that has traditionally been discounted, delegitimized, or even penalized in educational and professional contexts. Translanguaging changes the denominator of the language equation by adding more parts to the whole, and also radically changes the sum from a privileged, monolingual one to a plural, mixed many. Metrolingualism (Pennycook & Otsuji, 2015) goes beyond multilingualism by expanding linguistic resources to include semiotic assemblages and spatial repertoires. Language is viewed as an emergent property that defies counting by having a whole that is not only greater than the sum of its parts but also only fully present as an interactive complex.

These models share a focus on the power lines that construct and valorize language use in terms of legitimacy and privilege, and they seek greater inclusivity in order to provide more accurate models of how languages are used in, and contribute to, our communities. Such inclusivity may not seem radical at first – after all, linguistics has a long tradition of recognizing *langue* and *parole* and distinguishing between descriptive and prescriptive models – but does problematize many of the assumptions and decisions we make as researchers and teachers of language and challenge what counts as a variety or a language use, and how we should account for their contributions to the community. The pedagogical math seems clear: more accurate sociolinguistic accounts of how languages are used in our communities will add to our ability to help students develop intercultural competence and communication skills.

Metrolingual Maps Project

This chapter describes a project in which students explore language use in their communities in order to gain a better understanding of their sociolinguistic realities. By creating 'metrolingual maps', students learn how to document and analyze complex language use and inventory linguistic resources in their communities. The description is based on four iterations of the project, two in Asian settings (Japan and South Korea) and two in a European setting (Sweden). The two projects in Asia were completed by undergraduate university students as part of courses that focused on intercultural communication and English-language learning. One of the European projects was done by undergraduate university students in an academic literacy course for students in an international program, and the other by adult students in a language center for immigrants. The projects were regular class activities and were not part of a research study.

Background and rationale

The metrolingual maps project began as an attempt to incorporate more inclusive linguistic models in my undergraduate language courses in order to address a perceived mismatch between the descriptions of language and language use used in the classroom and the sociolinguistic realities of the community. The constellation of language varieties, language use, identities, topics, functions, and situations, etc. that comprised the English the students were learning in the classroom was useful, but it excluded much of the language use in the community and gave the students a distorted view of the sociolinguistic realities of their community. The discrepancy seemed to reinforce prejudice and negative social and linguistic attitudes, and lead to exclusionary practices that undermined both teaching and learning. Students did not get exposure to the language use they were likely to encounter in their professional lives, and there was a strong belief that linguistic proficiency in a universal, 'good' variety would facilitate intercultural competence and communication. The lack of inclusivity also contributed to the othering of the very people the students would actually be interacting with in the future in their communities. Academic discussions of issues related to language and integration helped, as did the contributions of fields such as World Englishes, but still failed to fully account for the linguistic diversity and its contributions to the community. It seemed clear that students would benefit from greater awareness of the sociolinguistic makeup of their community, as well as first-hand experience of how languages are used together and in context. With this in mind, I began designing class activities and projects which eventually became the multiple iterations of the metrolingual maps project on which this chapter is based.

Goals and student learning objectives

The purpose of the metrolingual maps project described below is to increase students' awareness of languages and language use in their communities and familiarize them with the sociolinguistic realities they may encounter in the future. The project also aims to introduce students to different ways of describing languages and language use, and to facilitate informed discussions about how languages are counted, who decides what counts, and how linguistic resources and their contributions to the community are accounted for. Specifically, students learn how to inventory linguistic resources and observe, document, and critically analyze complex language use. Student learning outcomes include:

- Understand different perspectives on language.
- Demonstrate understanding of basic sociolinguistic concepts.
- Apply sociolinguistic theory to observed language use.
- Observe and analyze language use in context.
- Identify and give examples of language variation in their local community.
- Give examples of the relationship between language use and context.
- Recognize relationship between language use and social structures.
- Identify and define language attitudes in their local community.
- Discuss the role and function of privileged and marginalized languages and language use in their community.
- Compare classroom language use and language use in the community.
- Gain a better understanding of how languages are used in the community.

The critical objective of the project is to highlight 'hidden' linguistic resources and language practices in order to empower marginalized language use and emphasize its importance to the community. Ultimately, the project aims to increase intercultural competence and communication skills by giving the students first-hand experience of their sociolinguistic realities and a better understanding of what they and their languages could and should do in and for the community.

Procedural step-by-step description

The project consists of a preparation stage, a data collection stage, a data analysis stage, and a presentation stage (see Table 10.1). Depending on the context and level of the students, the project requires about four to eight 90-minute lessons. No previous knowledge of sociolinguistics is required.

Students are assigned an area of their local community and asked to document and analyze how languages are used. Following a brief

Table 10.1 Steps for the metrolingual maps project

Preparation (1–2 lessons)	Students review key concepts, prepare research questions, conduct demographic research, and choose sites for observation
Data collection (1–2 lessons)	Students visit research sites, observe, take field notes, and conduct interviews
Data analysis (1–2 lessons)	Students discuss and analyze the results
Presentation (1–2 lessons)	Students present their findings in spoken or written presentations

introduction to the concepts of multilingualism and metrolingualism, the students develop a simple research framework. Using observations, interviews, and demographic data, students inventory languages in the community and document their use. After collecting the data, the students construct 'metrolingual maps' of their assigned areas and present the analysis of their observations.

Preparation (1–2 lessons)

In the preparation stage, students work in groups to design a simple research strategy. After a brief introduction to basic models of demographic research, observation, field notes, and interviews, the students brainstorm research questions. When the students have a set of research questions, they research the demographics of their community and create a research plan. The demographic research gives the students an idea of what languages are spoken in their community and helps them choose suitable sites for observation in their assigned areas. If the observations are to be done inside a business (e.g. a convenience store or supermarket, students talk to the manager to explain their project and ask for permission to observe).[1] If interviews are to be conducted, students prepare questions and a simple consent form. The students then design a simple mixed-method plan for collecting data (typically a combination of observations and interviews or surveys). Finally, groups share and revise their research plans based on peer and teacher feedback.

Data collection (1–2 lessons)

In the data collection stage, the groups visit the selected sites to observe and take notes. The field notes can be quite simple, but the goal is to identify what languages are used, how frequently, by whom, in what situations, for what purposes, etc. If possible, the notes record instances of code-switching, code-mixing, and translanguaging, and other modes of complex language use. Groups may also choose to interview participants in the interactions, or other subjects with knowledge of the situation.

Data analysis (1–2 lessons)

Once the data has been collected, the students begin the analysis by inventorying the languages, varieties, activities, and functions they observed. The observations are compiled in the form of a simple 'metrolingual map' that represents the observed language use in context. Based on the basic map, the students discuss the results. What is surprising, confusing, or interesting? Are some languages used for specific purposes? Who uses what language, and for what purposes? Are some languages used together? The analysis can lead to questions such as how different activities are valued and what the consequences are for the languages, and students may also consider inconsistencies and linguistic, economic, or social prejudices. Are some languages considered better or more important than others? Are some languages allowed or not allowed to 'do' certain things? Do languages get credit for the work they actually do? The students are also asked to discuss how their current language and communication skills align with the sociolinguistic contexts they observe.

Presentation (1–2 lessons)

In the final stage of the project, students present their findings in class in different forms, including actual 'maps' that show what languages are used, by whom, and for what purposes. As mentioned, the maps and presentations can be relatively simple, (e.g. general language inventories, or more sophisticated, e.g. by detailing instances of translanguaging, code-switching, etc.). The presentations are followed by a question-and-answer session and class discussion.

Assessment

The students receive formative assessment and feedback throughout the project. The research questions and research plans are peer-reviewed and reviewed by the teacher. Questions for analysis are shared, and initial analysis results are discussed in class. The final presentations, a brief research report and a group presentation, are assessed using a simple rubric that focuses on content, organization, and presentation skills. The project as a whole is assessed using some or all of the learning objectives listed above.

Classroom portraits: Observing commerce at the konbini *and multilingual housekeeping*

Creating metrolingual maps is an accessible activity that allows students with little or no previous knowledge of sociolinguistics to engage in meaningful discussions of the diversity and functions of language in their community. What starts as a very simple inventory can lead to reflections on intercultural competence and how language teaching and learning align with the sociolinguistic realities of a community, and to observations of correlations among language, power, and identity.

One group of students observing interactions at a convenience store (*konbini*) in Japan found examples of transactions involving up to five languages. Chinese was used by two customers to choose what to buy, English and Japanese were used to complete the purchase, and Japanese and Tagalog were used to price-check one of the items (see Figure 10.1). The students were surprised by the findings. While they knew from their demographic research that there are numerous speakers of Chinese and Tagalog in Japan, they had expected English to be the main *lingua franca*, and they had not expected so much Japanese to be used. The observation

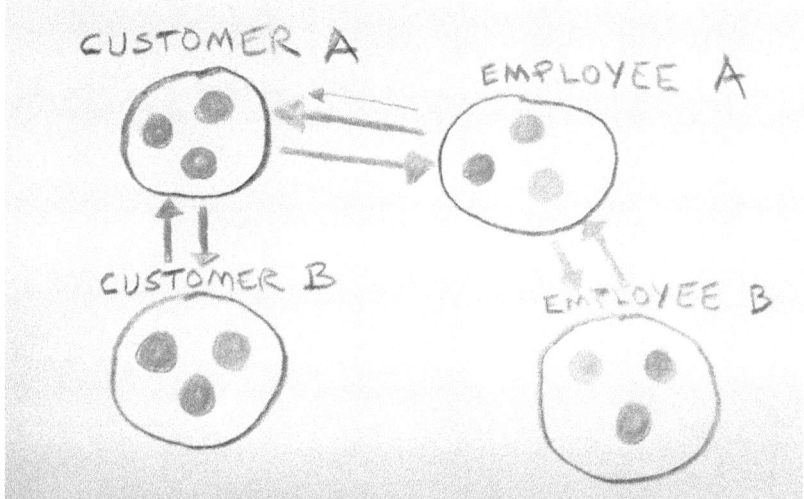

Figure 10.1 Commerce at the *konbini*
Note. Re-creation of student map. The circles represent the people observed in the interaction and the colors represent languages. Languages are referred to as 'language red' etc. in order to minimize assumptions about proficiency, functions, and value. The arrows indicate interactions.

also led the students to reflect on what they were learning about English and intercultural communication. In their presentation, the students stated that the project had made them rethink what intercultural competence means and question their own ability to navigate complex cross-cultural and multilingual interactions. They added that their limited exposure to different English varieties and topics and situations beyond those commonly used in their English classes made them feel less confident and somewhat uncomfortable when faced with a real-life cross-cultural context.

Metrolingual mapping can also lead to discussion of power structures. A group focusing on a sector including a hotel in Sweden documented the use of Swedish, English, Arabic, and German (see Figure 10.2), and identified activities such as greeting and processing guests, cleaning the rooms, making staff rosters, and so on. The group then correlated instances of language use and activities – greeting and processing guests was done in Swedish, English, and German; ordering supplies was done in Swedish; cleaning the rooms was done in Arabic and Thai, etc. The analysis also noted the identity of the speakers (e.g. receptionists, guests, managers, cleaning staff, and so on) (see Figure 10.3). In the analysis, the group began to notice and discuss the relationship between different languages and their relative functions and power. In the presentation, the students raised questions about why languages such as Arabic and Thai are included in demographic statistics but rarely described or mentioned as working languages in media and public discourses.

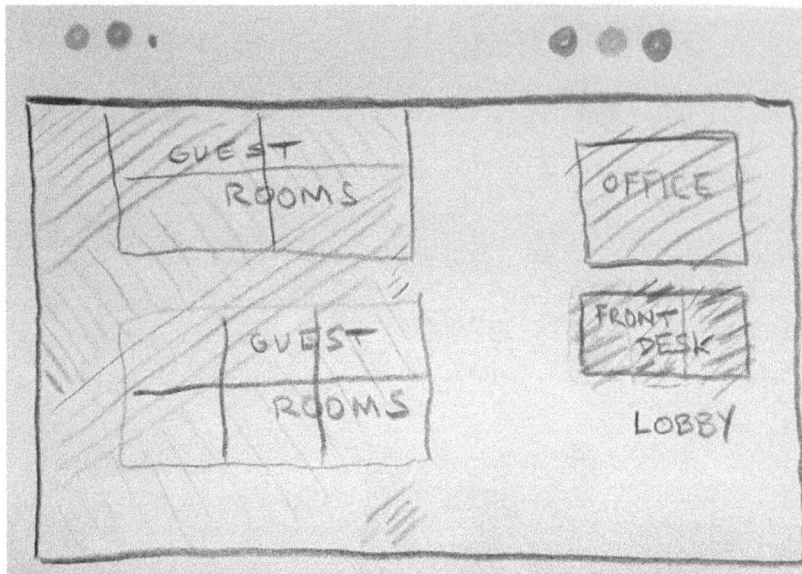

Figure 10.2 Multilingual housekeeping (1)
Note. Re-creation of student map. The colors represent languages and the shaded areas indicate where the languages were observed. Languages are referred to as 'language red' etc. in order to minimize assumptions about proficiency, functions, and value.

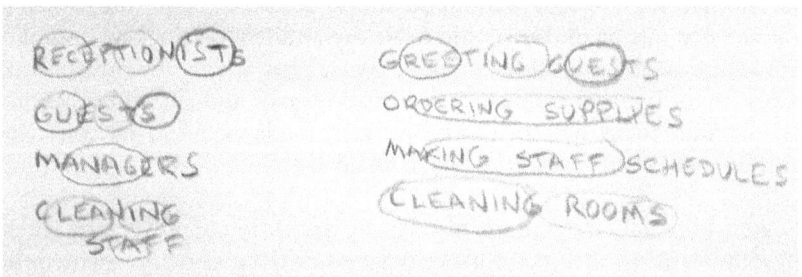

Figure 10.3 Multilingual housekeeping (2)
Note. Re-creation of student map. The colors represent languages and the circles indicate by whom the languages were used and for what purposes. Languages are referred to as 'language red' etc. in order to minimize assumptions about proficiency, functions, and value.

Post-Activity Thoughts, Reflections, Discussion

The classroom examples suggest that the metrolingual maps project increases awareness and give students a better sense of what languages do in the community. After completing the project, students often express surprise and interest as they realize that more languages are used, in more ways, than they had expected. Knowing that 13% of a community speaks a language has value but doesn't represent or explain the way the language is being used or how it contributes to community activities. Observing the language used in context, however, leads to a deeper and more useful understanding. Class discussion suggests that the metrolingual maps project encourages students to view linguistic competence as contingent, piecemeal, and complex rather than individual, complete, and uniform. For example, the group who observed the interactions in the Swedish hotel noticed that much of the language use was mixed, fragmentary, and context-dependent. They concluded that comprehension requires not only linguistic proficiency, but also professional expertise, practical experience, and cross-cultural competence.

The metrolingual maps projects also reveals how language use and language attitudes are affected by context. In the Asian settings, there was initially more focus on English and tourism, and students assumed that English would be the primary *lingua franca* and do most or all of the 'work' in cross-cultural interactions in the community. In the European settings, the focus was more on immigrants and integration, and students expected Swedish to be used. In their analysis, groups in both settings explained the expectations by pointing to media and public discourses (e.g. the premium put on English language learning and proficiency in Japan and the polarizing politics of immigration and integration in Sweden). However, the students also raised interesting questions: why do Swedish students, who are highly proficient in English and live in a relatively multicultural and multilingual setting, not assume that English would be the primary *lingua franca*? Similarly, why are Japanese students, who live in a relatively monocultural and monolingual country, surprised that so much Japanese is used in cross-cultural interactions?

Metrolingual maps do not provide a 'truer' or necessarily better overview of languages in a community, but they provide a more inclusive description of sociolinguistic realities that generates discussion and changes the way students count and account for languages in their community. The metrolingual maps project also suggests that maps are useful metaphors for researching and documenting language use since they literally position language use in the community. Unlike GPS, which tells us where we are and where to go, maps require us to position ourselves in relation to both the map and reality, an interesting way to experience the linguistic interplay of signs and signifiers.

Challenges

The metrolingual maps project is challenging, and it can be difficult for students to gain a comprehensive overview of the language use in their assigned area. The data collected tends to be fragmentary, incomplete, and lack resolution. In addition, students are limited to public areas such as stores and restaurants, and not able to access factories, hospitals, and construction sites. To remedy the latter, a strong emphasis needs to be put on including statistics, videos, and news reports related to the situation of foreign workers. Another significant challenge is to identify the languages being used. Students might not be able to identify a particular language; in other cases, it may be difficult to determine the extent to which languages are used, (e.g. in cases of translanguaging and other complex multilingual practices). It can also be difficult for students to correctly identify what the language is being used for. While it may be possible to link utterances and actions through casual observation, transcriptions and systematic interviews would reveal more accurate patterns. Despite these limitations, it seems clear that metrolingual maps are an effective way to increase student awareness of language use in their communities.

Advice and recommendations

Creating a metrolingual maps project in a high school or university language course does not need to be complicated or overwhelming. It is important to keep in mind that the objective is not to provide a totally accurate, complete map but to increase awareness of multilingualism and its contributions to our communities. The purpose can be achieved even with limited data collection and rudimentary analysis. Simplified versions are sufficient for the purposes of a course project. For a small project at the high school or university freshman student level, the study can be as simple as combining basic demographic research with limited field interviews or even observations of videos. Students might research the national and linguistic makeup of the local workforce and then follow up by interviewing staff at a convenience store in their community. Sectors and research sites such as restaurants, convenience stores, hotels, food markets, grocery stores, and other semi-public workplaces are suitable since they provide easy access. As mentioned above, factories, hospitals and healthcare facilities, and construction sites are more representative and appropriate for research purposes, but access is limited due to safety, privacy, confidentiality, and legal issues, etc. If field visits are impractical, or if even semi-public sites are difficult to access, teachers can facilitate by arranging class visits to one or more site, or by arranging online or face-to-face interviews with, or class visits from, staff or business owners in the community.

For teachers not content with how language is counted and accounted for in their classrooms, the metrolingual maps project can be used to increase inclusivity and stimulate discussion of language use in the community. In addition, the project can serve as an accessible and practical introduction to basic concepts of sociolinguistics and sociolinguistic research. By learning how to observe and analyze language use in context, students develop their ability to interpret and adapt to communicative settings. First-hand experience of multicultural and multilingual sociolinguistic realities also helps students gain confidence and develop attitudes and strategies for effective and appropriate communication that will ultimately increase their intercultural competence. Exploring the language use of their community exposes students to alternative, more inclusive ways of counting and accounting for language use, and shows them that in actual community settings, all is not one and one is not all when it comes to language use.

Note

(1) Class projects involving surveys, observations, interviews etc. may constitute somewhat of a gray area as far as ethical and legal research considerations in some academic institutions. In the projects on which this chapter is based, different procedures were followed depending on the institution. In all the projects, no recordings were made, no identifying data was collected, data was only used for classroom presentations, and all data was deleted after the project was completed.

References

Adler-Kassner, L. and Harrington, S. (2002) *Basic Writing as a Political Act: Public Conversations about Writing and Literacies*. Hampton Press.
Ben-Rafael, E. and Ben-Rafael, M. (2015) Linguistic landscapes in an era of multiple globalizations. *Linguistic Landscape* 1 (1–2), 19–37. https://doi.org/10.1075/ll.1.1-2.02ben
Canagarajah, S. (2011) Codemeshing in academic writing: Identifying teachable strategies of translanguaging. *The Modern Language Journal* 95 (3), 401–417.
Cummins, J. (2008) Teaching for transfer: Challenging the two solitudes assumptions in bilingual education. In N.H. Hornberger (ed.) *Encyclopedia of Language and Education* (pp. 1528–1538). Springer.
García, O. and Li, W. (2014) *Translanguaging: Language, Bilingualism and Education*. Palgrave Macmillan.
Huzar, T. (2014) Neoliberalism, democracy and the library as a radically inclusive space. *IFLA Conference Paper*, 1–9. Retrieved from http://library.ifla.org/835/
Kumaravadivelu, B. (2003) Critical language pedagogy: A postmethod perspective on English language teaching. *World Englishes* 22 (4), 539–550.
Pennycook, A. (2001) *Critical Applied Linguistics*. Routledge.
Pennycook, A. and Otsuji, E. (2015) *Metrolingualism: Language in the City*. Routledge.
Shohamy, E. and Gorter, D. (eds) (2009) *Linguistic Landscape: Expanding the Scenery*. Routledge.
Wangdi, J. and Savski, K. (2023) Linguistic landscape, critical language awareness and critical thinking: Promoting learner agency in discourses about language. *Language Awareness* 32 (3), 443–464. https://doi.org/10.1080/09658416.2022.2115052

11 The Dialogic Griot: Advocating for Communities through Story Mapping

Valerie A. Gray

> *The greatness of a community is most accurately measured by the*
> *compassionate actions of its members.*
> Coretta Scott King, 16 January 2000

Introduction: Transformative Storytelling through Radical Inclusivity, Critical Language Awareness, and Inclusive Andragogical Practices

When instructors provide authentic and lasting opportunities for students to partake in a dialogic learning community, they can transform the learning community through cultural synthesis (Freire, 1993: 160–161) to produce transformative and inclusive andragogical practices. *Radical transformation* andragogy is a philosophy and methodology that is embedded throughout the curricula to disrupt the power and privilege structures that are often inherent to the college learning community. Radical transformation shifts and redirects approaches and emphases in adult learning to reflect curricula that centers equity, agency, inclusion, and empowerment. The purpose of radical transformation is to establish learning communities that inform, advocate for, and support students in their learning community (Gannon, 2021). Intentionality is essential for sustainable radical transformation. The first step in this process is for instructors to participate in an honest and reflective interrogation and assessment of their inclusive andragogical practices. *Inclusive andragogical practices* refer to designing course materials and implementing assessment strategies that are accessible to all students, yet considers the pedagogical needs of each student (Florian & Spratt, 2013). This perspective acknowledges the importance of including learners in the decision-making process and fostering a learning community in which each student is welcomed. Consequently, students are encouraged to participate and may choose multiple ways to showcase their knowledge throughout a semester.

Instructors who take on radical inclusivity ensure that everyone, regardless of their intersectionality, are included in the fight for justice (Sengeh, 2023: xii). In addition, as an andragogical construct, radical inclusivity values the insight and perspectives of all learners. Discussions of radical inclusivity cannot fully take place without acknowledging the history of systemic conditions which are barriers instructors often implement that may alter the academic achievements of marginalized students. It is those policies and procedures applied to learning communities that can exclude students from participating in course discourse, decision making, and full participation.

This chapter analyzes how radical transformation, critical language awareness, and inclusive andragogical practices prompted me to rethink the necessity of assigning a traditional literary analytical report for my second-level African American literature course. It is now a transformative dialogic assignment that uses Esri/ArcGIS StoryMap as the cornerstone media. I will provide an overview of my introduction to Esri/ArcGIS geospatial tools – the frameworks upon which radical inclusivity for this assignment emerged – connections to African American literature that I have identified, and how it all converges to place radical inclusivity and critical language awareness at the center of student narrative discourse.

An Overview of Esri/ArcGIS

Esri (Environmental Systems Research Institute, Inc.) ArcGIS (Geographic Information System) is a group of web and cloud-based geospatial software with various mapping and narrating options. StoryMaps help students understand local issues and situations to offer solutions to make their communities more equitable, liveable, workable, and just (Kerski, 2024). Users and developers create, organize, analyze, visualize, collaborate, and share information from thousands of datasets and subjects. Over 7000 colleges and universities use the platforms of Esri ArcGIS. Esri provides free mapping software to schools from kindergarten to the twelfth grade. College students have free access to ArcGIS platforms purchased by their college or university. There is also an open option in which users can sign up for a free account to create maps, apps, and additional content, making this software accessible in availability and universal learning. Kerski (2021) has identified 10 pedagogical benefits for using GIS software to transform learning communities.

- Spatial thinking
- Critical thinking
- Project-based learning
- Geographic and scientific inquiry
- Data fluency

- Community connection
- Mobile teams
- Career pathways
- Content knowledge
- Agentic opportunities

StoryMaps is one of the most used software in the Esri ArcGIS suite. My exposure to StoryMaps began in August 2019, when I embarked on my journey into the digital technology platform of Esri/ArcGIS. My colleague Professor Nicole Ernst, who teaches geospatial technology, invited me to attend an Esri Educators conference in Huntington, West Virginia. There, I was introduced to the ArcGIS platforms to use data to critically examine the where and the why of spatial learning. From the outset, I was fascinated by the critical pedagogical enhancements the ArcGIS platforms provide to engage students.

My journey with training and using Esri/ArcGIS tools continues, but I am not alone. Professor Ernst established a GeoAcademy to educate faculty from various disciplines. This expansion in use of emerging technologies and approaches supports the transformation of the ways in which knowledge, methodologies, and processes are delivered for both the instructor and the student. In addition, it empowers faculty and students to experiment with emerging technologies in cross-functional and collaborative ways to foster knowledge-sharing (Bucăța & Tileagă, 2024). As faculty learn about and develop pedagogy through ArcGIS, they experience a radical andragogical transformation.

Figure 11.1 presents key elements of an inclusive learning perspective that centers learners. It was adapted from a figure that first appeared in a faculty toolkit on inclusion and diversity that I designed for faculty at the college where I teach. Each hexagon centers learners in an inclusive teaching practice with methods of how the practice can be used in the learning community. Its purpose is for faculty to analyze how these practices may assist them with instructional approaches for their learning communities.

The learner-perspective requires dedication to diffuse barriers that may enter the learning community. Research by Metz (2021) further supports the need to value a learner-perspective approach by acknowledging the value and knowledge students bring to their learning communities.

Introduction to and Context of the Course

ENGL 217 is a survey course that introduces learners to African American authors who wrote and published from 1746 to the present. The catalog description for the course states:

> Examines race, class, gender, and politics as they are portrayed in African-American literature from colonial times to the present. This course emphasizes the ways in which African-American writers have

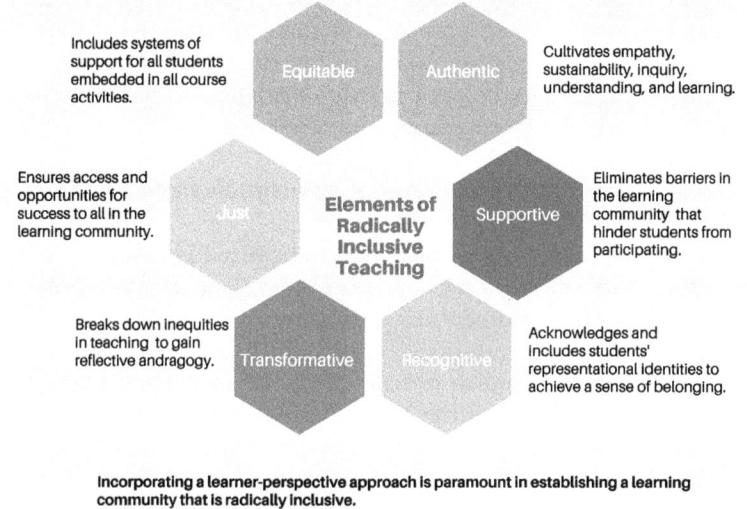

Figure 11.1 Elements of radically inclusive teaching practices

created and integrated literary traditions and construction into their works to depict the perils and the promise of reconstruction, the migration to urban life, and the struggle for social justice (HACC College Catalog, 2023–24).

I have taught one section of ENGL 217 through online modality since 2015. Each semester, students bring their diverse perspectives and backgrounds to the learning community. What virtual and remote students desire is to have more impact in their learning communities. They do not want to learn in virtual obscurity. Therefore, every semester brings new ideas to transform my classes. The transformation is influenced by societal events and recommendations from students.

A research component, such as an analytical literary research paper, is a learning outcome for the course. The transformation that I have implemented is reimagining what an analytical literary research paper can be. The result is using the Esri ArcGIS StoryMaps platform as the catalyst for students to tell the story of change needed to transform their communities to equitable places.

The assignment: Story mapping change in your community

Developing assignments that foster agentic contributions from students builds critical thinking, reading, and writing skills in the literature classroom. Through their exploration and inspiration of African American authors of their choice, and through their use of ArcGIS StoryMaps, students propose solutions to issues in their community; students tell the nonfiction story of an issue or situation in their community that needs awareness, improvement, and resolution.

Connecting radical inclusivity and critical language awareness to African American literature and story mapping

African American authors have used radicalized language to tell the stories of African American experiences. From Olaudah Equiano's use of subtle language to reinforce Africa as a civilized continent; to Phillis Wheatley's classical yet subversive poetry; to Paul Lawrence Dunbar's American vernacular English poetry that expresses Black love, pride, patriotism, and masking; to the social realism writing of Ida B. Wells Barnett that reported lynching and other atrocities in the US. They, as well as other authors, empower readers through their use of liberatory language in constructing an identity of resistance (hooks, 2010: 46).

In addition to celebrating the successes of African American experiences, students also experience the tribulations and trauma experienced by African Americans. Students are often transformed by their experiences. Critical language awareness is emphasized throughout the course in the context of honoring African American experiences and expressions. *Critical language awareness* (CLA) is a discourse that sets out to solve problems that impact communities, from a political, ideological, educational, social, racial, economical, and intersectional context (Tahiri & Muhaxheri, 2020). By reading and analyzing African American literature, students examine the situation, its cause and effect, its policy implications, and its historical impact on communities, in order to disrupt and to transform.

Learners express their appreciation for learning about African American authors; however, many students want to bring this knowledge and history to their communities. In this way, students are creating a learning community that promotes a *Sense of Responsibility Togetherness* (Mannarini & Fedi, 2009). Sense of Responsibility Togetherness determines the participants' level of interaction, motivation, and obligation (Mannarini & Fedi, 2009). This sense of responsibility provides space for acknowledging and honoring the knowledge, experience, and interests students bring to their learning environments and their communities.

The theory of Sense of Responsibility Togetherness is further supported through the research of Fredericks, Blumenfeld and Paris (2004) which focuses on student engagement in the togetherness process.

Students tell their story of improving their community in, for example, a social, cultural, or environmental context through researching, interviewing, and implementing a plan for justness. As stated by bell hooks, 'Telling stories is one of the ways that we can begin the process of building community' (2010: 49). As the dialogic griot, students are the creator, educator, historian, and storyteller. Thus, they are participants in sharing their critical language awareness.

Using the African American literary tradition of call and response promotes and requires students to collaborate with the instructor, classmates, student services (library and accommodation services, for example), and community members. In this way, call and response is being reinvented for the virtual space with the use of ArcGIS StoryMaps as the modality for their radically inclusive narrative. With such an intersectional approach, students connect learning to aspects of their lives that live beyond the classroom which expose the needs of their community and offer solutions through advocacy and action (Sengeh, 2023: 137–165).

Connecting setting and mapping to the African American literary experience

There are two historical and literary elements that are analogous to make story maps ideal for ENGL 217 and booster students' application of critical language awareness: setting and precedent.

Setting is an important literary device for all literary genres. However, setting is particularly important to the African diasporic experience because of its history of forced displacement experienced by millions; from capture, to enslavement, to banishment, to Jim Crow, to red lining, to gentrification. Setting has a direct link to spatiality and place-based pedagogy as it relates the geographic location of learners and educators (Yemini *et al.*, 2025). The tenets of GIS is for the user to inquire the *why* and the *where* to a research question or problem. This criterion is dedicated to the students' application of critical language through the use of the story map. StoryMaps help students understand local issues and situations to take action. This interconnectedness is described by Kerski (2024) as 'place-ify'.

Story mapping has historic application in the African American literary tradition. For example, in the 20th century scholar, author, and sociologist Dr W.E.B. Du Bois documented the Black experience in the exhibit 'The Ameican Negro at Paris 1900'. The exhibit was composed of dozens of charts, maps, and models; hundreds of photographs, books, and documents; all narrating the diasporic experiences of African Americans. The exhibit included documents of the African slave trade; contributions to history; contributions to their communities; contributions to industries, agriculture, education, medicine, and economies; service in the military; and place-based topics that included Black codes of Georgia, migration patterns, and exhibits from Historically Black Colleges and Universities (HBCU). The award-winning exhibit was curated by Mr Thomas J. Calloway (Du Bois, 1900, Special Collection and University Archives).

I argue that this was an epochal moment in story mapping through the lens of critical language awareness, as the exhibit allowed international and domestic audiences to experience voices of African American culture and history. As Du Bois described the exhibit, 'We have thus, it may be seen, an honest, straightforward exhibit of a small nation of people, picturing their life and without apology or gloss, and above all made by themselves' (1900: 577). This exhibit is, itself, an act of radical inclusivity.

Du Bois was a map maker. Figure 11.2 depicts a map of the United States Du Bois prepared to tell the story of migration of African Americans

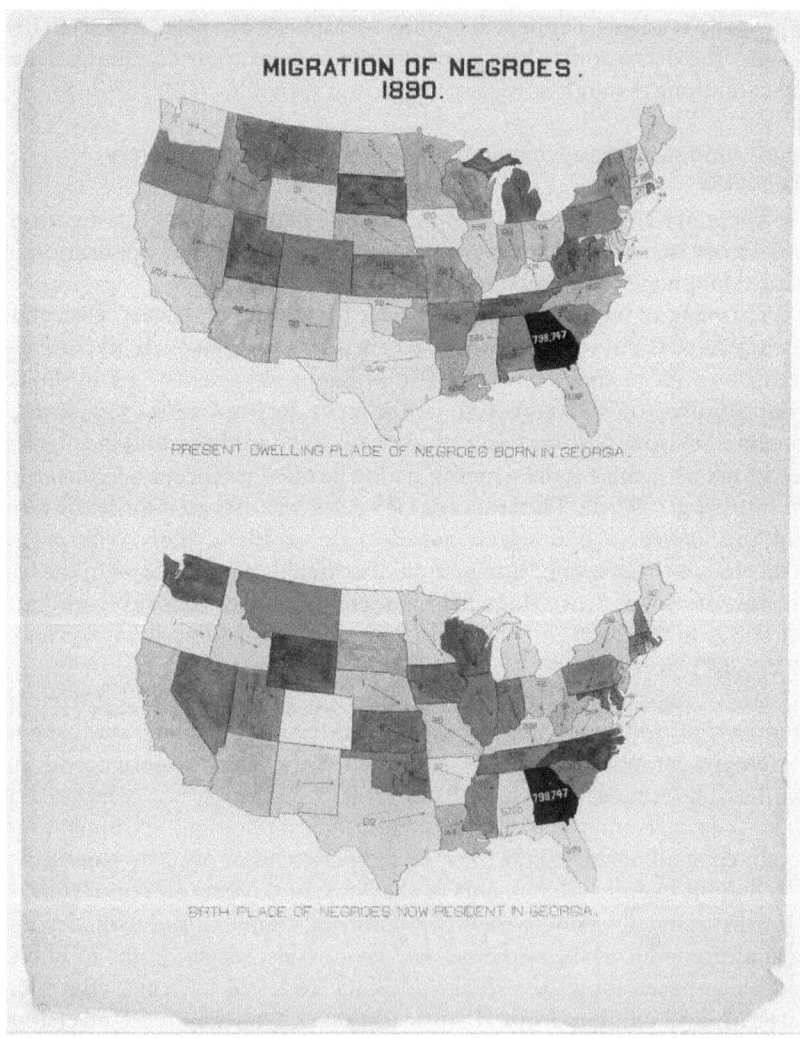

Figure 11.2 Migration of Negroes, 1890

Du Bois, W.E.B. (ca. 1900) *[The Georgia Negro] Migration of Negroes*. Paris, ca. 1900. [Photograph] Retrieved from the Library of Congress, https://tile.loc.gov/storage-services/service/pnp/ppmsca/33800/33870v.jpg.

born in Georgia residing in 1890 and another map showing where African Americans living in Georgia in 1890 were born.

When this example of a 19th century is presented to students, they understand the impact of their narrative and the direct correlation between Du Bois's story mapping using old media technology and story mapping in my African American literature course in which students use the new media technology of ArcGIS StoryMaps. Within ArcGIS StoryMaps, users are able to incorporate maps and design features to support their discourse, all of which are accessible within a story map template. Users may upload photographs, images, and audio to add individual emphasis. However, maps are at the center of the story. Features include maps that highlight key locations, based on search criteria that the user inputs in a search box. Based on the search results, users choose a base map on which to author a map. Users can layer their information on a map and/or generate information from sources within ArcGIS, such as Living Atlas and US Census data. Figure 11.3 shows the map generated as a result of a search in Living Atlas that I conducted to model results similar to the map designed by W.E.B. Du Bois. Search words included African Americans in Georgia.

Note that this map coordinates with the map drawn by W.E.B. Du Bois. By clicking on any location on the map, a pop-up screen will appear with, in this case, details about the African American population in Dougherty County, Georgia. Introducing the work of W.E.B. Du Bois to students serves several andragogical purposes. First, it solidifies the use of story mapping as an agent for change. I provide the work of W.E.B. Du

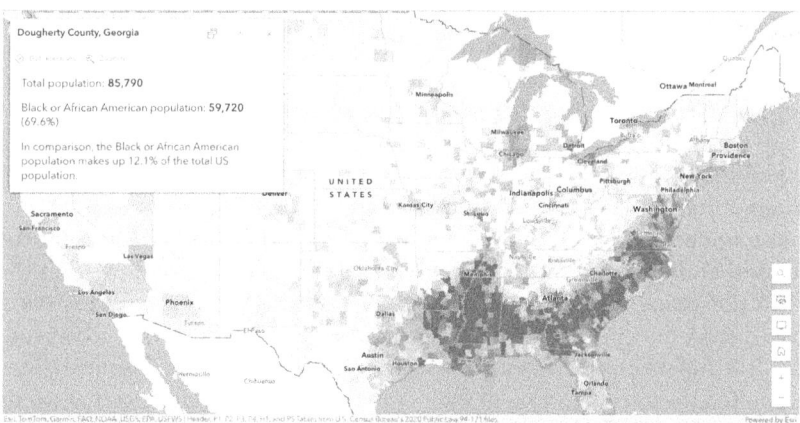

Figure 11.3 Percentage of population who are Black or African American (Non-Hispanic or Latino) – 2020 Census

The data are from the decennial 2020 Census, and sourced by the US Census Bureau for all states plus D.C. and Puerto Rico. The attributes come from the 2020 Public Law 94–171 (P.L. 94–171) tables. For full metadata including data processing notes, visit this group of ArcGIS Living Atlas layers. Source: US Census Bureau, Esri.

Bois in the Paris Exposition as an inspiration to students. In addition, through this discussion, students' use of critical reading, writing, and thinking question and expose inequities in their communities by identifying false and misleading claims, and misplaced arguments about their communities (Gates, 2001: 2430).

Introducing StoryMaps in the course

The likelihood that students have had experience with StoryMaps is slim. Therefore, it is necessary to introduce students to this new media. The course begins during the late-start session, running for 12 weeks. I introduce students to ArcGIS StoryMaps the first day of the semester via the course syllabus and lecture notes. I have found this step important so that students are introduced to the technology and its design elements before full discussions begin during week six. By week six, students log onto their student system to access StoryMaps, and identify a literature work of interest with which they share a personal connection; one that also aligns with the community change they want to make or inequalities they want to identify; one that serves as inspiration for reimagining their community.

Developing a StoryMap is intuitive; however, allowing time in the course schedule to account for a learning curve is necessary. The initial time commitment to complete a tutorial ranges from 30 to 60 minutes. Regardless of how rapidly a student may be able to learn this new medium, students may enter the experience with slight trepidation due to inexperience. Therefore, it is important to have support strategies in place.

The Derek Bok Center for Teaching and Learning (2021) classifies equitable and inclusive teaching as being cognizant, aware, responsive, and intentional to the dynamics that shape classroom experiences and impact learning (*Equitable & Inclusive Teaching*). A new approach and new technology can certainly change the dynamics of a learning environment. I have found that involving other members of the learning community is essential. A college librarian is embedded in the course to assist students with source selections and guidance on MLA format for citation and documentation. The librarian has a discussion thread in the LMS (Learning management system). As part of their class participation grade, students must communicate with the librarian at least twice during the drafting process. Students must explain their topic, the literature that prompted their reimagining of their community, the social issue that needs to be resolved, and the community in which the issue resides. They end the initial post with research questions to commence the discussion with the librarian.

During the finals week of each semester, students have the option of participating in a student academic celebration during which they present their work to a college-wide community audience. The extra credit opportunity is a student's choice. Should they participate, an additional ten points will be added to the final story map grade. The optional extra credit opportunity provides another opportunity for students to exercise their agentic power (Goldina *et al.*, 2020).

Story mapping change in your community assignment assessment

The story map is assessed through a formal rubric and narrative remarks. The remarks include comments of encouragement, kudos, and suggestions for ways to strengthen the story map. Since this is a new experience for most students, if there are areas in which the assignment does not meet expectations, I discuss those areas with students and offer an opportunity to revise their story map.

Each criterion on the rubric includes a list of objectives that students may use as a checklist as they draft their story map (see Table 11.1). The intention is to provide students with additional points to analyze their story map.

Story mapping in action: The student as a griot

The advantage to using StoryMaps is that it encourages the voice of the griot – the storyteller. For example, a student's story map discussed building equity in communities and provided suggestions for implementation. The story map centered on the struggle for dignity, visibility, and voice for Black youth in their community. The literature that sparked the topic was Gwendolyn Brooks' poem, *Boy Breaking Glass*. Every aspect, including the background thematic picture of shattered glass, supported the theme and thesis. The text of the story map began with an insightful overview of the poem, with relevant thematic connections with the poem, to the lack of local services for youth in African American communities.

The issue that the student wanted to discuss was to suggest a location for a community center. Supporting ArcGIS maps included a census report to show the percentage of African Americans in the community; and a perspective map to show the businesses in the neighborhood in which the student identified as the best location for the center. Both maps were interactive, allowing viewers to input additional criteria for additional results to expand the story.

The story map narrative revealed the student's knowledge of critical language awareness through insightful discussions regarding marginalization, discrimination, emotional impact, racial oppression, dismantling systems of racism; exploring coping mechanisms, confinement, and racial trauma.

To partake in community engagement and agency, the student presented the story map at a student festival. The student expressed that the choice to share the story map stemmed from the desire to inform the community rather than to receive extra credit for doing so.

Table 11.1 Story mapping change in your community rubric

Criteria	Score
Connections: The student describes and connects with literary work, issues, and community (37.5 pts.) Includes, but not limited to: • Analyze and critique works of literature for better understanding for community engagement • Connect themes in African American literature and the relevant history and culture that apply to your topic • Read critically and discuss literature for better understanding of how history has influenced African American literature	Exceeds expectations (34–37.5): The narrative is consistently focused, clear, purposeful, and always meets the needs of the audience and the creator's analysis. It is enhanced by well-placed, vivid, rich detail that captures the reader's interest. The narrative is a well-told, fully developed story of a situation that exists in the community. It displays insight of some depth and demonstrates substantial self-reflection and self-awareness. Meets expectations (30–33): The narrative is generally clear, focused, purposeful, adequately developed, and usually meets the needs of the audience. It is enhanced by some detail that catches the reader's attention and is told in a way that makes significance evident. The narrative shows evidence of the writer's insight and shows some self-reflection and self-awareness. Almost meets expectations (29–26): The narrative is partially clear and focused but not consistently so, and the writer may lose sight of audience needs and purpose. Detail is sketchy and not particularly vivid or engaging, and the narrative is not fully developed. The significance of the situation in the community is unclear, so the narrative therefore shows little evidence of insight, self-reflection, or self-awareness. Does not meet expectations (25.5–22.5): The narrative lacks focus and purpose, leaving the audience confused. Little to no effective detail in the narrative fails to engage audience interest, and the narrative is inadequately developed. The narrative leaves the reader with many questions about the significance of the community situation. Insight, self-reflection, and self-awareness are minimal or absent. _____ No attempt (22–0)

(Continued)

Table 11.1 (Continued)

Criteria	Score
Organization: Organization of story map that includes introduction, body, and conclusion supported by multimedia and reliable sources from the library databases (37.5 pts.) Includes, but not limited to: • Defines the community situation and the literary work that inspired the story map's focus and research criteria • Apply learning of African American literature beyond the classroom • Formulate ideas and to stimulate critical thinking • Maintain focus throughout the story map	Exceeds expectations (34–37.5): Narrative components connect clearly to one another. The narrative creatively engages the reader with a consistently strong internal structure that organizes the story and purposefully moves the reader easily through the text. Meets expectations (30–33): The narrative engages the reader and has a distinct structure that moves the reader easily through a progression of logically-sequenced paragraphs. Almost meets expectations (29–26): The narrative has a discernible structure but is not organized in a consistently effective manner, causing some confusion and difficulty in easily following the text. Does not meet expectations (25.5–22.5): The narrative lacks cohesive structure. Organization and sequencing are haphazard and ineffective, which leaves the reader confused and unable to follow the text and connections. _____ No attempt (22–0)
Voice: Narrative that includes your language, positionality, and intersectionalities (37.5 pts.) Includes, but not limited to: • Demonstrate knowledge of the various rhetorical devices used in African-American literature • Display the place-based needs and lived experiences of members in your community • Demonstrate analysis of African American writers • Understood the role that collaboration plays amongst community members in community development. • Connect your narrative to the literature	Exceeds expectations (34–37.5): The energy and tone of the language forcefully drive the narrative, making the text lively, expressive, and engaging. Descriptions and examples are strong. Includes the voices of community members. Meets expectations (29–26): The tone of the language reveals the writer's personality and makes the narrative interesting and informative. Elements of examples and descriptions appear. Almost meets expectations (25.5–22.5): The language and tone of the narrative are somewhat clichéd or lack energy and/or authenticity. Vague descriptions and examples. Does not meet expectations (26–22.5): The language and tone are flat, inexpressive, and unengaging. Examples and descriptions are excluded from the narrative.

(Continued)

Table 11.1 (*Continued*)

Criteria	Score
Research: MLA format for citation and documentation, includes details and descriptions, and maps with relevant data sets that support and connect with literature, community, and solutions to problems and/or inequities (37.5 pts.) Includes, but not limited to: • Synthesize how works produced by African Americans have influenced literature • Use the library and other information sources to research relevant literary criticism, history, and culture • Include maps from ArcGIS StoryMaps • Include interviews and data from community members • Support points with reliable primary and secondary sources	Exceeds expectations (34–37.5): Complete use of academic sources. Includes discussion of interviews with community members. No errors in MLA citation and documentation. Meets expectations (30–33): Complete use of academic sources. Includes discussion of interviews with community members. Citations and documentation correctly written with occasional errors. Almost meets expectations (29–26): Citations and documentation are incomplete. Vague representation of interviews with community members. Does not meet expectations (25.5–22.5): Some sources not listed on the documentation page or missing in-text citations. No representation from community members. _____ No attempt (0–22)
Student completed the reflective analysis (10 pts.)	
Score on this StoryMap literature and Community Project	

The importance of student introspection

A sense of belonging validates a student's personal belief that their presence and contributions within the learning community are valued as an accepted member (Trujillo & Tanne, 2014). A reflective narrative is included as an assignment criterion. The reflective narrative for the story map is an extension of reflective elements embedded throughout the course. For example, there are guided questions for journal responses; however, students are encouraged to also include their personal reflections and connections to the literature. The purpose of the reflective narrative is for students to interrogate their decision-making and the impact all the elements intertwined in the story map had on learning, from drafting to completion. They reflect on their experiences with researching, designing, and writing; and how they foresee the potential impact the story map may have on their language awareness and community building. Therefore, learners experience using their language to transform meaning and understanding, through action and reflection (Freire, 1993: 68). By completing this reflective narrative, students form their role as an agent in their learning community by highlighting their critical language awareness through a culturally and socially responsive perspective (Holmes, 2020).

Application of radically inclusive teaching to this assignment and your discipline

Figure 11.1 presents key elements of an inclusive learning perspective that centers learners. It was adapted from a figure that first appeared in a faculty toolkit on inclusion and diversity that I designed for faculty at the college where I teach. Each hexagon centers learners in an inclusive teaching practice with methods of how the practice can be used in the learning community. Its purpose is for faculty to analyze how these practices may assist them with instructional approaches for their learning communities.

Figure 11.4 expounds on these learner practices by explaining how I apply them to the story mapping 'change in your community' assignment. The contextualized sections in bold define how each element applies to the literary and community story map. However, this model of radically inclusive teaching practices is applicable to all disciplines and may be modified for assignments across the curriculum.

My reflections on the lessons learned

Radically inclusive teaching practices open up opportunities for critical thinking and critical language awareness. Students have discussed subjects in story maps that include stopping police brutality; helping the unhoused; honoring a loved one by opening a community center to support Black youth; maintaining contact with community leaders to apply for grants to improve the conditions of vulnerable members of the community; advocacy work in the community; and advocating to the local

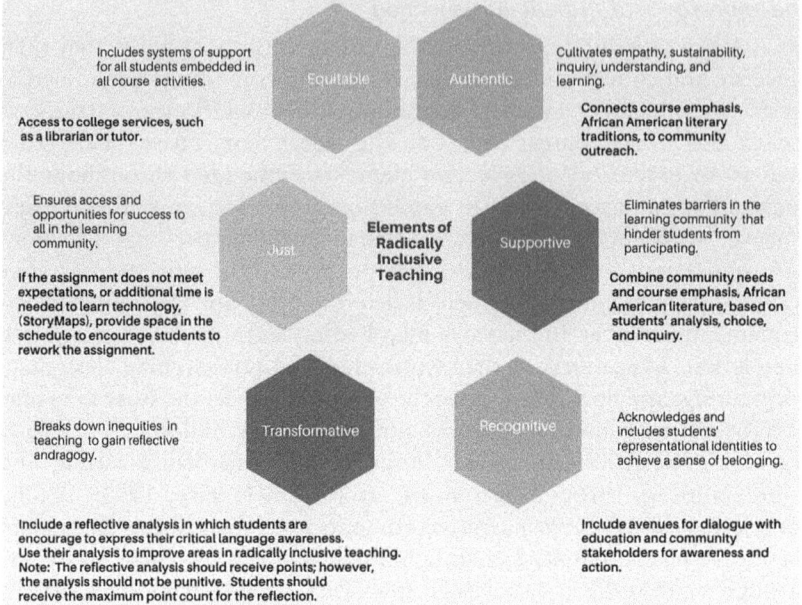

Figure 11.4 Elements of radically inclusive teaching practices in context

school board for more mental health resources. Each semester, I am always impressed with the ways in which students express their thoughts and ideas to connect with community members using StoryMaps. Regarding ArcGIS StoryMaps, the main obstacle students encountered was learning how to add maps to enhance their narrative. Once they were able to overcome this obstacle, they found StoryMaps to be a great platform to connect interests with community advocacy, and passion into actionable initiatives.

A student voiced their appreciation for the assignment and having agency to make decisions. However, the student realized that agency does not occur in all spaces. The student is a member of a marginalized group and felt their community was stifling and did not welcome the voice of marginalized members. The student expressed that they could not come up with the solution alone and not having the connection with their community is discouraging. In such cases, it is vital to assist students with finding contacts and resources that are available to assist, to encourage, and to empower.

I understand the value of introducing StoryMaps during the first week of class so that students will be familiar with its capabilities and role in the course. Informing students of the story map assignment the first week of class and letting them define its value for them will assist in cultivating an environment of openness and collaboration.

Granted, I have been working with ArcGIS platforms for more than five years; however, I am by no means an expert user. You do not need to be an expert user either. There are tutorials to get you started on the technical side. It is possible to build a story map with information pertinent to critical language awareness and social justice topics such as voter registration, mental health, or adult homecare. However, before you reach that point in your exploration, consider the pros and cons of implementing an activity that highlights radical inclusivity using ArcGIS StoryMaps. To get started, develop course materials using ArcGIS. Explain to students why they are using StoryMaps as the medium and its implication for the assignment. Introduce ArcGIS StoryMaps early in the course with a low-stake assignment, such as documenting their process of logging onto StoryMaps and uploading a map. To support a community of story map authors, schedule conferences with students to make the process less daunting.

With such an intersectional approach, students connect learning to aspects of their lives beyond the classroom that expose the needs of their community and offer solutions through advocacy and action (Sengeh, 2023: 137–165).

A call to readers

What do you want students to do with the information they receive every week? What do you want students to do with the information they receive after taking your course? What do your students do with the information they receive after taking your course? How do their experiences in their learning communities transform them? Of course, we want our learners to apply what they have learned throughout their lives. But how can we build an assignment that will have an impact not only for the student but also for their community? This is the call. What will be your response and your students' response?

References

Bucăța, G. and Tileagă, C. (2024) Digital renaissance in education: Unveiling the transformative potential of digitization in educational institutions. *Land Forces Academy Review* 29 (1), 20–37. https://doi.org/10.2478/raft-2024-0003

Derek Bok Center for Teaching and Learning. (2021) *Equitable & Inclusive Teaching.* Harvard University. https://bokcenter.harvard.edu/

Du Bois, W.E.B. (William Edward Burghardt), 1868–1963. *The American Negro at Paris W. E. B. Du Bois Papers (MS 312).* Special Collections and University Archives, University of Massachusetts Amherst Libraries. http://credo.library.umass.edu/view/full/mums312-b215-i231

Du Bois, W.E.B. (ca. 1900) *[The Georgia Negro] Migration of Negroes.* Paris, France, *ca. 1900.* [Photograph] Retrieved from the Library of Congress. https://www.loc.gov/item/2013650427/

Florian, L. and Spratt, J. (2013) Enacting inclusion: A framework for interrogating inclusive practice. *European Journal of Special Needs Education* 28 (2), 119–35.

Fredricks, J.A., Blumenfeld, P.C. and Paris, A.H. (2004) School engagement: Potential of the concept, state of the evidence. *Review of Educational Research* 74 (1), 59–109. https://psycnet.apa.org/doi/10.3102/00346543074001059

Freire, P. (1993) *Pedagogy of the Oppressed*. Continuum.

Gannon, K. (2021) *Inclusive Andragogical Practices*. Your faculty toolkit for inclusion and diversity. https://arcg.is/0eG9PD

Gates, H.L. (2001) Talking black: Critical signs of the times. In V. Leitch, W. Cain, L. Finke and B. Johnson (eds) *The Norton Anthology of Theory and Criticism* (1st edn, pp. 2424–2432). W.W. Norton & Company. (Original work published 1988.)

Goldina, A., Licona, P. and Ricci, P.L. (2020) Creating extra credit assignments that challenge, inspire, and empower students. *HAPS Educator*, special issue (August), 86–89.

Harrisburg Area Community College (HACC) Central Pennsylvania Community College (2023) *2023–2024 Harrisburg Area Community College Catalog*. https://sites.google.com/hacc.edu/2023-24-course-catalog/home

Holmes, A.G.D. (2020) Researcher positionality: A consideration of its influence and place in qualitative research – A new researcher guide. *International Journal of Education* 5 (4), 1–10. https://doi.org/10.34293/education.v8i4.3232

hooks, b. (2010) *Teaching Critical Thinking: Practical Wisdom*. Routledge.

Kerski, J. (2021) *Top 10 Educational Benefits for Students who Use GIS*. Esri Education. https://www.esri.com/about/newsroom/arcwatch/top-10-educational-benefits-for-students-who-use-gis/

Kerski, J. (2024) *From Data Collection to a Dashboard to a Story Map*. [Workshop]. GeoEd'24, 11–13 June, Louisville, Kentucky. https://storymaps.arcgis.com/stories/10547e1f28604252b15a2655ae60cff6

Mannarini, T. and Fedi, A. (2009) Multiple senses of community: The experience and meaning of community. *Journal of Community Psychology* 37 (2), 211–227. https://doi.org/10.1002/jcop.20289

Metz, M. (2021) Pedagogical content knowledge for teaching critical language awareness: The importance of valuing student knowledge. *Urban Education* 56 (9), 1456–1484. https://doi.org/10.1177/0042085918756714

Sengeh, D. (2023) *Radical Inclusion: Seven Steps to Help You Create a More Just Workplace, Home, and World*. Flatiron Books.

Tahiri, L. and Muhaxheri, N. (2020) Stylistics as a tool for critical language awareness. *Journal of Language and Linguistic Studies* 16 (4), 1735–1746. https://doi.org/10.17263/jlls.850989

Trujillo, G. and Tanne, K.D. (2014) Considering the role of affect in learning: Monitoring student's self-efficacy, sense of belonging, and science identity. *CBE – Life Sciences Education* 13 (1), 6–15.

Yemini, M., Engel, L. and Ben Simon, A. (2025) Place-based education – A systematic review of literature. *Educational Review* 77 (2), 640–660. https://doi.org/10.1080/00131911.2023.2177260

Part 4

What Does Radical Inclusivity Look Like in Institutional and Programmatic Contexts?

12 Exploring NCTE Position Statements as Opportunities for Critical Awareness and Inclusivity

Kristene K. McClure and Rodrigo Martinez

Background: Exploring Praxis in an Undergraduate Course

In this chapter, we – McClure, the instructor of the undergraduate course explained below, and Martinez, a pre-service English Language Arts teacher enrolled in the course in his final semester before graduation – describe and reflect on an activity intended to increase student awareness of linguistic and cultural diversity in a range of writing classrooms, especially in the secondary english teacher education setting. The activity stems in part from Kubota and Miller's (2017) call for work to deliberately narrow the theory–practice gap between academic research and real-time teaching practices, with the goal of 'speaking truth to people [by] communicating ideas with undergraduates and people in the community in accessible ways' (2017: 149).

The exigency of this truth-speaking is a direct response to recent attempts by numerous state-level legislative bodies, including the Georgia General Assembly, to erase reference to and therefore emphasis on notions of diversity, equity, and inclusion (DEI) and critical language awareness (CLA) in state educator standards (Georgia Coalition for Education Justice, n.d.). While the specific goings-on in Georgia obviously have the most ramifications for Georgia schools, we understand that Georgia was not the first state to enact such changes, coming after, for example, Florida's so-called 'Don't Say Gay' bill (Parental Rights in Education, 2022), nor is it likely to be the last. So far, these policy changes have not been aimed at Georgia's public higher education system, where K-12 teachers are trained, but reports of similar so-called 'anti-woke'[1] legislation in nearby states are on the rise (Quinn, 2024). Nevertheless, it is our hope that teacher preparation courses will continue to serve as sites of critical awareness where DEI and CLA approaches, such as the one detailed in this chapter, can be introduced and modeled for prospective language and writing teachers. Echoing Nguyen (2019), we 'teach from a position that knowledge is not neutral' and we aim for 'a refusal of the alienation and divisions of activities or skills…as well as for a *sliding under* institutional or state overpresence' (2019: 116, emphasis in original).

Introduction and Context of the Course

While radical inclusivity may be defined, envisioned, and enacted in multiple possible ways, a starting point for us was to hone in on two necessary elements of that definition as (1) inherently and intentionally *multiple* as well as, as much as possible, (2) *deliberate*. We explore these facets here, with initial emphasis on the latter, especially in light of the geographical/demographic specifics of our surrounding community, of which our school population serves as a microcosm, as well as in the class makeup and intentionally inclusive approaches to building all aspects of the course, not just the activity described in this chapter.

Geographical location and demographics

The undergraduate program in which we operate is located in Lawrenceville, the county seat of Gwinnett County, Georgia, a site that is noteworthy in part because of the demographic and political shifts that it has seen and that have made the county somewhat of a microcosm for potential shifts nationwide (Gringlas, 2022). Writing for the *Georgia Political Review*, undergraduate historian Andy Wyatt (2023) reported that:

> Gwinnett is incredibly [ethnically] diverse, tied with Alameda County, California, for the seventh-most diverse county in the U.S. It is also the most diverse county in the state of Georgia, with a diversity index of 75.1 percent. Nevertheless, just two decades ago, Gwinnett was not nearly as diverse as it is today. In 2000, the county was mostly White, at 67 percent of the population. 13 percent of residents were Black, 11 percent Hispanic, and 7 percent Asian. Since then, the county has rapidly diversified, and today, the county [only barely has] a White plurality. Thirty-two percent of residents are White, 31 percent Black, 22 percent Hispanic, and 14 percent Asian.

Ethnic diversity within the institution

This county-wide ethnic diversity is mirrored in our student population, as our institution, Georgia Gwinnett College (GGC) has consistently been ranked by *U.S. News & World Report* as the most ethnically diverse Southern regional college, corresponding with a consistent top 10 ranking in ethnic diversity among regional colleges in the nation (Georgia Gwinnett College, 2023). Additionally, in 2022, GGC was recognized as only the second Hispanic-Serving Institution (HSI) in Georgia (Sepulveda & Cade, 2022).

While ethnic diversity of the institution is not an inherent requirement for a faculty member wishing to incorporate a pedagogy of radical inclusivity, it helps that the school reaches such a broad demographic; beyond that, GGC is an access/nonselective institution, defined by Vanderbilt University as a school with at least an 80% acceptance rate (Doyle, 2010), and a Fall 2023 acceptance rate of 94% (*U.S. News & World Report*, 2024). Set against this backdrop of ethnic diversity and open access, the potential for radical inclusivity is essentially baked into the spirit and vision of GGC.

Education degrees at GGC

GGC offers numerous education-focused degrees, including the English Teacher Certification Program (TCP) where we do much of our work. The TCP degrees incorporate an introduction to educational theories beginning in the sophomore year, with emphasis moving in the junior year to practical teaching strategies, observations, and student-teaching demonstrations in the local secondary schools where students gain their required field experiences. Finally, in their senior year, teacher-trainees spend the first 10 weeks of their last semester fully immersed in student teaching, taking on the lead instructional role in their secondary English Language Arts (ELA) field placements. This practical entry into the full-time, albeit temporary, teaching role is a crucial step in the program, as much of the teacher-trainees' work gets refined through supervisor comments on lesson plans and conferences from formal observations, which all become an additional layer to the individual's story into their own classroom. In ENGL 3900: Theories and Practices for Teaching Writing, which is the course that houses the assignment described in this chapter, the intertwining threads of multiple stories, with narrators such as the teacher-trainees and the students in their classrooms, on-site mentor teachers and supervisors, and the undergraduate college faculty and mentors, combine in ways that can lead to radical development and transformation by all, not just by the novice teachers on the cusp of graduation. The NCTE Position Statements can thus contribute to a creative outlet and mindset for an inclusive student-centered classroom, crystalizing the theories that helped bring the teacher-trainees to a radically inclusive practice.

While TCP students enrolled in ENGL 3900 have usually had at least three prior semesters of field experience in their respective secondary placements, this course has students revisit past ideas about their general teaching philosophies and how those have evolved from a broad set of beliefs about teaching to more nuanced and actionable ideas about what they value in teaching writing. The program and this specific course intentionally strive to underscore the theory–practice connection, or praxis (e.g. Tinker Sachs, 2014) and to have teachers-in-training investigate 'scholarly knowledge [that may be] inaccessible to teachers or other stakeholders who [otherwise] have no opportunities to receive such learning experiences' (Kubota, 2023: 11).

One way that this scholarly knowledge can be made accessible and tangible to ELA teachers-in-training is through exploration of the extensive library of research-backed activities and position statements published by the National Council of Teachers of English (NCTE). This repository serves as the basis for the first major project in the course, as well as an introduction to 'critical approaches [that] problematize, examine, and transform power relations with a vision of constructing more equitable and just societies and relationships' (Kubota, 2023: 6).

Additional student enrollment in the course

The ENGL 3900 course is required in GGC's secondary education program for aspiring English Language Arts (ELA) teachers as well as for the Teaching English to Speakers of Other Languages (TESOL) Certification. However, it has been common in recent years for the course, with only completion of the first-year writing sequence as a prerequisite, to enroll more students taking the course as an elective than as one of these specific major or certificate requirements. The resulting mix of students across numerous education paths is an additional underlying way that the course serves as a space for openness and inclusivity, by being available to nearly any student with an interest in the course content.

Nevertheless, while having a course with minimal prerequisites may contribute at least nominally to a radically inclusive classroom ethos, creating a radically inclusive class environment requires deliberate and sustained course design to meet the needs of all students in the course. It is in this spirit that the notion of inclusivity is embedded from the earliest messaging in the course, with, for example, declarations from the instructor that 'Everyone is a teacher!' and intentional reference in every class session thereafter to all members of the course as teachers. Still, this heartfelt declaration is not always an easy sell without some further occasional coaxing; in particular, students who are in the course for reasons more of timing convenience than of overt interest in teaching may take a little more time to ease into this role, but class members are provided time and space to talk through some of their hesitations or misgivings, and the vast majority of students remain enrolled after the close of the drop.

Description of the Class Activity

Upon establishing the 'Everyone is a teacher!' ethos early in the course, we begin work on the major project-based activities in the course,[2] starting with the one highlighted in more detail in the remainder of this chapter: the Discussion Leader Activity on an NCTE Position Statement (hereafter, DLA).

Background and rationale of the activity

In the DLA, every student selects a position statement from the list on the NCTE website (National Council of Teachers of English, 1998–2024). Students then present their position statements over the course of the next three class weeks, with time allotted for all students to give detailed feedback on each presentation. This last point, insisting that all students adopt not only the presenter but also the evaluator role, adds another level of inclusivity to the project, as then all people in the course are not only students and teachers but also evaluators and assessors.

Activity goals and preparation

The DLA is intended as a gateway for students to accomplish the first of the course's four student learning outcomes, that 'students completing the course will be able to explain a range of major ideas and theories informing composition studies, writing pedagogy, and *inclusion and diversity in the classroom, especially the writing classroom*' (emphasis added). Rather than having pre-readings to contextualize the class activity, students are informed that the position statements themselves comprise the pre-readings that we will then continue to explore and connect to other course materials and assignments throughout the semester. This adds a degree of novelty to each iteration of the course, as topics covered in the DLAs vary from semester to semester.

Step-by-step description of the activity and assessment

The description below is based on a course that meets once weekly for 2.5 hours, but the activity can easily be adapted for classes meeting multiple times each week. Depending on the number of students in the course, it takes 2–3 weeks to complete, though that may also vary with changes to the expected presentation length.

(1) In week one of the course, the DLA is introduced as the first of three presentation/demonstration assignments scheduled throughout the 15-week semester. While not all position statements are equally suited for this activity due to their relative depth or applicability to a secondary ELA or TESOL writing classroom, the only position statements that are initially excluded from the available options are the three that are already built into the semester course structure, which are the statements on (a) Understanding and Teaching Writing: Guiding Principles (National Council of Teachers of English, 2018), (b) Professional Knowledge for the Teaching of Writing (National Council of Teachers of English, 2016), and (c) Students' Right to Their Own Language (Conference on College Composition & Communication, 2014).

(2) Throughout week two, students discuss interests that purposefully drive their position statement selection, and in some cases, students

who state interest in the same topic might pair up for a more detailed presentation. It is important here to note that not all position statements explore content that is inherently or overtly radically inclusive. For instance, while statements with titles that include reference to Ebonics, anti-racist ideals, or LGBTQ+ identities could be classified as inherently primed to be radically inclusive, other statements with broader content foci such as nonfiction literature or writing instruction in school may not, on the surface, seem as relevant to critical language awareness or radical inclusivity. However, in a course that regularly and deliberately infuses reference to meeting the needs of all participants, including the instructor, it is indeed possible to view many of the position statements through a critical or radical lens.

(3) Students are invited to review the instructor-designed assignment rubric and suggest updates, although this early in the semester, most students in this context, even relatively seasoned teacher-trainees in their last semester of the official education program, tend to shy away from suggesting rubric alterations.

(4) Based on stated preferences, the schedule of class presentations is then determined and spread out over the next three weeks of class. This class usually has 12–18 students enrolled, so there are four to six DLA presentations each week.

(5) At the start of each class day with DLA presentations, students see a list of presenters scheduled for that day and are provided with feedback forms to complete for each presentation. These forms are where the student audience members first get in-class experience with evaluating their peers, though this teacherly evaluation is framed not in terms of a grade or competitive scale against which students might judge each other. Rather, the feedback forms focus on how well evaluators grasp the concepts presented, what they want or need to know more about after the presentation, and how student presenters might improve their content design and delivery for the subsequent presentations in the course.

(6) Besides receiving detailed peer feedback on their DLA presentations, the instructor uses the previously-shared rubric to formally assess each student's performance on the activity.

(7) At the close of the last meeting when the DLA presentations are scheduled, students are invited to complete an anonymous survey on the activity overall, adding their opinions on the efficacy of the assignment design as far as meeting intended course outcomes, the effectiveness of the schedule of presentations, and any other insights on what they thought did or did not work well in the explanation and execution of the assignment. Feedback from this survey is then used to improve the activity for subsequent semesters. For instance, student comments from past iterations of the course have led to incorporating

more in-class discussion time about the overall goals of the NCTE position statements and about student-specific choices of topics to present. Additional student reflections on the activity are covered in detail below by Martinez, the co-author of this chapter who was also a student enrolled in the Spring 2024 iteration of the course.

Portrait of the Activity in Action: A Student's Perspective

This section, as identified in the heading, is an extended reflection by co-author Martinez, a graduating senior in the ENGL 3900 course. The content of this section was initially composed as a series of weekly reflections that were built into the overall course structure, though the reflection assignment for other students in the course focused more on synthesizing ideas from other course readings than on the kind of DLA-specific reflections explained below. Readers may note some repetition of ideas in the above description by McClure, but we hope that seeing this portrait through Martinez's eyes reinforces the importance of infusing student choice and voice in both the DLA itself and this chapter's explanation of it.

****

DLA overview: A student's perspective

As a student in my senior year at GGC, I took the ENGL 3900 course. As noted above, the course is an opportunity for student teachers to begin the transition from students to professionals. My understanding of the purpose of the assignment was for students to research and present a position statement published by the National Council of Teachers of English, paying particular attention to the connection to teaching writing as the class steers its future educators to pedagogical strategies and ideas about writing. Before addressing the assignment, I want to note the classroom's atmosphere and its effect on students. Some of my peers expressed excitement and had goals of becoming teachers, while others weren't sure that education was the path for them; they were enrolled in the class as an elective, perhaps based on availability, the time it was offered, or other individual preferences. However, the instructor made it clear that we were all teachers in her eyes. No matter the background in our college majors, life goals, abilities, talents, and so on, she persisted with the idea. This persistence in turn created an environment where everyone's inclusion was desired and needed in the conversation of teaching writing, making a lasting impression that we all had something unique to contribute to our learning. In this way, she set a base level of radical inclusivity for the class, modeling the mindset one should have as an educator and planting seedlings of the ideas and pedagogical techniques that foster radical inclusivity.

The instructor's modeling gave us a guide to rely and reflect on as a few of us each week stepped into a teaching role and others were reminded of the importance of student engagement, learning, assessment, and background. The students – those with us in the ENGL 3900 course and the ones we teach now or will teach – were to be at the forefront of our research and presentations. With these imagined audiences in mind, we understood that many of the NCTE position statements include some focus on critical awareness and inclusivity regarding differentiation of lesson plans, various modes of assessments and media, and so on. My peers took it one step further by presenting dilemmas and questions on student impact and brainstorming ideas to implement in future classroom settings.

Post-activity thoughts and reflections

As a future educator, I've been learning about the importance of student-based learning. I've encountered many words and phrases that emphasize inclusivity: differentiation, adaptation, cultural relevance, 'I can' statements, formatives, Maslow's hierarchy of needs, and so on. Some pedagogical strategies and theories are more direct than others in informing us that our thinking, planning, and services at large should always try to reach all our students as much as possible. I had some understanding of these inclusive concepts prior to this course, but the course and activity helped cement my actions going into the education profession, rather than just sporadically sprinkling in for inclusivity's sake.

One compelling aspect of the piece I presented, the NCTE's Teaching Storytelling Position Statement (National Council of Teachers of English, 2022a), is the speaker's inclusion or reach of the audience in creating a narrative. The DLA made me realize how unexpected and potentially radical the speaker–audience interplay can be. I had preconceived notions that oral storytellers told the same sequence of events they planned or were handed down from older generations, somehow passed down intact and not to be tampered with; however, stories are dynamic, and storytellers are quite dependent on the ebb and flow of their audience. If there is an unfavorable reaction, the teller will add a little more oomph to regain their attention. If the audience leans into their chairs, the teller may decide to further engage or even tease the audience with a twist. In an educational setting, the art form captures all varieties of students into its orbit through body movement, facial expressions, and tone intensity, creating a magical, engaging experience and presenting opportunities for different facets of learners' brains to be activated.

As the ENGL 3900 course focused on the theories and practices of teaching writing, we discussed the challenges teachers face concerning students' relationship with writing. We started by sharing our personal journeys, with many expressing struggles because of low confidence or a learning disability, among other reasons; however, the storytelling process and the skills it engenders can be applied to learning narrative writing. Educators can allow students who may have difficulty grasping certain elements of narrative writing to present their ideas in a different light. For example, students who are more vocal or verbal may need to orally tell their stories to understand the most important details they will want to later write, or students may need audience reactions to know where to enhance descriptive detailing. Crucially, as we learned throughout ENGL 3900, encouraging students by way of storytelling does not mean insistence on a monolingual perspective. In fact, multilingual students have access to multiple languages and cultures. Storytelling can be one way to empower multilingual learners (MLLs) and emphasize their contributions to everyone's learning by inspiring fellow students to steer their narratives based on their unique perspectives. In essence, the Teaching Storytelling Position Statement, one that did not have overt reference to critical elements of student identity, still taught me how radical inclusivity is a mindset that can be deliberately implemented in the ELA classroom.

What my peers and I learned

Our exploration of NCTE position statements in the DLA activity illustrated the importance of student diversity and inclusion, highlighting issues in education concerning traditionally marginalized students and how to adapt concepts within activities for different groups of students (e.g. MLLs, students with learning disabilities, and gifted students). Completing the DLA and co-authoring this chapter provided me with valuable insights into the challenges and possibilities of radical inclusivity. While I learned a lot from preparing my own presentation for the DLA, the class as a whole especially gained insights by listening to and participating in other students' presentations, which provided a helpful nudge to non-education majors to get into the mindset of a teacher when starting their teaching writing journey, and which aided future educators like myself in the process. With inspiration from their chosen position statement, my peers and I leaned into the opportunity to produce activities and discussions over student-centered learning, lesson planning, and classroom management.

For example, one of my peers presented the Position Statement on Writing Instruction in School (National Council of Teachers of English, 2022b). This statement points out that '[w]riting instruction focused on standardized tests fails to prepare a culturally diverse population…for the [future] writing they [might] do and, more broadly, to cultivate diverse communities of capable, engaged writers who write for their own purposes'. Also key to our growing grasp of radical inclusivity were points from this statement about the inherently classist nature of more traditional types of writing instruction, the dangers of student disengagement that teachers may face when too much emphasis is placed on Eurocentric language and writing norms, and the psychological threat of excluding families and communities based on their language use. As a class, we drew connections across other students' presentations, like the ones that explored Ebonics (National Council of Teachers of English, 2021) and Multimodal Literacies (National Council of Teachers of English, 2005), and gained a clearer understanding of the needs of students of different races, ethnicities, learning abilities, and languages. Many of us not only will be teaching in Gwinnett County but have also graduated from schools here, so some of our class conversations adjacent to the DLA stemmed from our personal experiences growing up in the county or, at large, metro Atlanta. A handful of my peers, including myself, are engaged in our pre-service fieldwork in the Gwinnett County Public School system, where our awareness of the county's diversity sparks the need and desire to be radically inclusive in all aspects of our profession.

Challenges of implementing the DLA in class: Martinez

The biggest obstacle I had as a student completing this assignment was in the small-group discussion activity I designed to accompany my Teaching Storytelling presentation. I assumed that my peers, especially the education majors, would catch on to the critical pieces of the process of storytelling and its elements in order to see how it can be related to an effective teaching strategy for students, especially for traditionally marginalized students who might benefit most when their teachers engage in radical inclusivity. However, although most of them saw the engagement and motivation aspect of storytelling for different kinds of learners (e.g. auditory, visual, kinesthetic), some still had a hard time seeing the practical usefulness of implementing storytelling into our standard units on teaching narrative writing. This led me to an important realization about trying to infuse inclusivity into lessons: reference to critical ideas really needs to be overt and deliberate, not something that we as teachers just assume everyone will catch on to.

A related drawback of the DLA that many students later identified as an area for improvement in the next iteration of the course was that, with 18 student presentations scheduled in only three weeks of class time, having a detailed discussion on any single topic or presentation was not really feasible. Still, in the time I've had to reflect since participating in this activity, I've identified some areas where I as the student presenter might have approached the assignment a bit differently. First, I shouldn't have assumed, because I mentioned the elements of storytelling and compared them to that of narrative writing, that my peers, especially the non-education majors, would just magically see how the concept of storytelling can be differentiated and radically inclusive. It can take many years of trial and error for educators to feel that their classes are spaces where students' needs and wants are mostly met, and I certainly am one educator-in-training that still needs more of that time and practice. I suppose I could've explained in more detail the practical connections, like how the elements and processes of storytelling can be an effective way to teach narrative writing, and then taken it a step further to explore more connections to radical inclusivity. Next time! Maybe I will have an opportunity some day to approach this lesson as the instructor rather than as the student or student-teacher.

Advice for implementing the DLA in various contexts: McClure

This ENGL 3900 activity is one that I have been honing for a few years, and the vast and growing repository of position statements coupled with the range of students who enroll in the course makes this DLA look and feel substantively different each time I teach the course. Still, I can think of a few ways interested readers might adapt this to their contexts:

(1) First, regardless of teaching context, a key consideration to successful implementation of this activity is a keen awareness of time. This includes the time needed to introduce the repository to students as well as the time needed for student presenters to do justice to their topics and ensure that the D, i.e. Discussion, in the DLA is at the forefront, so that this does not just become a series of 10-minute presentations, one after the other, with minimal opportunity for real-time reflection. One possible approach across contexts that respects the time needed for discussion and reflection is for the instructor to carefully curate the position statements to be covered in the DLA, perhaps based initially on only one or two rather than all of the 30 categories established on the webpage that lists all of the position statements (National Council of Teachers of English, 1998–2024). Another approach to help with leaving adequate time for discussion and reflection is to have students work in pairs or other small groups rather than as individual presenters.
(2) The activity can also work well in TESOL contexts. Here too, rather than introducing the assignment as one in which students choose among nearly any of the position statements, the instructor can narrow this down to those statements that focus specifically on, for instance, multilingual learners or second-language writing.
(3) This activity, as I designed it, is geared for a class in which, invariably, some students do not realistically intend to become teachers, since some undergraduate English majors or minors end up taking the course simply out of convenience based on the day or time it is offered. However, adapting the course for a group in which all students have access as the instructor to their own classrooms could involve adding a follow-up component that has students adapt their DLA, originally

designed for and presented to an audience of their college peers, to the respective classroom where they are working as the primary instructor or doing their student teaching. Taking Martinez's case as an example, this could mean that in conjunction with presenting the Teaching Storytelling Position Statement to his college classmates, he could then create a related lesson geared for his class of 10th grade MLLs, which becomes another facet of the DLA course project.

Notes

(1) The term *anti-woke* as used here means the opposite of 'aware of and actively attentive to important societal facts and issues (especially issues of racial and social justice)' (Merriam-Webster, n.d.). For a more detailed history of the term *woke* and how it has evolved since it first appeared in American blues singer Leadbelly's song 'Scottsboro Boys', see Robinson (2022). While some may see the term *anti-woke* as polarizing, a Florida law that followed the 'Don't Say Gay' bill was literally named the Stop W.O.K.E. (Wrong to Our Kids and Employees) Act, immediately showing how the historically Black slang term *woke* has been co-opted and steered into the negative connotation it has among many US political conservatives.

(2) Beyond weekly meetings that require regular written reflections on course readings, the course requires completion of five major projects: (1) the Discussion Leader Activity on an NCTE Position Statement, which is detailed in this chapter; (2) an interview with an educator who regularly assigns writing; (3) a presentation of a writing lesson created during the course of the semester; (4) a research project on a student-selected topic pertinent to teaching writing; and (5) a research-supported philosophy of teaching writing, first drafted early in the semester and then updated with sources explored in course readings as well as student-determined sources gleaned through the completion of the previous projects.

References

Conference on College Composition & Communication (2014) Students' right to their own language (with bibliography). CCCC. https://cccc.ncte.org/cccc/resources/positions/srtolsummary

Doyle, W.R. (2010) Open-access colleges responsible for greatest gains in graduation rates. Policy Alert. The National Center for Public Policy and Higher Education. https://files.eric.ed.gov/fulltext/ED508992.pdf

Georgia Coalition for Education Justice. (n.d.) GaPSC DEI open letter. https://docs.google.com/document/d/1LgAnUSH1u4eq-a-xM2vgbYjrsRQdInSGRsj7e0M93S4/edit

Georgia Gwinnett College (2023) Georgia Gwinnett College is most ethnically diverse Southern regional college. *GGC News*, 18 September. https://www.ggc.edu/about-ggc/news/ggc-most-ethnically-diverse-southern-regional-college-for-10th-straight-year-in-us-news-world-report-ranking

Gringlas, S. (2022) One of the country's fastest changing political landscapes is in suburban Atlanta. *NPR Morning Edition*, 31 March. https://www.npr.org/2022/03/31/1089885271/one-of-the-countrys-fastest-changing-political-landscapes-is-in-suburban-atlanta#:~:text=GRINGLAS%3A%20Li%20says%20Gwinnett%20County,the%20suburbs%20of%20the%20South.

Kubota, R. (2023) Linking research to transforming the real world: Critical language studies for the next 20 years. *Critical Inquiry in Language Studies* 20 (1), 4–19. https://doi.org/10.1080/15427587.2022.2159826

Kubota, R. and Miller, E.R. (2017) Re-examining and re-envisioning criticality in language studies: Theories and praxis. *Critical Inquiry in Language Studies* 14 (2–3), 129–157. https://doi.org/10.1080/15427587.2017.1290500

Merriam-Webster (n.d.) Woke. Merriam-Webster.com dictionary. Retrieved 23 May 2024, from https://www.merriam-webster.com/dictionary/woke

National Council of Teachers of English (1998–2024) Resources. NCTE. https://ncte.org/resources/position-statements/

National Council of Teachers of English (2005) Multimodal literacies. NCTE. https://www.readwritethink.org/professional-development/professional-library/position-statement-multimodal-literacies

National Council of Teachers of English (2016) Professional knowledge for the teaching of writing. NCTE. https://ncte.org/statement/teaching-writing/

National Council of Teachers of English (2018) Understanding and teaching writing: Guiding principles. NCTE. https://ncte.org/statement/teachingcomposition/

National Council of Teachers of English (2021) CCCC statement on Ebonics. NCTE. https://ncte.org/statement/ebonics/

National Council of Teachers of English (2022a) Teaching storytelling position statement. NCTE. https://ncte.org/statement/teaching-storytelling-position-statements/

National Council of Teachers of English (2022b) Position statement on writing instruction in school. NCTE. https://ncte.org/statement/statement-on-writing-instruction-in-school/

Nguyen, M.T. (2019) Our students are radical *because* they live in the real world. In J. Mink (ed.) *Teaching Resistance: Radicals, Revolutionaries, and Cultural Subversives in the Classroom* (pp. 115–117). PM Press.

Parental Rights in Education, Fla. CS/CS/HB 1557 (2022) https://www.flsenate.gov/Session/Bill/2022/1557

Quinn, R. (2024) Virginia officials scrutinize two universities' DEI course syllabi. *Inside Higher Ed*, 18 March. https://www.insidehighered.com/news/diversity/2024/03/18/va-officials-scrutinize-2-universities-dei-course-syllabi

Robinson, I. (2022) How woke went from 'Black' to 'bad'. *NAACP Legal Defense Fund*, 26 August. https://www.naacpldf.org/woke-black-bad/

Sepulveda, D. and Cade, B. (2022) GGC designated as a Hispanic serving institution. *GGC College News*, 7 October. https://generalspace.ggc.edu/server/api/core/bitstreams/af868bb0-06d1-4da0-b146-ed1f0e4f3bf6/content

Tinker Sachs, G. (2014) Reclaiming praxis: A tribute to Paulo Freire! *Ubiquity: The Journal of Literature, Literacy, and the Arts, Praxis Strand* 1 (1), 1–8. https://core.ac.uk/download/71427392.pdf

U.S. News & World Report (2024) Georgia Gwinnett College admissions. https://www.usnews.com/best-colleges/georgia-gwinnett-college-41429/applying

Wyatt, A. (2023) Realignment in Gwinnett County: Part I. *Georgia Political Review*, 28 November. https://georgiapoliticalreview.com/realignment-in-gwinnett-county-part-i/

13 Trauma-Informed Practice in a Radically Inclusive Classroom

Elizabeth S. Coleman

Background

I have long been a believer in the transformative value of education and its power to bring people out of darkness. While that sounds grand, I know that if it were not for supportive educators in my teenage years, I would not have the privilege to sit and write this today. Long before I even heard the term transformative pedagogy, I was fundamentally aware of what education could do, and as I honed my practice and endured tumultuous times, which I knew were also impacting my students, my interest in trauma-informed practice increased. From where I sit, trauma-informed education, radical inclusivity and transformative practice cannot be separated.

I work primarily from a position of transformative pedagogy as put forward by Paulo Freire and bell hooks. Transformative pedagogy sits in opposition to the banking method according to which educators deposit knowledge. Rather, learners can take an inquiry-based approach and explore ideas to construct their own meanings. hooks comments that students expect that education connects to their lives and that many of them show up with noticeably 'wounded...psyches' (hooks, 1994: 19); transformative pedagogy provides a way to prioritize personal experiences and allow for the inclusion of intersectional identities. As Freire notes, it is only by speaking our truth that we can transform the world (Freire, 1978/1970: 61). Within this pedagogy, we can incorporate the concept of radical inclusivity. Radical inclusivity here means accepting all individuals regardless of their identity and establishing ways to include those who are often marginalized through their differences. It is a valuing of all individuals as whole people with unique needs, ideas, and experiences. This transformative practice opens the path to radical inclusivity and critical language awareness as it makes space for everyone, regardless of how they show up. Both in *Teaching to Transgress* and *Teaching*

Community, hooks engages in conversations with her colleague Ron Scapp; in *Teaching Community* Scapp notes that educators 'cannot assume that because they hold valuable information that students need to know this will automatically lead to a feeling of community' (hooks, 2004: 109). Scapp continues that if we are to find unity in diversity, we must commit to community through the cultivation of civility and courage (hooks, 2004: 112). This strength in diversity is a direct benefit of radical inclusivity.

Within my practice, it seems both illogical and impossible to separate radical inclusivity and trauma-informed practice. It is not possible for learners to feel included if they do not feel safe and supported. Sadly, the institution in which I work does not prioritize inclusivity or trauma-informed practice, favoring a more direct academic position. My classroom practice is a response to the challenges my learners encounter and the wider environment they live in.

Radical inclusivity and critical language awareness

By radical inclusivity I mean the acceptance of all those Freire would consider oppressed. Adams, Bell and Griffin (2007: 3) define oppression as 'the fusion of institutional and systemic discrimination, personal bias, bigotry, and social prejudice in a complex web of relationships and structures that shade most aspects of life in our society'. Within our classrooms we cultivate communities, and within those protected spaces it is our duty to ensure no one is neglected or abandoned. This requires us to actively strive to support our learners, ensuring we meet both their social and educational needs. hooks comments, 'educators are poorly prepared when we actually confront diversity. This is why so many of us stubbornly cling to old patterns' (1994: 41). hooks continues that it is crucial to learn ways to relate to diverse students and those we are not used to interacting with. This may be a challenge on both sides, and hooks notes students may be baffled by the inclusion of topics other than language usage in an English class (1994: 42), yet these topics that get them talking back, both as replies and backchat, ultimately enhance their world view.

Critical language awareness (CLA) has been in operation since the 1980s, developing out of what has been termed activist teachers' ideas around making classrooms more inclusive. CLA has developed alongside social change, shifts in power structures, and language utilization. Fairclough terms CLA as 'a prerequisite for democratic citizenship' (1992: 3) implying that unless we engage with it, we cannot achieve an egalitarian position. Within classrooms characterized by radical inclusivity and transformative pedagogy, this position is vital for learners to feel valued within the educational community. hooks notes that in order for us to reach a position in which our learners share with us, we must also be vulnerable: 'Professors who expect students to share confessional narratives but who are themselves unwilling to share are exercising power in a manner that could be coercive' (1994: 21). She also finds that if we exercise vulnerability we will develop as people and educators. To promote radical inclusivity and acceptance, I conduct a circle activity in which my students share their core values and ideas. The activity leader may join as a participant and share their ideas with the students, or they may share them preceding the activity which allows them to both model the task and to offer up a part of themselves.

As highlighted by Rosa and Flores (2017), language classrooms come with the expectation of respectability politics: we must behave in a way that is condoned by the academy. Critics state that if minorities don't discuss their minority status, then they will be above being targeted, i.e. we should simply all use the sanitized and sanctioned language of the academic classroom. However, CLA offers us a way past this by allowing a critical analysis of the implicit and explicit meanings of what is said. If we are to move to a democratic classroom then we must look at how we can raise silenced voices. Within my classroom, this democratizing principle of CLA is applied to give a voice to students otherwise unable to share their ideas and identities. It is a tool through which we can overcome the censorship of the academy.

What's trauma got to do with it?

The APA (2020) defines trauma as an emotional response to an event, but it is more than this; it is insidious. It lives in our bodies and has the ability to completely derail us, with the APA (2018) noting that it affects a survivor's ability to view the world as safe and just.

When we consider what trauma is, we must examine the three Es of trauma: Event(s), Experience, and Effect(s). The event refers to what happened, that is the harm or threat that an individual experienced. Experience connects to how that individual processes the event; do they classify it as a major or minor thing, is it disruptive or not? The effects of trauma depend partly on the experience of it and can vary in length. An event may be insignificant and easily overcome, or major and easily overcome. More than likely though, major events will be disruptive and lead to long-term effects. Effects may include the inability to form meaningful relationships, trouble managing stress, and cognitive dysfunction (Coleman, 2020). Students who cannot process information, relate to their peers, or handle stress have the potential to become lost in the academy. Van Der Kolk (2015) relays a story of a young woman who found that her trauma impacted her ability to follow a lesson, noting that she would easily become lost in her lesson if she momentarily lost her focus:

> Imagine being in a classroom, and the teacher comes in and says 'Good morning. Turn to page two-seventy-two. Do problems one to five'. If you're even a fraction of a second off, it's just a jumble. It was impossible to concentrate. (2015: 325)

Being trauma-informed means educators know this and seek to avoid perpetuating further harm (Carello & Butler, 2015). Trauma-informed thinking, like transformative pedagogy and radical inclusivity, recognizes the unique experiences of individuals. It asks us to 'understand the ways in which violence, victimization, and other traumatic experiences may have impacted the lives of individuals' (Carello & Butler, 2015: 264) and accommodate their needs in a healing manner. As outlined by SAMHSA (2014), trauma-informed practice incorporates six key factors:

(1) Safety
(2) Trustworthiness and transparency
(3) Peer support
(4) Collaboration and mutuality
(5) Empowerment, voice and choice
(6) Cultural issues

How does this look in the classroom? *Safety and trustworthiness* are important in terms of students knowing where they stand; do we do the things they say we will? Do we offer the same consideration and permissions to all learners? Are we approachable as a source of support, comfort and safety in a crisis? In times of crisis or when suffering trauma, strong bonds between educators and students have been shown to increase resilience. Additionally, how an instructor acts serves as a model for members of the classroom. If we model healthy emotional and social behavior, we can achieve healthy, motivated classroom environments that facilitate learning; students who perceive their instructor to be sensitive to their needs achieve better academic outcomes (Jennings, 2019).

In the classroom, we talk about *peers* as those in the same educational cohort, and these peers are important, but within trauma work, *peers* refer to those who have similar experiences. *Peer support* is vital for those with trauma to know they are not alone. Within the framework of radical inclusivity, we accept learners however they show up – one way being with trauma – and we look at how we make the space safer for them. We must encourage inclusive environments in our classrooms that allow those with traumas to connect.

Mutuality is an area in which we see the inclusion of CLA approaches. *Mutuality* at its core is about removing power imbalances and creating a level playing field for all involved. In the classroom this means that we create space for everyone to speak and lead, we find room for students to co-teach and share their ideas. For democratic citizenship to exist, expression must be authentic. Within a classroom, although an instructor is there to run the class, they must not confer on themselves unnecessary levels of power. Through the transformative and radical approaches to seeing all people as valuable and worthy of contributing, we can see that in line with CLA, we are able to move away from the traditional power structure that says teachers lead and students absorb ideas without input.

CLA also relates to *empowerment and voice*: we must not police the language our learners use, although we should be mindful of language that may cause harm to other members of the community. Allowing learners to critique language and its application is vital in ensuring a safe space that facilitates democratic classroom citizenship. Much has been made of appropriate classroom language over the years, but forcing learners to use sanitized vocabulary and limiting the topics we discuss does not serve anyone in the long run. What our students need is for their language to serve them; they need to be able to express themselves about things that really matter. Banning topics from the classroom or limiting the manner in which they can be discussed leaves learners to investigate them on their own or feeling ashamed of their ideas and identity. In terms of minoritized identities, this shame and exclusion perpetuates trauma rather than creating a more comfortable environment. When it comes to avoiding potential harm to others, moving learners into a radically inclusive space will enhance their acceptance of diversity.

Educators must also be mindful that what they say matters; part of trauma-informed practice is also to avoid retraumatizing survivors and in this regard, it is necessary to know that some language and topics will be problematic for some learners. Try to avoid language that is known to be triggering to members of the group and, should whole topics be problematic, where possible offer learners the chance to be absent from that input. During a 2023 reading course, my students were set to cover the topic of earthquakes with the vocabulary from this text being included in an upcoming exam. Considering that the university was in special measures following an earthquake in February 2023, which impacted the families of numerous students and left the whole nation ill at ease, it would have been unfair to ask learners to attend this class. Students were warned that this topic was coming up and that they could be absent, and the vocabulary was provided in an alternative manner. Forcing learners to attend this session would have harmed rather than benefited them.

The last key factor of trauma-informed practice, *culture* (as well as history and gender), links closely to radical inclusivity. This principle asks that we move beyond stereotypes, recognize people as whole and complex and look at ways in which elements of culture and background can be used in the healing process. In our radically inclusive classrooms, this again asks us to accept people as they are not as we perceive them to be.

Teaching Context

Why is a trauma-informed radical approach needed?

Trauma covers a wide range of presentations and circumstances, but as an educator in a worsening social climate, it is vital for me to work in a way that recognizes the background and difficulties learners bring into the classroom. During my time teaching in Türkiye, the sociopolitical climate here has become increasingly conservative and minority communities have less freedom than they previously did. To understand how Türkiye arrived at its present position, and to see why learners arrive in university classrooms with a high affective load, it's necessary to consider the events that have occurred here in recent years.

In 2013, Istanbul witnessed the Gezi Park Uprising, akin to the Occupy movements of the time. The Gezi protests arose in response to plans for urban development in the park and began with a sit-in. Protestors were forcibly removed from the park, later returning to set up a protest camp. The camp was violently cleared two weeks later, but protests continued to rage nationwide. At this point, public anger was no longer about the loss of a park, but about wider environmental concerns, the increasing authoritarian ideas of President Erdoğan (seen through extended controls on alcohol and social debates on public displays of affection), and the nation's involvement in Syria. When the protests were quashed in August 2013 more than 8000 people had been injured by state forces, including up to 22 deaths, and 3000+ people had been arrested (Amnesty International, 2013). The state's response to these protests is seen as a turning point in Türkiye's freedom. Since this time, arrests for insulting the president have become semi-regular and large social gatherings are often prohibited.

A failed military coup in 2016 saw further repression of the people by the state. On the night of 15 July 2016, the Peace at Home Council (*Yurtta Sulh Konseyi*), which included members of Türkiye's judiciary and military, staged a coup to oust President Erdoğan, noting the loss of human rights, democracy, and secularism in Türkiye as their reasons for action. The president called on supporters to rise against this attack on the state; conflict ensued, and the coup ultimately failed. Meanwhile, 300 people had lost their lives and 2000+ were injured. The coup attempt was alleged to have been backed by Islamic scholar Fethullah Gülen, who was already exiled in the USA, having left Türkiye in 1999 for medical treatment and later been tried in absentia for promotion of Islamist ideas in a then secular state. Followers of Gülen worked closely with Erdoğan's Justice and Development party (AKP, *Adalet ve Kalkınm partisi*), with the AKP regime even acquitting Gülen in 2008 when Erdoğan was Prime Minister. However, the two groups parted ways in 2011 and have endured an acrimonious relationship ever since. Following the coup attempt, those seen as connected to Gülen were ousted from their positions. 40,000 detentions were made and 160,000 people lost their jobs including more than 30,000 in the education sector with 1500 of those being deans of university departments (BBC News, 2016). Fifteen universities were dissolved.

The Academics for Peace movement (BAK, Barış için Akedemisyenler) began in 2012 with 200 signatories from 50 universities signing a petition to support Kurdish hunger strikers requesting an improvement in prison conditions and the right to speak in Kurdish at their trials. In 2016 BAK developed another petition against the treatment of Kurds, this time extending to the curtailing of rights of citizens in Eastern Anatolia through the use of curfews and weaponry (Barış için Akedemisyenler, 2016: para. 1). This petition received signatures from over 1200 Turkish academics and more than 300 from overseas, notably including Noam Chomsky and Judith Butler (Kural, 2016: para. 5). The state branded the signatories terrorists and investigations were opened into all the domestic participants (Weaver, 2016: para. 8). Since then, academics have been wary of engaging in politics, yet our students need us more than ever.

All these events sit against an atmosphere of femicide, Kurdish suppression, anti-LGBTQ+ sentiment and an increasing anti-foreigner attitude of both the state and the people. In recent years Turkish residents have lost their freedom and socialization due to emergency measures around the Covid-19 pandemic and the 2023 earthquake. That is to say, people were forced into isolation at home with only digital communication as a means of connection. It is fair to say that students are arriving in classrooms exhausted from spending their developmental years in this environment. With all these events in mind, it seems necessary to me that we employ a trauma-informed practice in our classrooms.

Trauma-informed pedagogy allows for the development of safe spaces in which learners feel upheld and supported. Recognizing that students have unique issues that may provoke certain behaviours or necessitate extra accommodations allows teachers to include learners who might otherwise be excluded.

Within my practice, it is illogical and impossible to separate radical inclusivity and trauma-informed practice. Learners must first feel seen and acknowledged before they can feel truly safe. Thus, the activity detailed below is designed to hand back power to learners. It has been utilized with groups of university students where English is either their second or third language.

Course context

Learners in this program are first-year university students at a private foundation university in Istanbul, Türkiye. All students wishing to enter a university program here, with the exception of some vocational and associate degree courses, must demonstrate at least a CEFR B2 level proficiency in English as mandated by the National Council of Higher Education (YÖK). If students are not able to demonstrate this proficiency upon registration or via the university's own proficiency exam, they are required to undergo an English preparatory course known as *hazarlık*. This course is designed to bring all learners to the B2 level in one academic year.

Students in this programme are mostly 18–22 years old, although some mature students may be present. Often these mature students will be international students who are completing a second degree after relocating to Türkiye. Thus, students have a mix of L1s, making English a *lingua franca* across the cohort.

Within the university, there is currently an even split between international and home students, with some classes consisting entirely of international learners. 2023–2024 enrolment in preparatory English classes at this institution totalled around 3000 students. At this university, students are organized into classes depending on their future major. Considering this, the activities below have been carried out only with students who will enter medical faculties. Classrooms at the university are English-only to create an immersive environment.

Activity

Circles of affirmation

This activity does not come with a set of learning outcomes and is not designed for assessment; the aim is for students to express themselves authentically and build community. If you are working on a particular topic or lexical set, a provision may be included in the procedure to direct students to focus on that theme or utilize that target language. Feedback can be shared in later sessions. As it centers the learners, this practice can be beneficially employed on days when the class seems to be in a slump or has hit a wall of some kind. Using it in these circumstances can give students a feeling of control they may otherwise be lacking. As there is no set outcome for this activity, there is no rubric or marking scheme. The activity is successful if learners have produced some independent ideas and listened to their partners.

This activity is an opportunity for learners to express themselves freely, sharing ideas about themselves or what is important to them. Having a supportive classroom atmosphere is vital for participants to feel safe to do this, as this can be a vulnerable practice. Therefore, it is not recommended that it be used with groups of learners who have newly met. Establishing a general environment of inclusivity first will assist participants to feel safe to make honest disclosures during circle time. For students to have a reasonable number of partners, allow at least 30 minutes for the main activity.

Prior to the activity, allow learners a short time to reflect on what they consider to be their core values (or if limiting the topic, their beliefs related to it). Explain to them that their core values are the beliefs they hold that are of key importance to them and are unshakable. In ELT classrooms with a shared first language the term may be explained to the participants in their L1. If this is not possible, students may translate the term into their own L1s for a better understanding or engage in peer teaching in which the term is explained in L1 by stronger students who have grasped the concept. It is also recommended that the activity leader offers a core value of their own both as a model and to position themself on the same level of vulnerability as the learners thereby reducing the coercive power referred to by hooks (1994: 21).

Procedure:

(1) Clear all furniture to the edges of the room. Ask half the class to stand in a circle in the centre of the room facing out toward the walls; they will not be able to see each other.
(2) Ask the second half of the students to form a circle around the first group, this time facing inwards. Each student should be facing a partner.
(3) Set a time limit of 5 minutes. Instruct the students in the inner circle to share one or two core values with their partner. Once this has been shared, the outer partner shares core values of their own. Partners should not comment on the value their partner shares but should listen openly. They may ask questions to expand their understanding.

Instructors/facilitators should also not interfere in these conversations. However, monitoring for ideas that may need discussion at a later stage is important. If students are not comfortable sharing intimate thoughts, allow them to offer what they can.

(1) Once the time is up, the students in the outer circle rotate one person to the left (clockwise) so that they are facing a different partner.
(2) Give students the same time limit of 5 minutes and instruct them to share their values with their new partner. Again, begin with the inner person.
(3) Repeat this process allowing at least five turns.
(4) Once students have spoken to the allotted number of partners, thank them for their sharing and arrange them into small groups (5–6 people).
(5) In these small groups, learners will share what they have learned about each other. Give learners around 10 minutes to discuss these ideas together.
(6) After the time is up, bring the whole class back together and ask if there is anything that the learners would like to share. At this time, you may also bring up any topics you heard mentioned that you would like to discuss with your students.

In this stage, continue your position of not interfering with the learners' offerings as long as no harm is being caused, e.g. no discriminatory language is being used. Allow students to share freely how they feel about what is happening around them and what is important to them.

Student responses

Students tend to enjoy this activity as it gets them up and out of their chairs and gives them a chance to discuss something other than target language or grammar. Within my lessons, this activity is used after the discussion or introduction of social topics (e.g. homelessness, addiction) in reading or listening lessons. Within the materials that we currently use, gender and gendered behavior are frequent topics which they have a lot to say about. Students like to have the opportunity to express their ideas without being interrupted by an opposing view, although we often discuss some common ideas afterwards as a whole class. As many of the classes I teach are multicultural, we find that we get some conflicting ideas on what the roles of men and women are. This is a good reminder for us all that there are different ways of seeing things and different ways of being. It also allows students to gain insight into the perspectives and practices of other cultures.

While topics such as gender roles are often fun and light-hearted, not all topics leave us so joyful. In response to one particular activity in which they were asked what they would like to change about the country, students suggested among other things 'end honor killings', 'make education and healthcare free', and 'no censorship'. These are factors that speak to the heart of what ails them. They know we cannot speak freely on all topics, even in an open classroom, and they have already learnt at a young age how hard it is to be a woman in this society. In these moments, there is nothing I can say that will bring comfort, but I am able to listen while they share their feelings and make suggestions. Here lies the point of radically accepting people as they are: we create space for hurt to express itself and allow peers to acknowledge their shared feelings and find a way through together.

This idea of censorship is one of the hardest to combat when doing an activity such as this and this is why there must be an atmosphere of trust if difficult topics are to be tackled. While I disagree with the idea of prohibiting topics outright, in a climate such as Türkiye it is necessary to avoid politics at least. Educators facilitating this activity must be mindful of similar issues in their context and judge accordingly what is safe to discuss.

This activity can function as an opportunity for learners to practice their active listening skills and truly hear what their peers are saying. Moving from the exchange of ideas to a discussion allows participants to practice key techniques of active listening such as summarizing and paraphrasing and asking questions to expand the conversation and clarify the ideas being shared. Within discussions, students need to be mindful not to debate the validity of anyone's identity if this is a topic that comes up. Payne (2023) highlights that active listening allows for conflict reduction, greater understanding and enhanced communication. In classrooms where there is discordance among learners, or where minority groups are ostracized, this more harmonious position moves students towards a position of radical inclusivity in which they accept each other however they show up in the classroom, including moving towards acceptance of minority identities.

Alternatives

The statements that participants share in these circles may be affirmations about their self and self-worth, their ideals, or their ideas about society. The choice of subjects can be directed by the teacher or facilitator and related to the topics currently being discussed in the classroom. Affirmations about oneself tie in with discussions on personalities and characteristics of people, and statements about social change can be fitted into sociological themes. Language can also be adjusted to match the level of the learners. If learners are not able to discuss sociopolitical topics, they may focus on sharing ideas about themselves. This is also true in relation to the age of the students; young learners would be better suited to sharing ideas about themselves rather than broader sociological topics. Facilitators should also bear in mind the political climate in which they find themselves. Sadly, there are environments in which discussing political topics may put the students and instructor at risk. In this case, again it is best to stick to having learners affirm ideas about themselves.

Space may also be a concern when carrying out this activity. In this case, students may be lined up in two rows facing each other with one row moving along by one each time and the person at one end moving to join the far end to maintain pairs. If this is still unsuitable, or in the case of a very large class, students may be grouped in small clusters to exchange their affirmations. In this case, it is also possible to do this activity seated as there will be no requirement for learners to change their places. In these small discussion-like groups, your students will have less opportunity to share their ideas, but it will be possible for you to allow more time for the activity so learners can ask further questions of each other. This smaller-scale practice may also be beneficial for students who are reluctant to speak in a whole class environment, as it creates a cosier, and therefore possibly safer environment, in which they can speak to fewer people overall and have the opportunity to hear several other people speak before offering something of themselves.

Expansion

These circles of affirmation are a jumping-off point for further activities. With stronger ELT groups, and/or in reading and writing classrooms, it is possible to extend this activity into text/discourse analysis. Drawing out some of the ideas suggested by the students, (have them) source articles or audio-visual media on the same themes. These materials can be read and discussed with a CLA lens; offer questions such as *What is the author's intention? Who is backing this text? Is this a blanched text?* Once the material has been analysed learners may respond to the piece in writing. This may be a direct response, a critique, or perhaps an article in support of the original media and the style of writing can be matched to the present aims of a class's writing curriculum. Critical analysis can also be applied to the language used by activity participants during the discussions. Students should be encouraged to examine where their ideas come from and how the language they use can impact others and make them feel either welcome or excluded. Here educators can draw upon the trauma-informed principles of *safety* and *peer support* while highlighting the importance of being inclusive and critically aware of language usage.

Moving Forward

If educators are to create safe and welcoming spaces within their classrooms, they must be accepting of all identities and all the baggage that people bring with them on their journeys through life. The application of trauma-informed practices within a radically inclusive context sets out a way for students to be fully embraced and supported in their learning environments.

Radical inclusivity necessitates not only that we examine our structures of power through the application of critical language awareness, but that we also follow the lead set by Freire and hooks and move into a position of transformative pedagogy in which diverse identities are allowed to speak and lead educational content. hooks noted that education is a practice of freedom when the possibility of the classroom is utilized to challenge perceptions and approach things with open hearts and minds, something she asks we demand of ourselves and others (1994: 207). Education is indeed transformative, and those open hearts must extend to creating space and practices that support members of the academy in trauma. Fostering safe spaces in which students and educators can be vulnerable requires us to approach education with a praxis of radical empathy that pulls together trauma-informed practice, critical language awareness and radical inclusivity. It is only then that we can effectively serve our students.

References

Adams, M., Bell, L.A. and Griffin, P. (2007) *Teaching for Diversity and Social Justice*. Routledge.
American Psychological Association. (2018) Trauma. *APA Dictionary of Psychology*. https://dictionary.apa.org/trauma
American Psychological Association. (2020) Trauma. https://www.apa.org/topics/trauma/
Amnesty International. (2013) Gezi Park protests: Brutal denial of the right to peaceful assembly in Turkey. https://www.amnesty.org/en/wp-content/uploads/2021/06/eur440222013en.pdf
Barış için, A. (2016) We will not be a party to this crime! (in English, French, German, Spanish, Arabic, Russian, Greek). https://barisicinakademisyenler.net/node/63

BBC News (2016) Turkey coup: Purge widens to education sector. *BBC*, 19 July. https://www.bbc.com/news/world-europe-36838347

Carello, J. and Butler, L.D. (2015) Practicing what we teach: Trauma-informed educational practice. *Journal of Teaching in Social Work* 35 (3), 262–278.

Coleman, E.S. (2020) Why trauma informed teaching matters. *TESOL Turkey Professional Magazine* 5, 4–6.

Fairclough, N. (ed.) (1992) *Critical Language Awareness*. Routledge.

Freire, P. (1978/1970) *Pedagogy of the Oppressed*. Penguin Books.

hooks, b. (1994) *Teaching to Transgress: Education as the Practice of Freedom*. Routledge.

hooks, b. (2004) *Teaching Community*. Routledge.

Jennings, P.A. (2019) Teaching in a trauma-sensitive classroom: What educators can do to support students. *The American Educator* 43 (2), 12–17.

Kural, B. (2016). Academics: We will not be a party to this crime. *Bianet*, 11 January. https://bianet.org/haber/academics-we-will-not-be-a-party-to-this-crime-170978

Payne, Y. (2023) Active listening: Definition, benefits, techniques & challenges. *IIENSTITU*, 11 March. https://www.iienstitu.com/en/blog/active-listening-definition-benefits-techniques-challenges

Rosa, J. and Flores, N. (2017) Do you hear what I hear? Radicolinguistic ideologies and culturally sustaining pedagogies. In D. Paris and H.S. Alim (eds) *Culturally Sustaining Pedagogies: Teaching and Learning for Justice in a Changing World* (pp. 175–190). Teachers College Press.

Substance Abuse and Mental Health Services Administration (2014) SAMHSA's concept of trauma and guidance for a trauma-informed approach. https://library.samhsa.gov/sites/default/files/sma14-4884.pdf

Van Der Kolk, B. (2015) *The Body Keeps Score*. Penguin Books.

Weaver, M. (2016) Turkey rounds up academics who signed petition denouncing attacks on Kurds. *The Guardian*, 15 January. https://www.theguardian.com/world/2016/jan/15/turkey-rounds-up-academics-who-signed-petition-denouncing-attacks-on-kurds

14 Sparking Critical Awareness of Language Variation, Accent and Ideology through an Allyship Approach

Vance Schaefer and Tamara Warhol

Background

We advocate adding 'radical inclusivity' as an additional R to the traditional 3Rs of reading, (w)riting, and 'rithmetic, making the four Rs a critical part of a person's education. We define radical inclusivity as including the voices and speech styles of all people, particularly those of marginalized groups, in a coalition that reflects the reality of society and thereby, benefits learners in their social interactions, careers, and lives.

Communicative repertoire

If you talk to a man in a language he understands, that goes to his head. If you talk to him in his language, that goes to his heart (paraphrase of Nelson Mandela quote). The same can be said of speakers' various speech styles in a single language. Speakers possess a communicative repertoire of speech styles and select among them (i.e. translanguage) to express identities, relationships, and stances. Speech styles include (im)politeness registers, regional dialects, and sociolects indexing race/ethnicity, gender, LGBTQIA+ sexuality, neurodivergence, and more and may additionally vary by genres (i.e. participating in religion, vocations, etc.).

Knowing the forms of speech styles is part of a speaker's linguistic competence (Chomsky, 1965). Forms include a word's shape (i.e. morphology), the inventory of words (i.e. lexicon), pronunciation (i.e. phonology), how words are put together into phrases (i.e. syntax), and meaning (i.e. semantics). These varying forms may constitute different languages (codes) and/or different speech styles of one language. For example, in standard American English or General American (GA) taught in school, we learn 'aren't' rather than 'ain't', 'between you and me' rather than 'between you and I', or 'library' rather than 'libary'. We also may learn 'the government **is** accountable' rather than 'the government **are** accountable', or 'I don't know anything' rather than 'I don't know nothing'. While English teachers may prescribe these GA forms, the alternative forms may be used in different speech styles: 'ain't' in Southern American Englishes (SAE) or African American (Vernacular) Englishes [AA(V)E], the hypercorrective 'between you and I' when some speakers wish to sound formal or educated, 'libary' in casual speech or dialect, 'the government are' in some British Englishes, and 'I don't know nothing' in casual speech, AA(V)E, or perhaps when wanting to be humorous while speaking GA.

In addition to knowing the forms of speech styles or languages, speakers need to know the functions of speech styles. Knowing the functions of speech styles is part of a speaker's communicative competence (Hymes, 1966). Functions include when, where, to whom, why, and how to use these styles or shift to another speech style. That is, in what situations do we use these speech styles (e.g. formal/informal circumstances) and for what effect do we use them (e.g. solidarity, sarcasm, humor, etc.). Using or shifting among speech styles can reflect the relationships between speakers, the formality of the situation, the speaker's stance, the speaker's identity and willingness to converge or diverge from their interlocutor (i.e. accommodation; Giles, 1973), and more. Consequently, the usage of a particular speech style or switching to another speech style carries social meaning; that is, it is a pragmatic act. Communicative competence requires speakers to use an array of speech styles in order to avoid using inappropriate language with unintentional social consequences (Bardovi-Harlig & Mahan-Taylor, 2003). Speakers need to recognize these potential meanings and the social consequences of not using the socially-expected speech styles.

Standard language ideology

However, language learners, whether first or second language speakers, are expected to learn standard language (e.g. white, middle-class, heteronormative, cisgender speech; Kretschmar, 2004; Wells, 1982), erasing the voices of non-standard, marginalized variant speakers. Yet, everyone uses some form of non-standard language or even full-blown non-standard speech styles at times. In response, an allyship approach is adopted in teaching speech styles and their corresponding accents. An allyship approach as a part of radical inclusivity asserts that each individual speaker needs to learn various speech styles in order to successfully navigate society and their careers, especially as they themselves use an array of speech styles and encounter many speech styles in their daily interactions.

In other words, the reality of society is that diverse people with diverse speech styles exist. We encounter people with various speech styles, including native and non-native ones, in our daily lives. We hear them on TV. We read their books. We work with them. We teach them. We learn from them. We appeal to them in advertisements for products/services, political campaigns, and more. As such, in a modern, multicultural society, speakers need to learn oracy skills beyond the basics of public speaking and covering the communicative repertoire of speech styles. Speakers need to understand the forms and functions of various speech styles, including those of their own. An awareness of a communicative repertoire of speech styles and how these styles might be used as part of communicative competence can benefit learners in more persuasively expressing their ideas and more effectively understanding others.

One crucial aspect of speech styles concerns pronunciation and accent. Pronunciation can play an outsized role in communication and the arts. Stress, rhyme, alliteration, and other phonological features are harnessed in rap music, poetry, prose, speeches, advertising jingles, famous sayings, mnemonic devices, limericks, and more. Different accents are used in product advertising and political campaigns to appeal to different demographics as accents are perhaps the first noticed and/or principal marker of particular speech styles.

Additionally, social expectations may influence our pronunciation such as when we speak compared to when we read or when we read a passage versus a word list, e.g. enunciation, connected speech (Labov, 1972). We are also expected to read a situation and adjust our accent accordingly: We sound different in formal versus informal situations or when we speak to people who we identify as belonging to our social group or not (i.e. same generation, community, ethnicity, cf. convergence; Giles, 1973).

Accents, consequently, carry biases. For example, a white, male, middle-class, heteronormative, cisgender accent may be perceived as accentless in American society. Yet, everyone employs variation in their pronunciation. When our pronunciation does not fit what is expected, for example, using a so-called non-standard pronunciation, people may judge us negatively. Accents like speech styles can build and/or reinforce unequal social hierarchies (Lippi-Green, 2011). There are many communal accents that may be discriminated against: AA(V)E, SAE, neurodivergent, female (uptalk – rising pitch on statements, vocal fry – low crackling voice), LGBTQIA+, speakers with speech disorders (e.g. lisp, stutter), second language speakers of English, and more. The sexual identity of LGBTQIA+ members is often categorized by how listeners expect LGBTQIA voices (e.g. gay men) to sound, e.g. prosody, lisp, voice quality (cf. Sulpizio *et al.*, 2015) and in turn, lesbian-/gay-sounding individuals may be perceived as less competent for leadership roles (Fasoli & Hegarty, 2020). Similarly, accents associated to regions such as Southern American English or to racial/ethnic groups like African American (Vernacular)

English or Chicano English (i.e. English variety which may be spoken by Mexican-Americans and others) are generally recognizable by various phonological features (e.g. prosody, segment quality, voice quality), resulting in discrimination (e.g. telephone calls requesting housing; Purnell *et al.*, 1999). Likewise, the accents of speakers of English as an additional (foreign) language may be viewed negatively (Moyer, 2013). Visual cues may also impact accent perception: A non-white person may be perceived as having a non-standard accent when they do not (Gutiérrez & Amengual, 2016) or a non-native accent – although they do not – which in turn lowers comprehension (e.g. Asian face; Rubin, 1992). Additionally, accent triggers race-based stereotyping (i.e. accents evoke stereotyped physical appearances; Kurinec & Weaver, 2021). Fortunately, experience with different individuals using multiple language styles may mitigate biases (Gutiérrez & Amengual, 2016). Furthermore, learners may not wish to acquire a standard language accent but one that more aligns with their identity, that is to say, their ethnicity, race, and/or with their desire to pass or cross, among other reasons (see Cutler, 2014, for an overview).

In response, critical language awareness (CLA) is key to deconstructing the linguistic features of accent and their current associations to various language ideologies of privilege, power, legitimacy, uniformity (lack of diversity), equity, marginalization, exclusion, discrimination, and more. CLA is a pedagogical approach to language learning that focuses on intersectionality, with the goal of promoting agency, self-reflection, and social justice (Shapiro, 2022). CLA pedagogy encourages students to investigate multilingualism and variation; critically analyze discourse about race, class, gender, sexuality, disability etc., and enact resistance to oppression through their own linguistic choices (Leeman, 2018). As many speakers lack a proficient understanding of the phonological features of accent in English and/or other languages and a weak awareness of accent biases, there is an urgency to implementing a CLA-informed pedagogical framework toward radical inclusivity in language teacher education concerning accents and pronunciation.

As a part of CLA, we advocate an *allyship approach* to radical inclusivity in teaching as everyone has an accent and uses variation in pronunciation and everyone uses several speech styles including marginalized ones. For these reasons, we approach the teaching of language variation on the basis that every speaker has an accent and encounters different speech styles and accents in life and therefore, needs exposure and training concerning various speech styles and accents.

The basic elements of an accent

Accents are composed of many pronunciation elements. To better understand an accent, speakers should know what basic phonological elements may make up an accent.

Segments – Consonants, vowels

Words are composed of consonants and vowels (i.e. segments). Some accents may not feature the same segments: Some may not have the sound /θ/ in 'thin' or /ð/ in 'then' [as represented by the international phonetic alphabet (IPA)]. Indeed, /θ/ in 'thin' in both native or non-native accents of English may be replaced by /t/, /s/, or /f/. Vowels may vary greatly among different accents (General American versus Received Pronunciation versus General Australian; Wells, 1982). Consonants may vary in pronunciation because of where and how the tongue moves, how the vocal folds vibrate (e.g. voiceless /t/ versus voiced /d/ where both are pronounced with tongue tip behind the teeth and stopping and then, perhaps releasing airflow), or if the soft palate/velum is lowered or lifted to create nasal or oral vowels respectively (compare /n/ versus /d/), or for vowels how high-low and forward-backward the tongue is positioned, how tense the tongue muscle is, or if the lips are rounded. Lastly, while the number and/or quality of consonants may vary among Englishes, vowel quality may vary much more widely (Wells, 1982).

Suprasegmentals – Word stress, intonation

Words in English have stress that differentiates 'desert' and 'dessert' where the vowel in an unstressed syllable might be shorter, lower-pitched, quieter, and lax (i.e. centralized to a /ə/, /ɪ/, or /ɛ/) versus in stressed syllables where the vowel is longer, higher-pitched, quieter, and retains its quality (i.e. not centralized unless it already is). Words vary by stress in phrases: content words are more stressed than function words (i.e. grammatical words such as determiners, prepositions, helping verbs, pronouns, etc.) as in *the* dog, *to* school, *am* eating, *it* works where underlined words are function words and less stressed comparatively. This can impact connected speech where functions words might be reduced: *wanna, gonna*. Usually, the last content word in a phrase is the most stressed (i.e. focus word), but stress is used to emphasize words that are not normally stressed in order to convey meaning: **He did it, not me**. Intonation also indicates statements, questions, etc.

Phonotactics

Speech styles may vary by phonotactics (i.e. allowed segmental sequences) where consonant clusters like 'months' or 'tests' may be reduced by cutting some consonants: deleting /θ/ in [mʌns] or final /t/ and /s/ in [tɛs]. Phonotactics may interact with connected speech; for example, final consonants may connect to the beginning of the following word: 'ask her' [æ.skɚ]/[ae.skər].

Phonological processes

Accents may be marked by phonological processes. For example, the /t/ in 'water' may be flapped [ɾ] to sound similar to a [d] in some regional dialects of English, or an /r/ may not be pronounced (i.e. non-rhotic or non-/r/ dialects, e.g. 'car' as [kaː]) or pronounced/inserted in non-rhotic dialects (e.g. linking /r/: four o'clock or intrusive /r/: draw[r]ing).

Rhetorical pronunciation – Intonational paragraphs

Focus words shift position (i.e. not necessarily the last content word in a thought group/phrase): *Today, we'll discuss **politics**. We'll first **overview** politics*. Also, speaking at length (e.g. public speeches) is marked by higher pitch, faster speech rate, and more to indicate new topics (i.e. intonational paragraphs; Wennerstrom, 1998). Moreover, public speaking varies by purpose, audience, identity, and more (e.g. African-American discourse, sermons, political speeches, etc.) and therefore, may feature different accents/phonology, lexicon, syntax, and pragmatics (see Schaefer & Abe, 2020, for an overview of pronunciation training in oral rhetoric).

Other elements

Other elements may interact with accent/pronunciation, marking speakers' accents as socially unexpected, thus, negatively. Some speakers may have speech disorders such as lisping, stuttering, and disfluency among others. Neurodivergent speakers may have flat intonation. Some speakers may use uptalk (or high terminal rising) or vocal fry (lowering voice to lowest register) which may be viewed negatively. There are also other voice modulations associated to particular social groups or attitudes such as a higher pitched, breathy, soft voice (i.e. fundie baby voice) used by some fundamentalist Christian women to show submissiveness and femininity (Bologna, 2024). Paralinguistics (e.g. gestures, body language, facial expressions) may accompany pronunciation: speakers may gesture on word stress or certain emphasized words such as *huuuuge* or *straaaaight*. These gestures or lack of gestures may mark speakers as being different.

Pedagogical framework

To teach about accent/pronunciation and promote CLA, we use an EXposure process pedagogical framework from Schaefer and Warhol (2020; see Table 14.1) and incorporate other teaching techniques. Explicit

Table 14.1 EXposure process (Schaefer & Warhol, 2020: 7)

Step	Activity types
EXplain	Instructor explains forms and functions.
EXamine	Learners study intensive samples, i.e. short examples.
EXperience	Learners read and/or listen to extensive samples for meaning.
EXperiment	Learners practice speech styles by doing activities using these speech styles.
EXplore	Learners discuss speech style issues: discrimination, linguistic profiling, passing, crossing, appropriation, etc.

instruction, discussion and guided exposure are key. Inclusivity is also crucial in learning speech styles and accents, i.e. including various voices etc. (cf. high variability phonetic training; Logan *et al.*, 1991). Given that shifting among speech styles (i.e. styleshifting) is a pragmatic act, we advocate pragmatics-focused task-based language teaching where socially-expected speech styles, including accent/pronunciation, must be used to successfully accomplish particular tasks. Alternatively, if socially-unexpected styles are used, learners discuss why speakers used those particular styles, potential consequences, and social expectations. The objective is to help learners add active and/or receptive speech styles to their current communicative repertoire rather than ask speakers to change or eliminate certain speech styles.

Lastly, instructors might use some of the International Phonetic Alphabet (IPA) to help learners understand pronunciation. Basic IPA knowledge can benefit students in understanding various accents in English and the spelling–pronunciation discrepancy in English and in learning second languages, e.g. Mandarin Chinese, Arabic, French, etc.

Context of the course

The accent lesson presented below is used in graduate courses on teaching language variation or second language (L2) phonology. These two courses are attended by graduate students in the Applied Linguistics and TESOL master's program or Second Language Studies doctoral program at the University of Mississippi. Students are mostly international students from Saudi Arabia, China, Japan, Tanzania, Pakistan, El Salvador and more. They have taught and will continue to teach English as a foreign language in their native country or are currently teaching their native language in the US. Many of the PhD students will teach and/or research second language studies and/or foreign language pedagogy at universities in the US or abroad.

Both courses are 14 weeks with one finals week. The teaching language variation course covers teaching various speech styles (e.g. gender, LGBTQIA+, neurodivergence), their features (e.g. phonology, lexicon, syntax, pragmatics, paralinguistics), and pedagogical approaches/methodology/techniques. The L2 phonology seminar covers phonology basics (e.g. articulatory phonetics, segments, suprasegmentals, phonotactics, phonological processes, generative phonology, optimality theory) and L2 phonology (perception, production, acquisition, encoding). Students apply what they have learned in final projects: (1) teaching particular speech styles or their features in a language of their choice; (2) teaching pronunciation features in a given language; (3) writing a research proposal concerning the L2 phonology of a target language/variant.

Description of class lesson activities

By adding radical inclusivity as an essential fourth R to the 3Rs of education, linguistic variation is introduced into the language classroom to (1) foster communicative competence to more effectively navigate multicultural communities and appeal to different demographics (e.g. advertising, public speaking), (2) harness artistic creativity through multi-variant exposure, and (3) validate learners' identities and empower them in faithfully expressing their multiple voices.

The lesson is implemented under an allyship approach by integrating a coalition of underrepresented varieties (e.g. Southern American English, African American English, LGBTQIA+, neurodivergence, non-native) and their accents into language classrooms. Our targeted learners (e.g. language instructors, both native and second language learners) are located in the American South. Consequently, we target Southern American Englishes (SAEs) and African American (Vernacular) Englishes [AA(V)Es]. Further motivation behind focusing on these two varieties is that they are both marginalized and valorized. On the one hand, traditional education prescribes against using SAE and AA(V)E accents, vocabulary, and syntax. On the other hand, with their large populations and cultural, economic, and political power, these two varieties are as prevalent and influential as many Englishes of entire countries, if not more so. Indeed, AA(V)E appears to influence the English of young speakers who use many AA(V)E words, pronunciation, and grammatical structures, e.g. 'y'all' used by many non-native AA(V)E-speaking or SAE-speaking social media influencers when texting followers.

This lesson jolts instructors into awareness of accent features, their functions, and social issues. The lesson models how language instructors might teach high school or university language students. The lesson rationale is that accents (pronunciation) are likely the most salient feature of speech styles in speaking and rhetoric (intonation, stress, pausing in public speaking; accents appealing to particular demographics). Yet, students are not generally taught the fundamentals of accents. Furthermore, with globalization, native speakers such as American English speakers need to understand non-native and other native accents to more effectively interact with other Americans, new Americans, and non-Americans. Accent training enhances speakers' communication and practical skills needed for academic and professional careers.

Using the Speech Accent Archive (https://accent.gmu.edu), students deconstruct accents by segments (vowels, consonants), suprasegmentals (stress, intonation), phonotactics (allowable consonant clusters), phonological processes (e.g. flapping, assimilation) (cf. Schaefer & Darcy, 2022), voice quality (narrators, characters), and social associations. They rate accents by accentedness (presence/absence), intelligibility (ability to understand meaning), comprehensibility (ease of understanding) (Munro

& Derwing, 1995), pleasantness, trustworthiness, and more (Lambert *et al.*, 1960). They then experience accents by watching TV show/movie scenes where accents are exploited to build character identities, relationships, comic effect, and more. Using an EXposure process (Schaefer & Warhol, 2020), students explain, examine, experience, experiment, and explore diverse accents. They hear accent samples; analyze forms, functions, and styleshifting; compare accents; and dub or perform dialogues in original and different accents. Students explore social nuances and issues. Scaffolding pre-/ongoing-/post-activities include focused explanations, sample accent deconstructions, accent comparisons, and short readings on accent biases.

The following task-support activities prepare students for deconstructing accents: (1) the Stella passage handout (see below) demonstrating how to mark the instructor's reading and their accent, (2) a series of exercises focused on each accent feature, (3) reading Schaefer and Darcy's (2022) chapter to help students analyze accents, and (4) discussing learners' experience perceiving accents, including how their accent is perceived.

Instructor- and self-assessments use rubrics created by the instructor and/or students to guide learning; creating rubrics builds awareness and knowledge. Assessments include task-support exercises: accent markings, impressionistic ratings, short interview transcriptions, guest interview+discussion, IPA transcriptions of short conversations, and more to understand and recognize various accents, including the students' accents, and their features, functions, and biases. We recommend instructors/students score overall work and/or each rubric criterion from 0–3, where 3 = work 70% to 100% fulfilled criterion; 2 = work was done but needs more detail, thought, application of ideas, etc. to fulfill criterion.; 1 = work was done but not relevant; and 0 = no attempt was made to do work.

Rationale behind the lesson

The following rationale motivates the lesson. Accents play a large, noticeable role marking speech styles. In turn, speech styles greatly influence communication. Yet, accents rarely seem to be covered in the classroom. One possible reason may be that the phonological features of accents may not be well understood by instructors. Yet, a basic understanding of accent features is required to help learners more effectively explore CLA. Additionally, instructors may not fully grasp the impact of accent(s) in society and communication. Therefore, to promote CLA among instructors/students of accents, their physical properties, and social impact, we advocate lessons on accents and other linguistic aspects of speech styles (e.g. vocabulary, grammar, pragmatics, paralinguistics – body language, facial expression). Accent lessons are introduced under an allyship approach where students are reminded that (1) everyone has an accent even those who think they speak standard English (i.e. 'I don't have an accent'), (2) a speaker's pronunciation varies at times by situations (i.e. speaking vs reading; reading passages vs word lists, etc.; Labov, 1972), and (3) any accent, including both marginalized (e.g. Southern American English, African American English, second language accents) and 'standard accents' (e.g. General American, Received Pronunciation), may be socially accepted and/or discriminated against. Consequently, our sample lesson covers accent features and social biases.

To clearly guide instructors and students and provide them with tangible goals, learning outcomes include being able to:

(1) identify, mark, describe, and analyze accent features, functions, style-shifting cues/effects;
(2) define, evaluate, and critically discuss standard language ideology (biases) and its impact on accents of General American, other standard Englishes, and marginalized Englishes.

The lesson plan in Table 14.2 follows the EXposure process to deconstruct accents and discuss their social associations. Instructors can modify activities, times, and steps (e.g. cut, re-order, merge, repeat), duplicating lessons for different accents. For American-English speakers, we recommend using General American first as a common reference point and then, to meet the needs of the learners followed by Southern American English, African American (Vernacular) English, or other English varieties such as other regional dialects, (im)politeness registers, and social varieties shaped by ethnicity, gender, sexuality, neurodivergence, socioeconomics, vocation, situation, genre, and more.

Narrative of lesson activity

The instructor leads the class in marking a passage by projecting it on a whiteboard and marking it for various pronunciation features along with the language teachers (LTs). The accent is deconstructed step-by-step by the LTs working in pairs or threes and then, as an entire class, particularly focusing on Southern American English features. Discussion involves a dialogue among LTs giving their impressions, providing feedback from their experience, and asking questions. Going through pronunciation features and asking the instructor questions allows LTs to learn the accent elements and how they differ. Features are compared to General American when discussing accent perception, accent biases, standard language ideology, etc. Discussions can be lively and so, the instructor should encourage LTs to be supportive of one another as they discuss their experiences with accent discrimination (e.g. non-American English accents), general accent biases, and accent intelligibility/comprehensibility issues, including SAE and AA(V)E accents in the local community. Lastly, as current/future research practitioners, LTs have

Table 14.1 Accent lesson under an EXposure process (cf. World Englishes; Schaefer & Darcy, 2022)

Time	Step-by-step procedure
SAE accent features	
5–10 minutes EXamine	LTs (Language Teachers = students) listen to the following passage once or more. *Please call Stella. Ask her to bring these things with her from the store: Six spoons of fresh snow peas, five thick slabs of blue cheese, and maybe a snack for her brother Bob. We also need a small plastic snake and a big toy frog for the kids. She can scoop these things into three red bags, and we will go meet her Wednesday at the train station.* (Weinberger, 2015, https://accent.gmu.edu/)
10–20 minutes EXamine	LTs identify the accent. LTs discuss how and why they can identify the accent, e.g. pronunciation features, past exposure, etc.

20–30 minutes EXamine	LTs look at the passage transcript and hear the passage again in the targeted accent. In this lesson, LTs listen to a Southern American (SAE) accent and compare it to a General American (GA) accent. LTs mark differences with GA. LTs work alone, in pairs, or small groups marking the transcript, and/or the instructor guides LTs in marking a transcript projected onto a whiteboard with a marker. LTs mark a transcript handout provided by the instructor.
	
	– LTs use the International Phonetic Alphabet (IPA) and mark differences in vowel/consonant quality. If they hear the vowel [æ] in 'c**a**n' as [ə], [ɛ], or [ɪ], they write the IPA symbol above/below that vowel. Or if they hear a [d] for [ð] in- '**the**', they write [d] and so on.
	– LTs mark word stress by placing an apostrophe before the (primary) stressed syllable, e.g. ['wɛnz.deɪ] ''**Wednes**day'. In this passage, few words differ in stress location. However, stress varies in word phrases: '**blue** cheese vs blue '**cheese**.
	– LTs mark intonation. Learners write a line that goes up for yes–no questions, lists, or high rising terminal/intonation (i.e. uptalk), or down for a statement or WH-questions.
	– LTs mark phonotactic differences. They mark reduced consonant clusters: 'kids' with lines through the deleted letter: [kɪz] 'ki~~d~~s'
	– LTs mark phonological processes, e.g. [t] or [d] is flapped. For 'meet her' learners write a flap symbol [ɾ] (i.e. a sound similar to [d] as /t/ in 'water' in GA) above 't' as the two words connect sounding like ['mi.ɾɚ]/['mi.ɾər] 'meter'. They mark connected words. For 'ask her' a curved line connects the end of 'ask' and the beginning of 'her'. They mark sounds of adjoining words that may become similar in sound (i.e. assimilation): 'big toy' [bɪk.tɔɪ].
	– LTs mark other features with comments or broad IPA transcription of SAE,
	  • voice quality: drawl (vowel breaking, i.e. diphthongization where two vowels are pronounced in one syllable, making vowels sound longer), twang (nasalization of vowels in the *pin-pen* merger, vowel breaking, and more, potentially giving a nasalized impression by subconsciously focusing on nasals), lilt (intonation)
	  • pin-pen merger: ['wɪnz,deɪ] 'Wednesday'
	  • monophthongization, i.e. two vowels in one syllable become one (long) vowel: [faːv] 'five'
	  • diphthongization (vowel breaking): [spəunz] 'spoons', [tchəɪz] 'cheese', [θəɪŋz] 'things', snack [snæək] 'snack', [kɪədz]/ [kiːdz] 'kids'.
	  • non-rhotic/r-less: [fɔ] 'for'
	  • rhotacized/r-colored vowels: [fɚ.ɚ]/[fər.ər] 'for her'

(*Continued*)

Table 14.1 *(Continued)*

Time	Step-by-step procedure
10–15 minutes EXperience	LTs try to read the passage in SAE, looking at their transcript.
Social aspects of SAE	
15–20 minutes EXperiment EXplore	LTs evaluate a variety of SAE accents for: (1) intelligibility (Can they understand the accent?) (2) comprehensibility (Is it easy to understand the accent?) (3) accentedness (How heavy is the accent, e.g. compared to GA?) (4) impression (listeners' subjective feeling(s) toward the accent, e.g. pleasantness, trustworthiness, etc. LTs discuss their impressions of the dialect. They discuss their image of the speaker, i.e. physically, socially, etc.
10–20 minutes EXplore	LTs discuss why GA or SAE might (not) be used in a variety of situations (e.g. formal, outside the South, etc.). That is, which accent might be more appropriate or welcomed etc. LTs who are GA/SAE native speakers discuss if they shift between accents (e.g. between SAE and GA) and if so, why (to what effect, what social pressure), when, how, what features, etc.
10–20 minutes EXplore	LTs discuss SAE varieties. LTs discuss possible (dis)similarities between SAEs spoken by white and black speakers. LTs discuss (dis)similarities between SAE and AA(V)E, e.g. pronunciation features, usage, effect, biases, etc.
10–20 minutes EXplore	LTs discuss when native speakers of GA or other non-SAE dialects speak SAE, e.g. appropriation, crossing, passing, etc.
10–20 minutes EXperience EXperiment EXplore	LTs discuss SAE usage in media, e.g. commercials, TV shows, movies, etc. LTs discuss why and how SAE may be used and for which products they might (not) use SAE in advertising and then, create a commercial using SAE. LTs watch videos concerning SAE and discuss the content: (1) LTs listen to variations in SAE accents and note phonological differences: https://www.youtube.com/watch?v=mNqY6ftqGq0 (2) LTs watch SAE used by Asian Americans and discuss the reaction of the host and audience: https://www.youtube.com/watch?v=OTLeNzroY8I
10–20 minutes EXperience	LTs hear, watch, and/or read other samples of SAE: country music, TV shows, movies, dialogue in novels, etc.

questions concerning teaching accents to native/non-native learners and offer ideas about what and how to teach accents. In turn, LTs can use this marking activity as a template for their own accent teaching.

Post-activity thoughts, reflections, and/or discussion of challenges

The instructor's own CLA improved based on the LT's reactions, comments, and discussion. The instructor gained insights into LTs' experience with accent perceptions/bias concerning their own accent and other accents. For example, students were frustrated that they had difficulty in understanding university local maintenance or cafeteria workers and Walmart clerks. Additionally, the instructor was surprised that while students seemed to know a lot about literacy (grammar, structure, etc.), they did not know much about oracy (accent features, phrasal stress, rhetorical usage) and tended to focus on segments.

LT's CLA also improved as they learned basic phonology concerning accents, biases, standard language ideology, pronunciation teaching methodology, teaching language variation, and more. Students could mark a sentence with its differing stress levels by word type (function, content, focus) and paragraphs by rhetorical intonation and then, could read the sentences and paragraphs aloud accordingly. Learners gained basic tools to analyze and teach accents and enhance awareness of accent biases. Students could use the IPA to mark different segmental pronunciation (e.g. [wɪf] 'with', [ra:t] 'right', [jɔ:l] 'y'all') and tease out potential biases by correlating intelligibility/comprehensibility scores with impressionistic scores of pleasantness, competency, etc.

Classroom challenges are that students vary in background, knowledge, and experiences: LTs have different levels of understanding phonology and accents and progress at different rates. LTs have different interests in topics, languages, etc. Not all features can be covered, and discussion may be limited. Sometimes LTs have much to discuss or sometimes only a little and so, time for discussion must be adjusted.

Lesson advice includes simplifying explanations and activities for learners who have little to no knowledge of phonology/linguistics and finding accent samples to fit students' backgrounds. More time needs to be devoted to activities on understanding accents and to discussion of LTs' thoughts. Perhaps, only one feature per class period should be discussed slowly and clearly. Indeed, accent explanations and practice might be adapted into a series of lessons to provide more scaffolding in an undergraduate language or international communication course. While we might recommend starting with familiar standards like General American, starting with a marginalized variety like Southern American English or African American English may spur greater interest. More interaction between the instructor and LTs working together on pronunciation teaching approaches/methods/techniques/lessons is likely ideal since the learners are language teachers (LTs). More time might be devoted to LTs sharing teaching ideas and experiences (accents in English, native language etc.; K-12 teaching) and asking questions.

References

Bardovi-Harlig, K. and Mahan-Taylor, R. (2003) Introduction to teaching pragmatics. *English Teaching Forum* 41 (3), 37–39.

Bologna, C. (2024) 'Fundie baby voice' seems to be everywhere now. Here's what you should know. *Huffpost*, 12 March. https://www.huffpost.com/entry/fundie-baby-voice_l_65eb6b2fe4b05ec1ccd9e9b9#

Chomsky, N. (1965) *Aspects of the Theory of Syntax*. MIT Press.

Cutler, C. (2014) Accentedness, 'passing' and crossing. In J. Levis and A. Moyer (eds) *Social Dynamics in Second Language Accent* (pp. 145–168). De Gruyter Mouton.

Fasoli, F. and Hegarty, P. (2020) A leader doesn't sound lesbian!: The impact of sexual orientation vocal cues on heterosexual persons' first impression and hiring decision. *Psychology of Women Quarterly* 44 (2), 234–255. https://doi.org/10.1177/0361684319891168

Giles, H. (1973) Accent mobility: A model and some data. *Anthropological Linguistics* 15 (2), 87–105.

Gutiérrez, M.E. and Amengual, M. (2016) Perceptions of standard and nonstandard language varieties: The influence of ethnicity and heritage language experience. *Heritage Language Journal* 13 (1), 55–79. https://doi.org/10.46538/hlj.13.1.3

Hymes, D. (1966) Two types of linguistic relativity. In W. Bright (ed.) *Sociolinguistics* (pp. 114–158). Mouton.

Kretschmar Jr, W.A. (2004) Standard American English pronunciation. In E.W. Schneider, K. Burridge, B. Kortmann, R. Mesthrie and C. Upton (eds) *A Handbook of Varieties of English Volume 1: Phonology* (pp. 257–269). Mouton de Gruyter.

Kurinec, C.A. and Weaver III, C.A. (2021) 'Sounding Black': Speech stereotypicality activates racial stereotypes and expectations about appearance. *Frontier Psychology* 12, 785283. https://doi.org/10.3389/fpsyg.2021.785283

Labov, W. (1972) Some principles of linguistic methodology. In W. Labov (ed.) *Language in Society* 1 (1), 97–120. https://doi.org/10.1017/S0047404500006576

Lambert, W.E., Hodgson, R.C., Gardner, R.C. and Fillenbaum, S. (1960) Evaluational reactions to spoken languages. *Journal of Abnormal and Social Psychology* 60 (1), 44–51. https://doi.org/10.1037/h0044430

Leeman, J. (2018) Critical language awareness and Spanish as a heritage language: Challenging linguistic subordination of US Latinxs. In K. Potowski (ed.) *Handbook of Spanish as a Minority/Heritage Language* (pp. 345–358). Routledge.

Lippi-Green, R. (2011) *English with an Accent* (2nd edn). Routledge.

Logan, J.S., Lively, S.E. and Pisoni, D.B. (1991) Training Japanese listeners to identify English /r/ and /l/: A first report. *Journal of the Acoustical Society of America* 89 (2), 874–886.

Moyer, A. (2013) *Foreign Accent: The Phenomenon of Non-Native Speech*. Cambridge University Press.

Munro, M.J. and Derwing, T.M. (1995) Foreign accent, comprehensibility, and intelligibility in the speech of second language learners. *Language Learning* 45 (1), 73–97.

Purnell, T., Idsardi, W. and Baugh, J. (1999) Perceptual and phonetic experiments on American English dialect identification. *Journal of Language and Social Psychology* 18 (1), 10–30. https://doi.org/10.1177/0261927X99018001002

Rubin, D.L. (1992) Nonlanguage factors affecting undergraduates' judgments of nonnative English-speaking teaching assistants. *Research in Higher Education* 33 (4), 511–531. https://doi.org/10.1007/BF00973770

Schaefer, V. and Abe, L. (2020) The art of imitation: How to use outlines to teach rhetorical prosody and structure. *English Teaching Forum* 58 (2), 2–13.

Schaefer, V. and Warhol, T. (2020) *There ain't no doubt about it*: Teaching EALs to recognize variation and switch/shift between varieties and registers is crucial to communicative competence. *TESOL Journal* 11 (3), e504. https://doi.org/10.1002/tesj.504

Schaefer, V. and Darcy, I. (2022) Speak locally, listen globally: Training listeners to understand the diverse accents of Englishes around the world. In M.D. Devereaux and C.C. Palmer (eds) *Teaching English Language Variation in the Global Classroom: Models and Lessons from Around the World* (pp. 113–122). Routledge. https://doi.org/10.4324/9781003124665-15

Shapiro, S. (2022) *Cultivating Critical Language Awareness in the Writing Classroom.* Taylor & Francis.

Sulpizio, S., Fasoli, F., Maass A., Paladino M.P., Vespignani, F., Eyssel, F. and Bentler, D. (2015) The sound of voice: Voice-based categorization of speakers' sexual orientation within and across languages. *PLoS ONE* 10 (7), e0128882. https://doi.org/10.1371/journal.pone.0128882

Weinberger, S. (2015) *Speech Accent Archive.* George Mason University. http://accent.gmu.edu

Wells, J.C. (1982) *Accents of English Volume 3: Beyond the British Isles.* Cambridge University Press.

Wennerstrom, A. (1998) Intonation as cohesion in academic discourse: A study of Chinese speakers of English. *Studies in Second Language Acquisition* 20 (1), 1–25.

15 Partnering with Students with Disabilities: Informed Practices and Support Networks

Abir Ward, Carroll Beauvais, Amy Bennett-Zendzian, Jessica Kent and Marie Satya McDonough

Introduction

For several years, faculty in the College of Arts and Sciences Writing Program (WP) at Boston University have been working to strengthen our department's diversity and inclusivity, with deliberate efforts to ensure equitable representation, accessibility, and cultural sensitivity for both students and instructors. These efforts were accelerated by the COVID-19 pandemic, with its urgent need to accommodate students with remote learning, but also predated it, including a 2017 faculty seminar titled 'Disability, Accommodation, and Universal Design'. Our program has embraced alternative assessment practices as well as Critical Language Awareness, emphasizing the importance of understanding how language can challenge power dynamics, ableism and discrimination. In 2022, WP faculty revisited disability and accommodation with another seminar, 'Partnering with Students with Disabilities', and discussed gaps in the system, including the continued pressure of unending labor for instructors, many of whom have disabilities themselves. At the seminar's end, the five of us came together to explore the potential for improving our pedagogical practices and the limitations to accessible pedagogies in higher education. In this chapter, we highlight best practices in inclusivity from the standpoint of 'partnership' with students informed by their – and our – experiences as people with disabilities, both hidden and visible.

The literature in disability studies

The literature in disability studies and inclusive teacher preparation emphasizes the importance of inclusive methodologies and pedagogies within the realm of education. Research on the transformative potential of disability studies in education (DSE) called for integrating DSE into teacher preparation programs to challenge conventional notions of disability and promote social justice (Ashby, 2012; Connor et al., 2008; Danforth & Gabel, 2007). Moreover, the complexities of implementing inclusive pedagogy within exclusionary schooling environments have been thoroughly explored, highlighting the need for teacher preparation programs to navigate these tensions through a DSE framework and targeted training opportunities (Erevelles, 2005, 2011; Freedman & Applebaum, 2019; Gilham & Tompkins, 2016; Lombardi et al., 2013; Naraian, 2021; Naraian & Schlessinger, 2017). In this context, researchers emphasized the cultivation of practical judgment and the disentanglement of disability from medical concepts in schooling practices. For example, Baglieri, Valle, Connor, and Gallagher (2011) challenged conventional understandings of disability within special education by advocating for a more expansive conceptual framework that incorporates broader social, cultural, and historical contexts. By contextualizing disability within larger societal structures, research highlights the importance of resisting static understandings of disability, recognizing the experience of disability in its nuance, and challenging social exclusion processes within education studies (Biklen, 2000; Goodley & Runswick-Cole, 2010; Mori & Orozco, 2021). As a result, the significance of the social model of disability and of anti-oppressive education in promoting equitable pedagogical approaches has taken center stage (Beckett, 2015; Bolt, 2004). Consequently, the need to push disability studies to the forefront of educational conversations has helped expand the research on students with disabilities and provide faculty training programs on inclusive education and disability (Brown, 2014; Carballo et al., 2019; Nusbaum & Steinborn, 2019).

Radical inclusivity in the writing classroom requires conceptualizing disability and accommodation broadly, addressing how trauma and neurodiversity affect learning. Trauma is defined not simply by specific events but by its effects on the brain, triggering physiological responses that hinder learning and cognitive functioning. A significant proportion of individuals, as demonstrated by a 2013 survey on Adverse Childhood Experiences (ACEs), have experienced potentially traumatizing events, highlighting the significance of trauma in educational contexts (see Figure 15.1). Neurodivergence, meanwhile, encompasses variations in cognitive, social, and emotional functioning within the brain, including conditions such as Attention-Deficit/Hyperactivity Disorder (ADHD), autism spectrum disorders (ASD), dyslexia, and anxiety. However, institutional support in the United States often places the burden of proof on learners to demonstrate their inability to access the curriculum due to neurodivergent diagnoses, thereby excluding individuals with undisclosed diagnoses, those who are undiagnosed or whose symptoms don't meet diagnostic criteria, and those lacking access to diagnostic resources (Bellis

> **Expanded List of ACEs**
>
> | | |
> |---|---|
> | Emotional Abuse | Experiencing Discrimination or Racism |
> | Physical Abuse | Witnessing Violence |
> | Sexual Abuse | Living in an Unsafe Neighborhood |
> | Emotional/Physical Neglect | Living in Foster Care |
> | Domestic Violence | Experiencing Bullying |
> | Single Parent Homes Due to Separation/Divorce | Serious Injury/Accident |
> | Substance Abuse in One or Both Parents | School Violence |
> | Incarcerated Parent(s) | Natural Disaster |
> | Parent(s) Suffering from Mental Illness | Forced Displacement |
> | Parent(s) Suffering from Chronic Illness | War/Terrorism/Political Violence |
>
> Sources: Felitti et al. (1998), The Philadelphia Urban ACE Survey (2013), Felter and Ayers (2016)

Figure 15.1 Expanded list of Adverse Childhood Experiences

et al., 2018). Moreover, this approach operates under the deficit model, perceiving differences as weaknesses and intervening accordingly. Shifting toward strength-based interventions and accommodations, such as the Twice Exceptional model, fosters holistic student development by nurturing both weaknesses and strengths. Trauma-informed pedagogy, supported by research on ACEs (Bellis *et al.*, 2018; Rao, 2019), similarly emphasizes creating supportive learning environments that acknowledge and accommodate students' diverse experiences. These inclusive approaches align with the ethos of prioritizing process over product in writing assessment and pedagogy (Luria, 2012; Vygotsky, 1978).

Imagining pedagogy that includes students with diverse learning needs and conditions brings us to the concept of Universal Design (UD), a framework that aligns with creating inclusive environments not just for certain individuals but for all participants in a learning ecosystem. As framed by Dolmage (2017), UD emphasizes designing products and environments to be accessible and usable by the widest range of individuals. UD is characterized by a set of principles that ensure designs are equitable, flexible, simple and intuitive, tolerant of error, and require low physical effort. Just as UD advocates for environments and products designed with the needs of all users in mind, inclusive teaching strategies, such as labor-based grading contracts, collaborative practices, and a focus on belonging, self-care, and communication, aim to create educational experiences that are accessible and equitable for all students. The strategies we present here are aligned with the ethos of UD, as they seek to remove barriers to learning and participation, ensuring that education is designed from the outset to support a diverse range of learners and learning needs.

Using Labor-Based Grading Contracts for Inclusive Assessment

Radical inclusivity asks us to recognize that each student has a unique trajectory, and the most effective grading paradigms allow us to meet them where they are rather than measure them against an ostensibly 'objective' standard. A basic inclusive gesture in our program is the use of a labor-based grading contract in lieu of traditional grading. It is well established that traditional grading does not measure learning in a meaningful way; nor does it increase motivation or the desire to learn (Schinske & Tanner, 2014). Rather, it penalizes disabled and otherwise marginalized students by assuming that all students enter our class from the same starting point and journey through it in the same way. When we level the classroom by removing barriers of class and 'college preparedness', we let our students know that we expect to differentiate for them in support of their best learning.

The grading contract widely adopted in our Writing Program guarantees students a grade of B+ if they are fully engaged in the course: they must attend class without missing more than one week, actively participate in all class activities, complete homework and major assignments on time, and show effort and investment in their work. Grades lower than a B+ occur when students do not meet the minimum contract requirements and are determined in conversation with students; grades higher than B+ reward students for additional contributions to their learning and the community's learning. Carroll (co-author of this chapter) has developed a gamified version of the grading contract in the form of a BINGO card (Figure 15.2). Each student can visually map their journey towards earning the grade they seek while choosing how to

QUICK LOOK AT CORE COMPONENTS W SIMPLIFIED OVERVIEW OF CRITERIA. PLEASE CONSULT ASSIGNMENT SHEETS FOR DETAILS.

B	Topic Proposal	See assignment sheet for details
I	Annotated Bibliography	See assignment sheet for details
N	Positioned Research Paper	See assignment sheet for details
G	Podcast Project	See assignment sheet for details
O	Citizenship, Community, & Compassion + Required Responses	• Regular, consistent, punctual attendance • Regular, consistent engagement in class • Full and equitable participation in your group's collaborative note taking responsibilities • Completion of three required responses
!	Portfolio	• Create portfolio on Digication (if necessary) • Three responses of your choice from the semester • Chosen featured assignment • Final Reflection

If you satisfactorily complete and meet expectations for all tasks on this page, you are guaranteed a B+ in the class.

B I N G O !

Attend an event & write a response	Listen to a podcast & write a response	Compassion Journal x 3	YOUR CHOICE	Extra peer review with writers' salon remarks and peer review worksheet
Visit CAS Writing Center and write a reflection	YOUR CHOICE	Reading & Research Journal x 3	Listen to a podcast & write a response	Attend an event & write a response
Reading & Research Journal x 3	Compassion Journal x 3	Create, maintain, and use a personalized **Tool Kit**	Extra peer review with writers' salon remarks and peer review worksheet	Visit CAS Writing Center and write a reflection
YOUR CHOICE	Reading & Research Journal x 3	Listen to a podcast & write a response	Attend an event & write a response	Compassion Journal x 3
Compassion Journal x 3	Visit CAS Writing Center and write a reflection	YOUR CHOICE	Reading & Research Journal x 3	Listen to a podcast & write a response

If you satisfactorily complete one BINGO on this page, your grade will improve to A-; if you complete two BINGOs, your grade will improve to A.

Figure 15.2 A gamified 'Bingo' grading contract

demonstrate their process and labor (Gameful Pedagogy, 2019). Options encourage forming a writing group or attending local events, expanding the classroom beyond the university walls and into the world. Students may also choose to reflect in video instead of writing and to engage creatively with drawing and other storytelling methods in lieu of creative writing. The 'Your Choice' Bingo spots reward student innovation and initiative, giving students more control over class instruction and creating self-directed learners.

Since students have different capabilities and availability, each of us provides a 'choose your own adventure' approach with many different ways to earn a higher grade, should the student wish to do so. For example, in Jessica's version (see Figure 15.3), 'Community Points' options have different values, from one to ten points; every fifteen Community Points raises a student's final semester grade by 1/3 of a letter grade. If they fulfill the grading contract, that means that they need 30 points to earn an A in the class. If they do not fulfill the contract, they can still use Community Points to raise their grade. The options include more classic academic assignments, like additional chances to practice their close-reading skills or engage with academic sources, as well as creative assignments, like cartooning workshops, and collaborative assignments such as helping absent students catch up with what they missed.

Community Points Opportunities: All assignment sheets are available on Blackboard. Here are the current Community Point assignments (more than 100 potential CPs):

To support you academically		
Opportunity	**Community Points**	**Due Date**
Close Reading B	5	2/1/24
Close Reading C	5	2/6/24
Exhibit Recommendations	2 each	2/8/24
Positionality Statement	3	2/13/24
Periodic Class Reflection	2 each	3/26/24; 4/23/24
Feedback on Feedback	3 each	TBD (approx. 1 week after feedback)
Sketchnotes on a Scholarly Source	3 each	4/2/24
Reflection on Librarians	3 each	Rolling until 4/25/24
Reflection on CAS Writing Center	3 each	Rolling until 4/25/24
Creative Failure Journal	1 each	Rolling until 4/25/24
Class Sketchnotes	1 each	Rolling until 4/25/24
Helping Absent Students	2 each	Rolling until 4/25/24
Final Reflective Letter	5	4/30/24
Top 30% Class Participation	5	N/A

To support you creatively		
Opportunity	**Community Points**	**Due Date**
Style Imitation	3 each	3/21/24
Thanks, Brian Eno	2 each	Rolling until 4/25/24
Lynda Barry Diary Exercise	1 each	Rolling until 4/25/24
Cartooning workshop	2 each	Rolling until 4/25/24
Songs to Draw To	1 per 5 drawings	Rolling until 4/25/24

To support your mental health		
Opportunity	**Community Points**	**Due Date**
Self-Care Journal	1 each	Rolling until 4/25/24

Many of your CP submissions occur on the Flip website, where you will post short videos. If you would prefer not to post videos, send me an email and we will set up an alternative submission process.

Figure 15.3 Community Point opportunities on Jessica's Spring 2024 syllabus

With respect to students and teachers with disabilities, the grading contract creates clear expectations and a reasonable threshold for success: students do not have to push themselves beyond their limit or compete with others to do well. The contract also eschews our often-implicit models of learning as progressing linearly, giving students space to explore and change (or not) at their own pace and in their own manner. This different conception of progress aligns with disability theory's embrace of non-normative 'crip time', and with its critique of models of the person that emphasize improvement and cure (Clare, 2017; Kafer, 2013). For disabled instructors, simplifying the grading process can reduce the emotional and mental strain of writing comments designed to justify grades (as well as tedious grade calculations).

That said, the grading contract is not without difficulties for those seeking a radically inclusive approach to disability. In particular, it tends to reward measures of engagement that are less accessible to students with disabilities: for example, what does the privileging of 'showing up' or being 'fully present' mean for students who are dealing with chronic pain that makes it difficult to come to class, or distracts them while they're there? Does replacing evaluations of the 'quality' of written work with the fact of it having been turned in on time unfairly disadvantage students whose medical needs might make turning work in on time more difficult? How does an emphasis on verbal participation impact students dealing with anxiety disorders, who might feel penalized for their reluctance to speak? Inoue (2023) addresses yet another concern: awarding higher grades for additional labor unfairly excludes students who cannot complete 'extra' work, whether because they need to work outside jobs or because their health prevents them from taking on additional tasks. While we hope that the abundance of choices for additional credit will allow neurodivergent, disabled, and working-class students to find options that will work for them, no system is perfect. Although some students enjoy the autonomy of the system, others can feel overwhelmed by the choices.

We continue to struggle with these questions and to seek ways to make our grading contracts more equitable. Here are some approaches we've tried:

- Marie has turned previously required assignments into additional labor units, so that students can earn an 'A' grade simply by fully completing all of the course's work.
- Jessica's grading contract allows students to request different values for their labor, accounting for the fact that the same assignment may demand a different amount of labor from one student versus another.
- Carroll employs a 'Lightning Round' in the final three weeks of the semester, allowing students to swap and move Bingo spots around to meet the criteria for earning an 'A'.
- Amy's 'time bank' allows students a predetermined amount of extra time (e.g. 24 hours per unit or 72 hours over the semester) to turn work

in late, giving them flexibility in managing their workflow while reducing the burden of responding to requests for extensions for the instructor.
- Instructors can develop policies that allow students to make up missed classes, in-class activities, and workshops. Several of us give Community Points to student volunteers who work with absent students to make up missed activities such as peer review. Amy records her classes; absent students send in a brief report affirming they've viewed it and ask any questions they may have about the material.
- Some pedagogical activities simply cannot be deadline-flexed, such as collaborative in-class activities. However, instructors can implement a 'drop the lowest' policy for these kinds of assignments, or allow additional labor activities to be used to make up assignments for which extensions don't make sense.
- Accommodation options can be made more or less flexible in accordance with an assignment's learning goals: for example, it may be easier to allow an alternative approach to oral or signed presentations in a course whose learning goals do not include oral or signed communication than in one that does.

More holistically, cultivating a classroom environment that feels safe and welcoming of difference can have an outsize impact on students' experience of our course requirements. We strive to keep our students in the learning or growth zone rather than in a panic zone in which their energy goes to managing stress (Vygotsky, 1978). Certainly, one lesson we have learned is that one size does not fit all, and that a dialogical approach in which learning goals and measures of their achievement are coarticulated with individual students best helps them thrive.

Building Classroom Community through Collaborative Practices

As we have detailed above, one of the affordances of labor-based grading contracts is that they can be explicitly designed to promote collaborative learning. Traditional grading systems 'individualize learning by associating the grade or rank with an individual performance', which runs the risk of 'eliding the collaborative nature of all literacy learning, ... ignoring the others in a course who likely collaborated or helped in the learning processes that produced that performance' (Inoue, 2023). In other words, since humans live and work in groups, it only makes sense that we emphasize community care as an essential component of learning. Therefore, in our grading contracts we explicitly include and reward collective care as labor, which may be called 'Class Citizenship' (Amy and Marie); 'Community Points' (Jessica); 'Citizenship, Community, and Compassion' (Carroll); 'Sawa', the Arabic word for together (Abir); or something similar. In this chapter, we refer to this set of practices as

'Community Points' for the sake of consistency. When students help each other out in this way, it increases the class's sense of community and creates a class culture of support rather than competition. We are partners in the learning process, working together to lift each other up.

Carroll facilitates a class climate of belonging informed by the Montessori practice of classroom agreements. Students co-create a Community Contract at the beginning of the semester by applying backwards design and metacognition, reflecting on previous learning experiences – the good, the bad, and the ugly – to brainstorm how they want to *feel* in the classroom. Most of us enjoy showing up when we are happy to see our peers (perhaps share a laugh with them), feel respected, and supported; when our community values our unique perspectives; and when we will not be judged for making mistakes. By collectively prioritizing the top four to five desired feelings, students work backwards to develop actions that they agree are necessary to maintaining these feelings and a community of belonging. For example, it's quite difficult to build a community of trust when no one shows up for class or no one shares their ideas or calls each other by name. Students self-assess and reflect on how they and their collective classmates are upholding their Community Contract throughout the semester.

In Amy's class, one way of earning Community Points is by going above and beyond base requirements on a semester-long collaborative class resource, specifically collaborative class notes (similar practices may include collaborative annotating and class wikis). Amy's practice was born of necessity when she had to teach remotely during pandemic lockdown: she began using Google docs, located on a shared class Google drive, as substitute whiteboards, allowing her to share her own notes, slides, and boardwork. She used them as a place for students to record notes during their small-group conversations in Zoom breakout rooms before reporting back to the class. She also incorporated knowledge-activating prompts such as 'What do you already know about writing effective introductions?' or 'Please type a discussion question for the reading today'. Given how effective this approach was in starting conversations and keeping everyone participating – including students who do have things to say but don't find it easy to speak up in front of a class – Amy continued this practice when in-person teaching resumed. Amy, Marie, and Carroll make the shared documents a foundational feature of their classes, and have set up a formal system of student responsibility for collaborative notetaking.

Here's how the collaborative notes work:

- At the start of the semester, students are put in teams that are 'on point' for notetaking in a designated shared document on particular days/weeks during the semester.
- Group members form a plan for how they will divide responsibilities during their assigned week(s).

- The instructor may paste in lecture notes, discussion prompts, links, slides, materials, images etc.
- During class, students can be asked to type responses to prompts in the notes document; it can also be used for record-keeping and reporting back during small-group work.
- All students are encouraged to contribute notes at any time, not just when assigned; contributions may be asynchronous with the class, and students may add notes in whatever form they prefer to take them, such as phone pictures of handwritten notes.

Of course the notes help students who miss class to catch up, but their usefulness extends beyond that. Some students love taking notes and are good at it, while others struggle or are unpracticed, so they benefit from sharing the task and from seeing what other students do. Shy or anxious students can contribute during class by typing in the document without speaking aloud. To broaden the inclusivity of this practice, consideration is warranted for multilingual and neurodiverse students, who are more likely to find notetaking a challenge on top of listening and processing. Allowing teams to divide notetaking responsibilities among themselves in accordance with their strengths can alleviate this issue. In another practice that lessens the burden on students by scaffolding notetaking skills, Amy and Abir seed the documents with lecture notes and material ahead of time, so that students may 'fill in the blanks'. Whether the seeded material is minimal or more extensive, it frees notetakers from feeling the responsibility of trying to transcribe everything the instructor says, and gives them something to build on.

In collaborative notetaking, radical inclusivity opens up UD to center the accommodation as a shared practice accessible to everyone. Amy reports that since she implemented this system, her students frequently mention their use of the collaborative notes in surveys and course evaluations, saying they often refer back to the notes even when they were present in class, especially while writing essays; many also describe being more focused and attentive in class when serving as notetakers. The notes need not be graded; our experience is that when classes are set up to reward additional labor efforts that benefit other students in the class, the quality of the final product is higher than might be expected for an ungraded task. Additional labor clauses in the grading contract can incentivize this and other types of classroom collaboration: students can volunteer to sub for assigned notetakers who are out sick; they can elaborate on the existing notes, collate and clean them up, or revise them for clarity, in order to earn Community Points. These efforts improve the usefulness of this shared resource, and what's more, it gives students a writing task where the instructor is not their primary audience, and where the goal is to *help others* understand the material. As we know, helping others learn improves the quality of one's own learning.

Fostering Belonging, Self-Care, and Communication

Under radical inclusion, belonging must encompass more than providing space for 'special needs', acknowledging that each learner contains multiple identities (Shapiro, 2020). Before students can be expected to embrace risk-taking in their processes, the classroom climate must be one of safety and belonging. Practices like contract grading and collaborative activities are one step in designing such a classroom climate, which is essential to building the skills of intrinsic motivation that process-oriented pedagogy fosters (Deci & Ryan, 2008).

In Carroll's classroom, one key practice for fostering a richer paradigm of belonging is the Open Needs Statement ('Compassionate teaching', n.d.). As shown in Figure 15.4, the Open Needs Statement invites students to bring their whole selves to the classroom, acknowledging life challenges that could impede learning and access to the curriculum. An Open Needs Statement is a great equalizer, releasing the burden of navigating systems to prove the need for accommodations and providing a pathway for partnership between the student and instructor to co-create a meaningful and accessible learning experience. Acknowledging that challenges, weaknesses, and strengths can exist without official diagnoses gives students the permission to advocate for their needs, also opening the door for first-generation students and non-native English speakers to advocate for accessibility with the professor. It's important to note here that the Open Needs Statement holds power only if we as instructors refer back to it throughout the semester and when students reach out to us for support. To make the Open Needs Statement meaningful, we must consider how to mitigate mere empty signaling and bring the action to (and elicit the action from) our students. Carroll asks students to directly share, either through a writing assignment or Google form, how she can best support them in achieving their goals and best work in the class at the start and

---

Open Needs Statement

Any students with circumstances they believe affects their ability to succeed in this course (e.g. difficulty affording food and/or accessing safe housing, mental health issues, sexual assault, reproductive healthcare, etc.) are encouraged to contact Boston University's office of Student Wellbeing, located at 930 Commonwealth Ave., Suite 1012. You may also use their website (https://www.bu.edu/studentwellbeing/find-wellbeing-resources/?dimensions=core-needs) for quick access to available services. If you feel comfortable, you may also notify me of challenges so that I can best support you in the classroom and assist you in locating the resources you need.

You may also find a longer list of student-centered resources and offices on campus (including but not limited to Student Wellbeing) at https://www.bu.edu/wpnet/files/2023/07/RESOURCES-1.pdf.

Figure 15.4 Open Needs Statement

middle of semester, directly referencing the Open Needs Statement. Engaging in dialogue about the Open Needs Statement in student conferences and assessments can also help instructors get a sense for who may need more pointed support but is reluctant to ask.

We also create alternative labor opportunities that center student wellbeing and self-regulation rather than the course's content, a practice that supports the student as a whole person. For example, Jessica's Self-Care Journal assignment (Figure 15.5) was born during the frantic weeks after Boston University switched to fully remote learning in March 2020. Their students (and colleagues) were barely hanging on, and Jessica wanted to give students a way to shift the conversation away from their immediate fears and toward plans for self-care. Today, the assignment continues to be one of the most popular Community Points choices among students; Jessica estimates that over the last nine semesters, about half of their students have chosen to complete it.

As shown in Figure 15.5, students post one video per week. The more videos they post, the more Community Points they earn. In each 3–5-minute video, they respond to these questions: What challenges are you facing this week (feel free to be vague about this if the topics are private)? How is your stress level? What are you currently doing for self-care (if anything)? What positive changes could you make to your self-care routine?

In end-of-semester reflections, students say that this exercise was very helpful to them and led to better habits, including the self-care basics of drinking water, sleeping, eating regular meals, taking their medications, and leaving their dorm rooms (though some students continually struggle with the basics). Some of them choose to continue posting videos after the semester ends, even though Jessica is no longer checking them. Some students have noted that they watch one another's videos and feel comforted to know they are not alone in their worries and stress. Crucially, the videos also help the instructor know whether an individual student might need accommodations and whether the entire student community is overwhelmed during a particular week. Sometimes Jessica has changed the modality of their teaching (from a lecture to something more hands-on, for example) as a result of watching the videos and realizing that students are unlikely to retain the lesson at that time. In this simple assignment, students reflect on practical changes they can make in the upcoming week to take care of their allostatic systems, build skills at self-regulating, and hopefully create a new habit of checking in and centering basic self-care within (a sometimes dehumanizing) academic culture.

Many students write about the difficulty of expressing compassion for themselves in the same way they do for others. Creating an opportunity for students to have this realization on their own terms, whether they know it or not, sows the seeds for reckoning with internalized ableism. Student evaluations state that this practice taught them not just about

Purpose:

This Community Points assignment is a metacognitive exercise that asks you to check in and reflect periodically about your self-care routine, or lack thereof. Hopefully it will help you pay attention to your needs so that you can take good care of yourself this semester.

Assignment:

On Flip, post at least three 3–5-minute videos in which you respond to the prompts on self-care. The more weeks you post a video, the more CPs you will earn.

What counts as self-care? Here are some ideas:

Physical:	sports, exercise, eat nutritional food, eat enough food, drink enough water, sleep enough (7-9 hours a night), sleep consistent hours, maintain good hygiene, maintain a clean living space, take medication as prescribed, avoid drugs and alcohol, take a bath, ground yourself with smells/tastes/textures, pet an animal
Social/Emotional:	build community at BU, go to therapy, check in with family and friends, set boundaries, find an emotional outlet, take the time you need to be alone, participate in clubs, listen to music, participate in your spiritual practice or community, end toxic relationships
Intellectual:	listen to a podcast, learn a new skill or hobby, go to a museum, read a book you enjoy, watch a documentary, do some creative writing, meditate, do a puzzle, make music, take a social media break, reflect on your most important values

This is just a start – part of the goal is to figure out what forms of self-care will work for you!

Process:

1. On our class Flip page, see the prompt under the "CP: Self-Care Journal" assignment.

2. Post 3–5-minute videos (each on a different week) responding to the following questions:

    - What challenges are you facing this week? (feel free to be vague about this if the topics are private)
    - How is your stress level?
    - What are you already doing this week for self-care (if anything)?
    - What positive changes could you make to your self-care routine?

How to earn points for CP assignment "Self-Care Journal":
- ☐ Each video is 3-5 minutes
- ☐ Each video is posted on a different week of the semester
- ☐ Videos respond to the four questions above

Figure 15.5 Self-Care Journal assignment sheet

writing, but also about bringing mindfulness into how they conduct their lives. In Carroll's class, intentional reflection and feedback are key to fostering a supportive learning environment. Students participate in 'Community Check-ins' to assess how well they are upholding their Community Contract, allowing Carroll to provide constructive feedback. This kind of open dialogue promotes a judgment-free, inclusive classroom atmosphere. Instructors also engage in self-assessment by collecting anonymous feedback from students on curriculum accessibility and instructional methods, collaborating with them to make adjustments. This approach models leadership based on vulnerability and accountability, enhancing trust and authenticity in the classroom.

We cannot assume achievement alone will give us insight into our students' learning profiles and abilities. The more opportunities for ownership we can provide, the more students feel they are valued, respected, and belong. The more choices we provide, the more our students experience control over how they engage in the content and meet objectives, while learning to listen to their own internal intelligence about how they best learn.

Concluding Reflections

In conclusion, our journey towards 'Partnering with Students with Disabilities' has been an eye-opening and transformative experience. Through collaborative exploration and meaningful dialogue, we have delved into the complexities of disability, accommodation, and inclusive pedagogy within the realm of higher education. This exploration brought forth the critical need to center both the voices and experiences of students with disabilities and our own experiences as instructors, whether our disabilities are visible or hidden. This commitment has led us to embrace several key strategies that enhance our pedagogical approaches and ensure an inclusive learning environment. Firstly, we have focused on using labor-based grading contracts for inclusive assessment – a method that prioritizes effort and growth over traditional metrics. This approach seeks to level the academic playing field and acknowledge the unique contributions of each student, thereby promoting equity. Secondly, building classroom community through collaborative practices has helped us design activities and assignments that encourage students to work together, share their diverse perspectives, and learn from one another. Such practices not only enhance learning outcomes but also foster a sense of belonging and mutual respect among students. Lastly, creating a supportive and welcoming classroom atmosphere helped us recognize the importance of ensuring students feel seen and valued, encouraging open communication, and promoting self-care and well-being within the academic environment. However, despite these focused efforts, we acknowledge the presence of challenges and systemic gaps, including ableist practices and the undue burden placed on instructors. Moving forward, we are dedicated to continuous reflection, adaptation, and advocacy to ensure that our pedagogical practices remain responsive, equitable, and supportive of all students, regardless of their abilities or backgrounds. Through our collective efforts, we aspire to cultivate a culture of partnership and empowerment, serving as a model for the university, where students with disabilities are not only accommodated but are actively engaged as valued members of our academic community. This vision drives us to push beyond existing boundaries and work towards a truly inclusive educational experience for every student.

References

Ashby, C. (2012) Disability studies and inclusive teacher preparation: A socially just path for teacher education. *Remedial and Special Education* 33 (2), 89–99. https://doi.org/10.1177/154079691203700204

Baglieri, S., Valle, J.W., Connor, D.J. and Gallagher, D.J. (2011) Disability studies in education: The need for a plurality of perspectives on disability. *Remedial and Special Education* 32 (4), 267–278. https://doi.org/10.1177/016146811111301001

Beckett, A. (2015) Anti-oppressive pedagogy and disability: Possibilities and challenges. *Ethnic and Racial Studies* 38 (13), 2341–2357. https://doi.org/10.1080/15017419.2013.835278

Bellis, M.A., Hughes, K., Ford, K., Hardcastle, K.A., Sharp, C.A., Wood, S. and Davies, A. (2018) Adverse childhood experiences and sources of childhood resilience: a retrospective study of their combined relationships with child health and educational attendance. *BMC Public Health* 18 (1), 1–12.

Biklen, D. (2000) Constructing inclusion: Lessons from critical, disability narratives. *Teachers College Record* 102 (2), 296–319. https://doi.org/10.1080/13603110050168032

Bolt, D. (2004) Disability and the rhetoric of inclusive higher education. *Discourse: Studies in the Cultural Politics of Education* 25 (1), 1–16. https://doi.org/10.1080/0309877042000298849

Brown, A.M.B. (2014) Situating disability within comparative education: A review of the literature. *Comparative Education Review* 58 (3), 492–515. https://files.eric.ed.gov/fulltext/EJ1055222.pdf

Carballo, R., Morgado, B. and Cortés-Vega, M. (2019) Transforming faculty conceptions of disability and inclusive education through a training programme. *International Journal of Inclusive Education* 23 (2), 194–209. https://doi.org/10.1080/13603116.2019.1579874

Clare, E. (2017) *Brilliant Imperfection: Grappling with Cure*. Duke University Press.

Compassionate teaching (n.d.) Academy for Teaching and Learning, Baylor University. https://atl.web.baylor.edu/guides/considering-students/compassionate-teaching

Connor, D., Gabel, S.L., Gallagher, D. and Morton, M. (2008) Disability studies and inclusive education: Implications for theory, research, and practice. *International Journal of Inclusive Education* 12 (5–6), 593–603. https://doi.org/10.1080/13603110802377482

Danforth, S. and Gabel, S.L. (2007) Vital questions facing disability studies in education. *Educational Philosophy and Theory* 39 (4), 384–396. https://doi.org/10.1111/j.1469-5812.2007.00315.x

Deci, E.L. and Ryan, R.M. (2008) Self-determination theory: A macrotheory of human motivation, development, and health. *Canadian Psychology/Psychologie canadienne* 49 (3), 182–185. https://doi.org/10.1037/a0012801

Dolmage, J.T. (2017) Universal design. In J.T. Dolamage (ed.) *Academic Ableism: Disability and Higher Education* (pp. 115–152). University of Michigan Press. http://www.jstor.org/stable/j.ctvr33d50.7

Erevelles, N. (2005) Understanding curriculum as normalizing text: Disability studies meet curriculum theory. *Journal of Curriculum Studies* 37 (4), 421–449. https://doi.org/10.1080/0022027032000276970

Erevelles, N. (2011) Disability and difference in global contexts: Enabling a transformative body politic. *British Journal of Sociology of Education* 32 (5), 699–710. https://doi.org/10.5860/choice.49-5982

Freedman, J.E. and Applebaum, A. (2019) Integrating disability studies pedagogy in teacher education. *Teacher Education and Special Education* 42 (1), 35–50.

Felitti, V.J., Anda, R.F., Nordenberg, D., Williamson, D.F., Spitz, A.M., Edwards, V., Koss, M.P. and Marks, J.S. (1998) Relationship of childhood abuse and household dysfunction to many of the leading causes of death in adults: The Adverse Childhood Experiences (ACE) study. *American Journal of Preventative Medicine* 14 (4), 245–258. https://doi.org/10.1016/S0749-3797(98)00017-8

Felter, J. and Ayers, L. (2016) *Incorporating Trauma Informed Practice and ACEs into Professional Curricula – A Toolkit*. Philadelphia ACE Task Force Workforce Development Workgroup. philadelphiaACEs.org

Gameful Pedagogy (2019) What is Gameful? https://www.gamefulpedagogy.com/what-is-gameful/

Gilham, C.M. and Tompkins, J. (2016) Inclusion reconceptualized: Pre-service teacher education and disability studies in education. *Canadian Journal of Education/Revue canadienne de l'éducation* 39 (4), 1–25. https://www.jstor.org/stable/10.2307/canajeducrevucan.39.4.08?seq=1&cid=pdf-reference#references_tab_contents

Goodley, D. and Runswick-Cole, K. (2010) Len Barton, inclusion and critical disability studies: Theorising disabled childhoods. *International Studies in Sociology of Education* 20 (4), 297–313. https://doi.org/10.1080/09620214.2010.530851

Inoue, A.B. (2023) *Cripping Labor-Based Grading for More Equity in Literacy Courses*. The WAC Clearinghouse, University Press of Colorado. https://doi.org/10.37514/PRA-B.2023.2203

Kafer, A. (2013) *Feminist, Queer, Crip*. Indiana University Press. https://www.jstor.org/stable/j.ctt16gz79x

Lombardi, A.R., Murray, C. and Dallas, B. (2013) University faculty attitudes toward disability and inclusive instruction: Comparing two institutions. *Journal of Postsecondary Education and Disability* 26 (3), 229–246.

Luria, A.R. (2012) *Higher Cortical Functions in Man*. Springer Science & Business Media.

Mori, A.A. and Orozco, I. (2021) Health sciences and inclusive pedagogy: A qualitative study exploring educational practices for students with disabilities at Spanish universities. *Health Education Research* 36 (2), 111–123. https://doi.org/10.1093/her/cyab017

Naraian, S. (2021) Making inclusion matter: Critical disability studies and teacher education. *Journal of Curriculum Studies* 53 (3), 381–398. https://doi.org/10.1080/00220272.2021.1882579

Naraian, S. and Schlessinger, S. (2017) When theory meets the 'reality of reality': Reviewing the sufficiency of the social model of disability as a foundation for teacher preparation for inclusive education. *Disability Studies Quarterly* 44 (1), 81–100.

Nusbaum, E.A. and Steinborn, M.L. (2019) A 'visibilizing' project: 'Seeing' the ontological erasure of disability in teacher education and social studies curricula. *Disability Studies Quarterly* 39 (4).

Public Health Management Corporation (2013) Findings from the Philadelphia Urban ACE Survey. philadelphiaACEs.org

Rao, K. (2019) Instructional design with UDL: Assessing learner variability in college courses. In S. Braken and K. Novak (eds) *Transforming Higher Education Through*

Universal Design for Learning (pp. 115–130). Routledge. http://doi.org.ezproxy.bu.edu/10.4324/9781351132077

Schinske, J. and Tanner, K. (2014) Teaching more by grading less (or differently). *CBE – Life Sciences Education* 13 (2), 159–166.

Shapiro, S. (2020) Inclusive pedagogy in the academic writing classroom: Cultivating communities of belonging. *Journal of Academic Writing* 10 (1), 154–164. https://doi.org/10.18552/joaw.v10i1.607

Vygotsky, L.S. (1978) *Mind in Society: The Development of Higher Psychological Processes*. Harvard University Press.

Afterword: Moving Forward with Shared Understanding and Responsibility

Gloria Park, Quanisha Charles, Shannon Tanghe and Marie Webb

As we near the completion of this edited collection, our hearts are full, yet the result of the 2024 US Presidential election continues to polarize our humanity. Our work, as represented here, is critical at this time and in the years to come in US history, and we hope to push forward with combatting all the hatred toward humanity such as racism, sexism, homophobia, ableism, and anti-immigration rhetoric, just to name a few. As language and writing educators, we have a social and ethical responsibility to focus on what matters in the lives of ALL people, but especially those who are marginalized by the global issues manifesting in our daily lives. Individuals from these marginalized and minoritized communities enter our classrooms every single day, and we hope that our edited collection can bring a ray of justice and equity for those who choose to learn with each of the contributing authors and editors of this volume. The purpose of this Moving Forward section is to offer both reflective and reflexive narratives on completing this edited volume, and to conclude with a set of questions that remain as we continue to uphold the framework of radical inclusivity.

Gloria's Learning by Doing Practices

I am forever indebted to the contributing chapter authors of this collection. I have learned so much from engaging in their chapters – not only in terms of the scholarship that anchors their practice, but the detailed intricacies of their pedagogy enacted in their classrooms/communities with their students as the central focus. Given the limited space of this edited collection and being mindful of being inclusive of all facets of teaching and learning, I am grateful to have chapters focusing on preparing writers all the way to challenging the institutional and programmatic barriers that create divisions in our educational landscape. Depending on what we teach and where we teach, the next four years will be tough because we have to continue to fight for who we are, who our students are and what we stand for as educators. My own imposter syndrome and vulnerability surface at times when my students and my colleagues need me the most. However, if I did not embrace these as part of my reflexivity practice, I may not be able to fully engage in humility and compassion that is at the core of what we do as educators. I will continue to learn from and with my students and colleagues from all walks of the educational and professional landscape. For me, learning will never cease no matter where I am and how long I have been in my field. I conclude with some questions that we all should tackle together:

- How does the concept and practice of radical inclusivity shift with the current climate? What do we as educators hope for during this time? How do we continue to engage in reflective and reflexive practices when times are tough and resources are meager?

Quanisha's Equity-Minded and Justice-Driven Practices

Reflecting on the chapters within the book is an important reminder that embodying radical inclusivity is a multifaceted approach and a universal endeavor that is equity-minded and justice-driven. Our contributing authors have nicely evinced myriad ways to practice antiracism, support trauma-informed pedagogy, embrace social-emotional learning, and engage translingual perspectives in the classroom, all via critical language awareness. I would be remiss to overlook that practicing radical inclusivity, while significant, does not need to be taken on alone or all at once. For practitioners seeking ways to embody such an approach, please practice with care, kindness, patience, and if possible, through collaborative spaces. Scaffold activities and maintain reflective journals that remind you to choose which battle you are ready to overcome in the classroom. Similarly, extend similar grace to your students. Consider labor-based grading contracts for inclusive assessments (Ward *et al.*, Chapter 15) as alternatives for students who struggle with standards and fitting into models. Co-create content with students and share ways in which pedagogical approaches and ways of learning are equity-minded and justice-driven. Reward along the way, whether it is through writing retreats or classroom writing workshops, and take time to celebrate small wins while acknowledging big outcomes. Remember that going beyond inclusion is a continuum that challenges us to seek exclusion, inequity, and injustice, and work towards a better world. Concepts of a better world will look different to everyone, but radical inclusivity envisages trust, safety, and hope that sustains and benefits all. Thus, I pose the following questions to conceptualize such a world:

- How can we be ethically and responsibly radically inclusive? What might effective radical inclusivity entail in techno-culture or in digital spaces that are AI-influenced?

Shannon's Collaborative and Inclusive Practices

Collaborating with the co-editors and co-authors of this book has felt like a true embodiment of radical inclusivity. Beyond just 'talking the talk', it is inspiring to read about the impactful work everyone is doing. Throughout this process, I have been impacted by the commitment and creativity of authors throughout the world who are actively cultivating radical inclusivity in their contexts. While the world continues to evolve, I find hope in each of the dedicated educators who have so willingly shared their radically inclusive practices. As I reflect on this book, I am reminded of Jennifer Gonzalez's 'marigold effect' (https://www.cultofpedagogy.com/marigolds/). This effect builds on the gardeners' secret of companion planting – growing certain plants near each other knowing those plants are mutually beneficial and will enhance growth for all surrounding plants. The marigolds protect neighboring plants from pests and weeds, helping them to grow strong and healthy, supported by the strength and encouragement of the marigold. I see all the contributing authors as a powerful field of marigolds–surrounding, supporting and encouraging, strengthening classrooms around the world. In their unique contexts, each author has planted seeds of change, nurtured these seedling ideas with care and patience, carefully tended to them, and watched them grow. Now, as the winds of collaboration blow, the seeds are being spread and carried to new environments, where they will take root and grow and flourish in new places. As these new seedlings take root, they will change as they adapt, evolve and grow into new, unique hybrids that flourish in new environments. These new seedlings will strengthen and become the new generation of marigolds that will also continue to evolve, grow and spread, continuing the cycle of radical inclusivity. Though, like any gardener knows (and my not-so-green thumb can certainly attest to), there will be challenges. There may be droughts, floods, rocky soil and cold winter days that hinder growth and development. However, by committing to radical inclusivity, together, we can navigate challenges and build a more inclusive community. With this spirit, we will continue to progress, both as individuals and as a collective radically inclusive community. As I think about this, I continue to reflect on this question:

- Specifically, what promotes the ongoing spread and nourishment of radically inclusive practices from teachers to students and throughout communities? How do we collaborate and share these ideas?

Marie's Call to Social Justice Language Instruction

I am proud to see the authors of this book advocating for teaching about language and writing from a social justice perspective. As demonstrated throughout each chapter of our work, many of us in the Global North see a continued need for educating our students and colleagues about critical language awareness. While global relevance of this topic may not seem interesting to some, I see our collection as an important work that recognizes the fact that language is at the root of all social power dynamics. Our students at all levels of language acquisition and educational backgrounds can and should be involved in the return to critical discussions of language use and usage as a basis for enacting and creating new social justice orientations and dispositions. Many of our students are as passionate as we are about understanding and learning the histories and emerging uses of social justice language and terminologies. New words and movements often occur rapidly and our students (alongside with us) are struggling to make sense of the limitations and power of such terminologies. Take the popularization of the word BIPOC in the news during the COVID pandemic as an example. While my American students may be more familiar with the term, my international students in the United States often have extremely limited cultural and historical knowledge about the acronym. While some readers may not see the relevance of teaching may not see the relevance of teaching social justice language within their immediate contexts, I urge them to consider the positive impacts that such learning can bring to English learners around the world. English holds significance as a *lingua franca*, therefore English can be our vehicle for global peace and social justice initiatives. While many of the contributing authors of this book have learned to engage in decolonized teaching practices by trial and error, I feel we all hold the belief that it is our shared duty to support one another in our endeavors to infuse our teaching with critical exploration of social justice language and peace education. In my own experiences, my students have expressed their appreciation of my efforts to acknowledge the inherent power dynamics at play with language as they learn to critically explore them. I have learned to become more vulnerable with my students about my racial and linguistic background, as a vehicle to build connection and shared belonging in my classroom spaces. I feel I have found and co-created a community with my students and the authors of this book. I no longer feel alone in my endeavors. Therefore I urge all readers to consider the following question and to return and unpack it throughout our lifetimes:

- As language users, how can we *all* return to our most basic experiences and recollections of language learning to draw upon our roots as a method of (re)transforming our relationships with linguistic justice and radically inclusive practices, and how can we do more to emphasize the importance of this individual and collective work?

Index

accent, 29, 55, 84, 93, 94, 119, 120, 181–195
access, xiv–xvii, 8, 59, 84, 112, 125, 134, 136, 137, 155, 158, 165, 196–198, 201, 204, 205, 208
advocacy, xv, xvii, xxiii, 21, 23, 30, 52, 112, 141, 149–151, 205, 209
affect, 76, 133, 176
African American literature, 140
agency, xiv, xvii, xxii, 3, 6, 30, 46, 52, 54, 72, 86, 87, 93, 111, 136, 145, 150, 184
Allyship Approach, 181–184, 188
andragogical, 136–138, 143
anti-racist pedagogy, 41, 46
asset, xv, xvii, xxiii, 35, 52, 94, 98, 99, 101, 105, 112

belonging, xxiii, 84, 85, 97, 112, 121, 149, 183, 198, 203, 205, 208, 215
bias, 37, 40, 44, 68, 75, 80, 82, 102, 111, 113, 169, 183, 184, 189–193

cartoons, 59–62, 66, 67, 200
class project, 114, 135
collaborative classroom practices, xxi, 42–46, 67, 74, 89, 138, 198, 200, 202–205, 208, 213, 214
communicative repertoire, 35–37, 72, 73, 87, 181–183, 187
community, xxi–xxiv, 6, 31, 62, 85, 90–93, 101–103, 114, 117, 125–134, 136, 138–141, 144–151, 169, 175, 200, 202–204, 208, 209, 214, 215
comprehensibility, 188, 190–193
conscientização, 68–73, 80–82
contract grading, 37, 205
creative fiction writing, 17–20, 27
Critical autoethnographic narrative (CAN), 85–94
critical incidents, 21, 90–94
critical pedagogy, xv, 3, 53, 64, 111, 112

criticality, 13, 14, 52, 59, 69, 79, 98

dialect variation, dialects, 7–14, 23, 24, 29, 34, 42, 43, 54, 55, 58–60, 72, 100–107, 110, 182, 184, 187, 188, 190–193
dialogic, 4, 136, 137
disability, 163, 196, 197, 201
discourse analysis, 3, 52, 56, 57, 178
discussion forums, 69, 72–77
diversity, 18, 25, 26, 31–33, 39–41, 46, 52, 54, 55, 59, 60, 67–69, 73, 75, 76, 99, 103, 104, 112, 127, 130, 155, 159, 169, 172
Du Bois, W.E.B., 141–143
duoethnography, xix, xxiii

educational inequality, xvi, 40
educator/(language) teacher preparation and education, 52, 69, 85–87, 89, 90, 94, 97–99, 107, 112, 113, 155, 184, 197
ESOL, TESOL, xiv, 107, 159, 165
Esri/ArcGIS, 137–139
First Year Composition (FYC), 31, 36, 37

flash fiction, 22–24, 29
formal written English, 7, 8, 12
freewrite, 8, 21, 34–37

Global Englishes, 23, 26
Global Thinking Routines, 117
glottonormativity, 68–76, 80–82

hooks, xiii, xxiii, 140, 168, 169, 176, 179
hope, xxiii, xxiv, 30, 85, 120, 155, 213, 214

identity lens, identity work, 85–87, 89–91, 93, 94
identity tensions, 91
inclusive assessment, 199

informal written English, 7, 8, 12
intelligibility, 188–193
intentionality, 136
intersectionality, intersectionalities, xx, xxiii, 21, 89, 90, 113, 116, 119, 137, 140, 141, 147, 151, 168, 184

labor-based contract grading, 34, 198–202, 208, 213
language discrimination, 39, 40, 51, 53, 55, 61, 77, 84, 114–120, 145, 184, 186, 190, 196
language ideologies, 3, 7, 11, 36, 85, 88, 91, 104, 109, 152, 184
language ideology, 7, 31, 35–37, 52, 55–57, 85, 86, 88, 91, 93, 104, 184
language knowledge, 7, 10, 14
language subordination, 55–57
language teaching methodology, 187, 193
language variation, 99–107, 110, 128, 183, 184, 187, 188, 192, 193
learning about Written Languages (LaWL), 40, 41, 46
learning community, 136, 138, 140, 144, 149
linguicism, 9, 111, 115, 118, 119
linguistic diversity, 52, 55, 59–62, 66–68, 75, 76, 80, 112, 127
linguistic justice, xv, 7, 36, 40, 52, 112, 215
linguistic landscapes, 68–70, 126
lived experiences, xix, 19, 35, 37, 77, 90, 120, 147

mentorship, xix, 20, 90, 94, 157
metacognition, 30–32, 35, 37, 203
metrolingualism, 126–134
multilingualism, xv, xix, xxii, xxiii, 19, 32–35, 39, 44, 58, 69, 70, 74–77, 82, 91, 97–100, 103, 107, 126, 129–134, 163, 184, 204

National Council of Teachers of English (NCTE), 157–163
neoliberalism, 39, 77
neurodiversity, 181, 183, 186–190, 197, 201, 204

ocularcentrism, 69, 79–81
oracy skills, 183, 193

pedagogizing identity, 92

peer support, 171, 179
personal values, 102, 149
place/place-ify, 137, 141
Plurilingualism, 74, 82
privilege, xiv, xxii, 5, 20, 30, 41, 43, 52, 68, 84, 90, 91, 111–117, 119, 120, 125, 126, 128, 136, 184
pronunciation, 181–193

radicality, 98, 101, 107
reading, 3–14, 17, 69, 144, 177, 178, 181, 189, 190, 200
reflective narrative, 86, 149, 150
register variation, 7, 8, 11–13, 186
rhetorical moves, 7–10, 40, 43
rural students, 17–21, 26

secondary education, 4, 5, 155, 159
self-care, xxvi, 198, 205, 206
social justice, xv, xxii, 3, 30, 31, 40–46, 111, 112, 139, 166, 214, 215
sociolinguistic diversity, 77, 126–130, 133
speech styles, 181–189
Standard Language Ideology, 12, 13, 31, 36, 52, 55, 56, 57, 101, 182, 190, 193
StoryMaps, 137–141, 144, 145, 150, 151
student empowerment, 136, 171, 172, 205
student narratives, 23, 67, 85, 137, 163
styleshifting, 187, 189, 190
systemic racism, 41, 44, 55

teacher/educator education and preparation, 52, 69, 85–87, 89, 90, 94, 97–99, 107, 112, 113, 155, 184, 197
teacher educator identity, 87, 92
teacher identity, 85, 87–89
teaching English to speakers of other languages (TESOL)/ESOL, xiv, 107, 159, 165
Theoretichal approach, 69, 70, 73, 77, 81
transformative pedagogy, 168, 171, 179
translanguaging, translanguage pedagogy, 3, 9, 11, 18, 21, 22, 23, 28, 29, 33, 34, 36, 64, 126, 129, 130, 134, 181
translingual pedagogy, 19, 53, 55
trauma-informed pedagogy, 174, 198
trauma-informed practice, 168, 169, 171–175, 177

writing pedagogy, 159

For Product Safety Concerns and Information please contact our EU Authorised Representative:

Easy Access System Europe

Mustamäe tee 50

10621 Tallinn

Estonia

gpsr.requests@easproject.com

www.ingramcontent.com/pod-product-compliance
Ingram Content Group UK Ltd.
Pitfield, Milton Keynes, MK11 3LW, UK
UKHW021839210426
5322IPUK00021B/361